THE TRUTH ABOUT THE '37 OSHAWA GM STRIKE

Tony Leah

THE TRUTH
ABOUT THE '37 OSHAWA GM STRIKE

They Made Cars and They Made Plans:
Reds, the Rank and File, and International
Solidarity Unionized GM

Baraka
Books
Montréal

ISBN 978-1-77186-365-0 pbk 978-1-77186-373-5; epub 978-1-77186-374-2 pdf

Cover photo (Oshawa Museum A016.12.8)
Cover by Gianni Caccia
Book Design by Folio infographie
Editing and proofreading: Robin Philpot, Anne Marie Marko, Elizabeth West

Legal Deposit, 4th quarter 2024
Bibliothèque et Archives nationales du Québec
Library and Archives Canada

Published by Baraka Books of Montreal
Printed and bound in Quebec

TRADE DISTRIBUTION & RETURNS
Canada – UTP Distribution: UTPdistribution.com
United States — Independent Publishers Group: IPGbook.com

We acknowledge the support from the Société de développement des entreprises culturelles (SODEC) and the Government of Quebec tax credit for book publishing administered by SODEC.

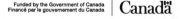

Dedication

This work is dedicated to the members of the UAW who, at the time of writing in the fall of 2023, were waging a strike, not just for themselves but, in the words of their President, "for the good of the entire working class." As Shawn Fain declared at the 2023 UAW Bargaining Convention, "We're here to come together to ready ourselves for the war against our one and only true enemy: multi-billion-dollar corporations and employers." With the Stand-Up Strike against the auto majors and an aggressive organizing campaign at non-union auto assembly plants, the members and new leadership of the UAW are showing a determination to return to the roots of radical industrial unionism established in the 1930s in places like Flint and Oshawa.

Acknowledgements

My goal in writing this book was to add to the understanding of a key event in Canadian labour history, with the hope of aiding those who are striving today to revive a class-conscious, militant labour movement. To whatever extent I have succeeded, it is because I have been able to build on the work of those who went before me, including labour historians Philip Foner, Roger Keeran and William Z. Foster. Among recent works, I was inspired and informed by Toni Gilpin's analysis of the heroism of the Farm Equipment Union.

Henry Kraus, James Napier, and Wyndham Mortimer were in the thick of the battle to establish industrial unionism in the North American auto industry, and their accounts helped me to understand the role of leadership and the relationship between union leaders, the left, and rank-and-file workers that enabled that battle to be won.

When I began my research, the too-little-recognized MA thesis of James Pendergest opened my eyes to the depth of engagement, understanding, and commitment of the GM workers in Oshawa in 1937. Pendergest's simple but profound commitment to finding and reporting the day-to-day events of the strike proves that meaningful historical analysis has to start with the basic facts.

I brought to my investigation the lessons I have learned over a lifetime of labour and political activism. My approach is guided by historical materialism, learned not just from works by Marx and Lenin, but from working with comrades who have helped me to understand and apply those principles to current events. Foremost among mentors and guides has been political analyst and radio host Phil Taylor, who provided critical insight to my research.

I particularly want to acknowledge the importance of my 40+ year career on the shop floor and engagement in union activities and struggles. I have gained an understanding of the labour movement, working class struggle, and the history and legacy of my Local union—UAW/CAW/Unifor Local 222—from rank-and-file workers and retirees, and union activists that would be hard to achieve any other way. Many members of Local 222 offered support, encouragement, and assistance during my research, and I particularly want to thank Don Nicholls, a great repository of historical knowledge, who read my 2023 MA thesis—on which this book is based—and provided helpful corrections and comments.

The foundation for this book was my 2023 MA thesis. My thesis adviser, David Goutor, was a constant source of support, encouragement, and challenging commentary, and helped me to strengthen my research, analysis, and writing. I also want to thank the other members of my thesis defense committee, Stephanie Ross and Wayne Lewchuk. The courses I took with them and other faculty members in the School of Labour Studies at McMaster University helped me develop greater academic rigour and analytical skills. It was a privilege to be part of an academic institution that has worked to bridge the silos of academia and the labour movement. I also appreciate my acceptance by a somewhat younger generation of students, and my brief but proud membership in CUPE Local 3906 as a teaching assistant.

The staff at the Oshawa Museum and the Walter P. Reuther Library (Wayne State University) provided excellent access and assistance to key research materials, and my thesis would have been poorer without their help.

Most of all, I want to thank my partner, Lorie King, for her support during the months when my concentration on research and writing put extra burdens on her. Lorie has a long-time commitment to the labour and progressive movements, and her love, collaboration, and support have enriched my life immeasurably, and in large part made this book possible.

Contents

List of Abbreviations

AAWA	Associated Automobile Workers of America
ACCL	All-Canadian Congress of Labour
AFL	American Federation of Labor
AIWA	Automotive Industrial Workers Association
AWIU	Auto Workers' Industrial Union
AWIU-BC	Auto Workers' Industrial Union of the Border Cities
AWU	Auto Workers Union
CBRE	Canadian Brotherhood of Railway Employees
CCF	Co-operative Commonwealth Federation
CDAC	Cleveland District Auto Council
CIO	Committee for Industrial Organization
CLDL	Canadian Labour Defence League
CPC	Communist Party of Canada
CPUSA	Communist Party of the United States of America
CWAW	Union of Carriage, Wagon and Automobile Workers
FE	United Farm Equipment Workers of America
ILD	International Labor Defense
IRA	Irish Republican Army
IWW	Industrial Workers of the World
MESA	Mechanics Educational Society of America
NUWA	National Unemployed Workers' Association
OBU	One Big Union
OCVI	Oshawa Collegiate and Vocational Institution
PAO	Public Archives of Ontario
PWOC	Packinghouse Workers Organizing Committee
RILU	Red International of Labour Unions
SWOC	Steel Workers Organizing Committee
TLC	Trades and Labour Congress of Canada
TTLC	Toronto District Trades and Labour Council

TUEL	Trade Union Education League
TUUL	Trade Union Unity League
UAAVW	United Automobile, Aircraft and Vehicle Workers' Union of America
UAW	United Automobile Workers of America (sometimes UAWA)
UE	United Electrical, Radio and Machine Workers of America
ULTA	Ukrainian Labor Temple Association
UPWA	United Packinghouse Workers of America
WRL	Walter P. Reuther Library, Wayne State University
WUL	Workers' Unity League of Canada

Introduction

On Saturday, April 17, 1937, *Toronto Daily Star* reporter Frederick Griffin spoke to a worker on strike against General Motors in Oshawa. It was the tenth day of the strike, and the worker, a chief steward, was steadfast. "We'll stick until our belts are up to the last notch. This strike has only begun. I've been through strikes in England that lasted three months, six months, nine months—and we won them. We'll win here."[1] Even though there was a possibility of a long strike at that point, another striker said "We hope it lasts a while yet. Every day gives us an education in labor-industrial matters we knew nothing about two weeks ago."[2] A few days earlier the same determination was expressed by Gertrude Gillard, one of 300 women strikers and a member of the union's bargaining committee, who told the *Star*, "Of course the girls will stick. They know what they're striking for and they'll see it through. None of them that I have talked to has ever suggested we go back to work or has ever expressed any doubt in the cause."[3]

These voices of rank-and-file workers and shop-floor union activists display courage and determination. More than that, they reveal the engagement of workers in the strike, their solidarity, and their remarkable understanding of the importance of the battle they were fighting, even while they were still in the middle of it. Until now, not enough has been done to seek out and highlight these voices in order to fully understand the events and lessons of the 1937 strike by General Motors autoworkers in Oshawa.

In fact, their voices have largely been obscured, and the true story of the strike has been subject to misrepresentation and omissions because of the wide acceptance of the account of academic historian Irving Abella. In the late 1960s and early 1970s, Abella constructed a narrative that the Oshawa strikers had received no significant support from their international union, the UAW. Abella minimized the contributions of Communist organizers in the tough years of organizing prior to the strike, and downplayed the role of rank-and-file workers in the events of the strike itself. The true story of the Oshawa 1937 strike ended up being replaced by a myth that is captured in the title of Abella's article in *Canadian Dimension*: "The CIO: Reluctant Invaders."[4]

I have been a Local 222 member since 1980, when it was still part of the UAW. I always had a keen interest in labour history, so I thought I had a pretty good grasp of the Oshawa 1937 strike. I had done a fair amount of reading, and also talked to veteran members of the Local. But when I started doing research for my MA thesis at the McMaster University School of Labour Studies,[5] I quickly realized that much of what I thought I knew was actually false. I went back to primary sources, particularly contemporary news accounts, and uncovered an incredibly rich account of the day-to-day twists and turns of the strike. The misrepresentations originating with Abella were overturned by the evidence that I pieced together, and I also learned many more details of the deep engagement of ordinary workers and rank-and-file leaders in building a union in which workers exercised their power on the shop floor and built solidarity in the community. I learned for the first time that in a workforce of 3,700 women and men, the UAW organizers had established a stewards' body of some 300 workers. The stewards built enough shop-floor power that they forced management to resolve workers' grievances—even before the strike, and thus before there was a collective agreement. This stewards' body played a critical role during the strike.

The Oshawa 1937 strike is widely recognized as a significant turning point in Canadian labour history—it is hailed as the strike that "established industrial unionism in Canada." Local 222 of the United Auto Workers (UAW) had been chartered on March 2, 1937, just a few weeks before the strike began. To be successful, Local 222 had to take on General Motors of Canada, which dominated the auto industry in Canada and was completely dominant in Oshawa and the surrounding region. Its parent company was the wealthiest corporation in the world at the time. The union also had to fight the Ontario government and Ontario Liberal Premier Mitch Hepburn, who was determined to prevent recognition of the UAW and the Committee for Industrial

Organization (CIO) to which it was affiliated. Hepburn attacked the UAW organizers as "foreign agitators." He told the *Toronto Daily Star* that it was "a fight to the finish" and that "we know that the Communists are standing by, by the thousands, ready to jump in at the first sign of disorder. If the C.I.O. wins in Oshawa, it has other plants it will step into. It will be in the mines, demoralize that industry and send stocks tumbling."[6] Almost all of the daily papers at the time backed Hepburn and his inflammatory accusations, and the resulting hostile climate posed even more challenges to the union.

It is important to examine the factors that contributed to the workers' success, despite the considerable forces arrayed against them.

The 1937 Oshawa strike took place at **a particular moment in history**. When an earthquake occurs, it is after many years of opposing forces building up until something gives. The battle in Oshawa in 1937 was part of a broader movement across North America that was shaking up relations between workers and corporate owners in major economic sectors. To understand the Oshawa strike, we need to investigate the origins of the industrial union movement and the class conflict it made manifest.

The events in Oshawa also took place at a tumultuous time in the world. Fascism was on the rise, and international rivalries were setting the stage for a world war. The Western capitalist powers were trying to respond to the deep economic crisis of the Depression, then in its eighth year. Popular movements in opposition to the devastation wreaked by the Depression, war, and fascism were calling into question the continuation of the capitalist system. At the same time, the Western powers felt challenged by the growing strength of the Soviet Union and rising movements against colonialism. Their responses not only included attempts to vilify, isolate, and undermine the Soviet Union, but also a renewed and expanded "red scare." Government repression included arrests, deportations, and other measures against labour and other activists who were seen as supporters of the communist movement or were just portrayed that way because they were challenging corporate power. These ongoing developments and conflicts, directly or indirectly, played a part in what occurred in Oshawa.

The Oshawa strike also occurred in a **particular place**. There was a long history of labour struggles in the Oshawa region, including earlier attempts to build unions. For many years the other protagonist in the strike, General Motors of Canada, had played a dominant role in the political and economic life of the region. By 1937, autoworkers in Oshawa and GM stood as widely recognized representatives of the class battle between workers and corporations that was taking place across North America.

Another key factor in the Oshawa strike was the conflict between contesting groups with different ideological outlooks who were vying for leadership of the workers' struggle in the years leading up to 1937, and during the strike itself.

Craft union leaders had long opposed attempts to establish an industrial model of unionism. Early attempts to establish unions on the basis of one union for all workers in an industry included the Knights of Labor, the Industrial Workers of the World (IWW), and the One Big Union (OBU). The Knights of Labor and the IWW began and were strongest in the U.S., but both played an important role in Canada. The Knights in particular had a significant following in the Oshawa area in the 1880s. The rapid decline of the Knights after 1886 was at least partly due to the Knights leadership's promotion of cooperation with industry, rather than a commitment to the interests of workers as a class. They opposed strikes and building workers' strength in the workplace. In the words of prominent labour historian Philip Foner:

> The basic cause [of the disintegration of the Order] was the breach between the leadership and the rank-and-file, a conflict already present in the K. of L. at its height in 1886 ... It was a conflict between two ideologies: the first of these based itself on the class struggle and the second on class collaboration.[7]

On the other hand, communists and many socialists advocated an approach based on class struggle rather than accommodation with corporations and governments, and played an important role in the development of Canadian unions. Socialists organized in Canada, both within the union movement and outside of it, in the late 1800s and early 1900s. The victory of the socialist revolution in Russia in 1917 was a boost for many of these groups and spurred the formation of the Communist Party of Canada (CPC) in 1921. The CPC had a presence in Oshawa dating from the mid-1920s. Communists gave a high priority to organizing workers, both within existing unions and in forming new ones. Their strategic approach emphasized shop-floor organizing and action. The Communists also took a broader working-class approach: organizing the unemployed and wider working-class communities, including immigrant and ethnic communities, opposing racism, and uniting male and female workers. The CPC had particular bases of support among immigrants from Eastern Europe and the U.K., especially skilled workers, who had participated in unions or left-wing political organizations like the Labour Party, Independent Labour Party, or Communist parties before emigrating. Notably, Communists also were part of an international movement with common policies and strategies, and a commitment to international solidarity. The role played by these left-wing organizations and activists in the broader movement for industrial unionism and in the workplaces and community of Oshawa was important in laying the foundation for the later successful unionization of General Motors.

There were other differences and conflicts within the labour movement that were important to understanding the 1937 strike. These included disputes over whether unions should be based solely in Canada, or should be "international," representing workers in the United States as well as Canada. It is also important to consider alternative models of union structure and organization, including the level of internal democracy, the approach to bargaining and demands, the involvement of rank-and-file workers, shop-floor presence, and political views and activities. There was significant overlap between advocates of "rank-and-file unionism," like many of the early CIO unions, and "class-struggle unionism" that was the goal of Communist organizers. While the term "rank and file" originally was used in a military context, to distinguish commissioned officers from the rest of the soldiers, it came to be applied to unions in the nineteenth century. There is a crucial difference to be noted: rank-and-file soldiers are expected to obey orders without question. On the other hand, advocates of rank-and-file unionism believe that the ordinary workers need to be fully engaged in all union activities, and that the rank and file should be making the decisions. The goal is much more than formal democratic structures, but real engagement and debate. It is characterized as tumultuous in this definition from *The Lexicon of Labor* by R. Emmett Murray:

Rank and fileism—The term given to a kind of tumultuous local participatory democracy practiced in the early CIO unions and even today by a few unions, most notably in some West Coast locals of the International Longshore and Warehouse Union.[8]

While not all advocates of rank-and-file unionism are socialists or communists, in practice, in unions where the left has played a significant role in the leadership there has been greater internal democracy, more engagement of members, and often greater militancy and exercise of workers' power in the workplace. Examples can be found in unions like the United Electrical Workers Union (UE), the United Packinghouse Workers of America (UPWA), and the Farm Equipment Workers Union (FE), and also in individual locals like UAW Local 248, among others.[9]

My approach to investigating this contested terrain has been to learn as much as possible about the day-to-day events of the strike. I have considered the positions and actions of the adversaries—both between union leaders, company, politicians, and media—but, also, within the union between people with different perspectives or ideologies. In all of this I have aimed to bring to the fore the voices, views, and actions of rank-and-file workers and shop floor union activists. I think their role is fundamentally important and is far too often given scant attention.

Misinterpreting Winning Strategies

Irving Abella's analysis, in his book *Nationalism, Communism, and Canadian Labour,* has greatly influenced the prevailing view of the events and significance of the 1937 Oshawa strike since it was published in 1973.[10] Abella's account of the Oshawa strike was reprised as a chapter in *On Strike: Six Key Labour Struggles in Canada 1919-1949.*[11] Much of the same material had also been published in Abella's 1969 essay in *Historical Papers.*[12] Abella also advanced his analysis of the Oshawa strike in a *Canadian Dimension* article with the provocative title "The CIO: Reluctant Invaders."[13] Most writers and researchers discussing the Oshawa strike since the publication of Abella's book have accepted his interpretation, generally without independent research or verification of his claims. Abella's influence has been so strong that even histories by leading researchers from the union itself have accepted some of his theses, particularly those of minimizing the role of the

UAW/CIO and cross-border internationalism in the victory. Abella made four main arguments. First, he claimed that the Oshawa workers received "not one penny of aid" from the international UAW or CIO.[14] Abella's criticism went far beyond saying that the UAW and CIO leadership provided insufficient support. He accused them of acting dishonestly and in bad faith, claiming they "bamboozled" workers in Oshawa with false promises.[15] Second, Abella argued the UAW was not necessary, since "what the Oshawa strikers achieved, they achieved on their own."[16] In fact, Abella argued that "the CIO connection was as harmful as it was helpful."[17] Third, Abella concluded that the strike ended because the workers were desperate, the union was "bankrupt," and "the union negotiating committee ... was ready to sign an agreement on almost any terms."[18] Finally, Abella argued that "the formation of the CIO doomed whatever possibility there remained of creating in Canada a labour movement, the majority of whose members belonged to Canadian unions."[19] To Abella, this "has allowed foreigners to control the labour movement in Canada," and is evidence of "the colonial mentality of the Canadian workingman."[20]

There is an ideological underpinning to Abella's analysis, particularly a deeply condescending view of rank-and-file workers, a commitment to a rather narrow Canadian nationalism, and evidence of anti-communism. Abella's dismissal of ordinary union members is laid out starkly in the preface to his book, where Abella claimed "The average union member, as almost all studies of the labour movement have shown, plays an unimportant role in the affairs of his union." Abella modified this only slightly with the qualification "Only at times when his own economic well-being is at stake— during strikes and collective bargaining negotiations—does he take more than a passing interest in the activities of his union. And this, of course, was especially true of the unionist in the 1930s and 1940s, when his immediate, and indeed sole concern was to achieve financial security."[21] Even with this disclaimer, Abella argued that what he believed were the most important issues to the labour movement—"the internal threat from the Communists and the external threat from the Americans"—were only of concern to the leadership.[22] Expanding on what he saw as the external threat, Abella argued that "few Canadian unionists considered the drawbacks of being forced to accept policies made for them by men in another country. Few saw the problems involved in having Canadian unionists subject to the whims and wishes of an American leadership."[23] It is noteworthy that Abella labelled the Communists as an "internal threat." Abella's view of the role of Communists in the lead-up to the strike is somewhat contradictory—at times acknowledging that they played a major role, at times declaring "they accomplished nothing." Still, he baldly stated that, to the leaders of Canadian unions "the Communists and their left-wing allies were indeed a menace." When Abella did recognize that Communists played an important role in the formation of CIO unions in Canada, he primarily credits them for being hard workers, but deprecates the importance of their strategic outlook, based on their ideology.[24] In the book's conclusion, Abella acknowledged that "the contribution of the Communists to the creation of the CIO in Canada was invaluable," and that it is doubtful that "the expulsions of the left-wing unions accomplished anything of benefit to the Congress."[25] What Abella misses is that the undemocratic purges of left-wing unions and union activists meant the solidification of a class-collaboration orientation in the leadership of the Canadian labour movement, and thus its long-term decline as a body fighting for the advancement of the Canadian working class. These biases influenced Abella's interpretation of the lead-up to the strike, and events during the strike—particularly the role of left-wing leadership, the engagement of rank-and-file workers and the community, and the value of the decision to organize under the auspices of the UAW/CIO; all of which were interconnected. Because of his biases, Abella paid scant attention to the role of rank-and-file workers. In particular, he barely mentioned the mass membership meetings and large stewards' meetings that took place during the strike. In contrast, James Pendergest pointed out the significance of many of those meetings. In fact, Abella seems to have not even understood who the stewards were or what role they played in the union's structure. Abella's ideological blinders may also be the reason that he failed to mention even once the existence and role of women strikers, and the women who were members of the local bargaining committees.

Two widely used texts on Canadian labour history accept key parts of Abella's analysis. In *Working-Class Experience: The Rise and Reconstitution of Canadian Labour, 1800-1980*, Bryan Palmer claimed that "Oshawa created a CIO presence in Canada in the absence of actual CIO organizers," and argued that the strike was won "through subterfuge" of the leaders denying affiliation with the CIO.[26] Palmer also stated that "the lack of funds and support from [John L.] Lewis retarded growth" of the CIO in Canada.[27] Palmer credited Abella for this analysis of the CIO, calling him "its historian."[28] Desmond Morton, in *Working People: An Illustrated History of the Canadian Labour Movement*, also echoed Abella's thesis that "well aware that they were penniless and that the militancy of their members was eroding fast, the Canadian leaders would have accepted almost anything."[29]

Charlotte Yates' book, *From Plant to Politics*, focussed on the history of the UAW in Canada from 1936 to 1984, when the Canadian section broke away to form the independent CAW. Yates' scholarship is detailed and well researched for the most part, but she accepted Abella's view of the Oshawa strike without critique.

> The real weak link in the strike was the union itself. The UAW was bankrupt[30] and unable to deliver on its pledges of financial support for Local 222's struggle ... [UAW International President Homer] Martin was determined to end the strike and refused a request to organize sympathy strikes to put greater pressure on General Motors. This decision, in combination with the lack of financial support from the International UAW, left the Local 222 bargaining committee desperate for a settlement.[31]

Laura Sefton MacDowell's article, *After the Strike—Labour Relations in Oshawa, 1937-1939*, was mainly concerned with the immediate aftermath of the strike, rather than the strike itself. MacDowell did, however, review the highlights of the strike, with a preface that reveals the extent to which Abella's interpretations have become perceived as established fact. MacDowell stated, "The Oshawa strike has been examined thoroughly," giving only one source for this assertion—Irving Abella, *On Strike*.[32] Her account of the end of the strike clearly echoed Abella.

> From an undercover agent Hepburn knew that CIO activity was increasing in other Ontario industries, that Local 222 was not receiving financial support from the UAW, despite union president Homer Martin's public promises, and that the local union was in trouble ... the union negotiating committee was anxious to conclude an agreement as soon as possible.[33]

By the 1990s the Abella narrative—that the Oshawa strike had been won without any real support from the CIO or UAW, that the UAW leadership had misled the Oshawa strikers with promises of financial assistance that could not be honoured, and that, before the strike was two weeks old, the negotiating committee and strike leadership were desperate to settle—was even repeated in publications of the union itself (after the 1985 decision of the Canadian section of the UAW to split, the union's name became the Canadian Auto Workers). Abella's article "Oshawa 1937" was used as a reading in CAW educational programs. *The Canadian Auto Workers: The Birth and Transformation of a Union*, the 1995 history of the union by Sam Gindin, at the time assistant to the CAW President, repeated these basic themes without questioning them:

> In order to boost morale, [Homer] Martin had promised financial assist-ance and sympathy strikes, neither of which he had discussed with the CIO or UAW executive boards and which he could not honour ... Charles Millard, the president of the Oshawa local and now a full-time CIO organ-izer, was equally nervous and anxious for a settlement.[34]

> The Oshawa strike was organized and ultimately won in Canada. The American UAW was too new and distracted by the events exploding in its own country to offer support by way of strike pay, cadres of organizers, or sympathy strikes.[35]

A few years later, the CAW produced an interactive CD-ROM of the union's history, *No Power Greater: How Autoworkers in Canada Built a Union and Made History*. The article on the Oshawa strike included this passage:

> On Monday, April 19, workers rejected the first offer of their bargaining committee. The deal included many of the workers' demands but would have required them to return to work before an agreement was signed. However, by the end of the week, workers voted to accept the second offer of a one-year agreement when it became evident that neither financial assistance nor sympathy strikes would come from the International union in the U.S..[36]

Abella's criticisms of the international UAW leadership were often stated with few or no sources cited. Abella heavily relied on interviews with a few key participants without acknowledging the limitations or biases of his interviewees. Even beyond that, Abella made assertions that are contradicted by some of his own evidence. Often, Abella seemed to put quotable phrases—"The CIO—the reluctant invaders," "not a penny of support," "workers needed jobs not unions,"—ahead of careful analysis.

THE CIO:
RELUCTANT INVADERS

by IRVING ABELLA

John L. Lewis

Most Canadians know that the vast majority of the organized workers of our country belong to American unions. What is less well known is what these workers think of the situation. The problem

be concentrated amongst a very few labour leaders. Though recently there have been some minor rumblings, the problem of the American domination of our labour movement has not yet seeped down to

Canadian Dimension Vol. 8 No. 6 (March-April 1972)

This book revisits the Oshawa 1937 strike, looking at its historical context, the preceding history of labour organizing that made it possible, and most importantly, a careful review of the day-to-day events of the strike that seeks out the voices and actions of the workers involved. The contending forces of workers, corporations, and a rabidly anti-union government that clashed in Oshawa in 1937 are largely the same ones we see in the battles going on in North America today. Understanding the factors that led to the success of the Oshawa strikers can provide lessons to those seeking to revive today's labour movement.

It is important to test Abella's assertions about the Oshawa strike with a careful review of the historical record. I believe this record shows convincingly that the role of the international leadership of the UAW was positive and important in the success of the strike, although much of this evidence has been given insufficient attention to date. There is also a rich record of the critical role of rank-and-file GM workers and particularly of the remarkable stewards' body they created in Oshawa that has been given far too little attention until now. The Oshawa 1937 strike is an inspiring story of real rank-and-file unionism and remarkable levels of engagement, solidarity, and democratic organization that has not yet been fully known or appreciated by either labour activists or academics.

Another goal of this book is to understand the historical factors that preceded the dramatic events of 1937 that were responsible for their ultimate ground-breaking success. Foremost of these factors is the history of years of efforts, unsuccessful strikes, and organizing that created the right conditions for success in 1937. Particularly important was the leadership of working-class organizers committed to a class struggle outlook. While Communists chose to step back from open leadership roles during the formation of Local 222 and during the historic strike, they still had an important influence through the principles they had long advocated. These principles include many that would now be considered features of rank-and-file unionism: industrial unionism, democratic engagement of rank-and-file workers, militancy on the shop floor, building solidarity within the workforce and in the community, international solidarity, and rejecting cooperation with corporations.

Chapter 1

The McLaughlins vs. The Workers

"The history of all hitherto existing society is the history of class struggles,"[1] so the foundations of the history of the Oshawa area must also be found in the battles between workers and the owners of industry in that Southern Ontario community. Of course, establishment histories often tell this story from the viewpoint of the dominant class and put corporate owners and the wealthy centre stage. But we know that the wealthy didn't construct the stage: it was the working class. It is particularly important in researching the history of Oshawa to seek out the stories of workers, their lives at work and in the community, and their struggles.

Histories of Oshawa often feature, sometimes to the point of glorification, the McLaughlin family. Robert McLaughlin began building cutters in a corner of his barn in 1864 and founded the McLaughlin Carriage Works in 1867. In 1878 the works was moved from Enniskillen to Oshawa, and by 1899 McLaughlin claimed to have "the largest carriage factory in Canada." Not only was Robert "a member of a powerful new class of brewers and distillers, sugar refiners, flour millers, cement makers, and steel manufacturers" in central Canada, he was also the Mayor of Oshawa.[2] An early example of government support that helped the McLaughlin family expand their wealth and influence occurred when a fire destroyed the McLaughlin Carriage Works in December 1899. The mayor of Gananoque offered McLaughlin the use of a vacant building to operate his business. In order to encourage the carriage works to remain in Oshawa, it was proposed the town provide a $50,000 loan to rebuild. To avoid the perception of a conflict of

The McLaughlin Carriage Works, Oshawa 1908, with the workers in front and in the windows. The transfer above Mary Street is to the left.
(The Robert McLaughlin Gallery, Bouckley Collection 0677)

interest, Robert resigned as mayor and accepted the loan. The original building had been well insured, and most of the carriages had already been sold and shipped for the Christmas trade, so the fire ended up being a windfall for McLaughlin.[3]

Robert's son, Robert Samuel (Sam) later became an Oshawa icon, even after the business was sold to General Motors in 1918. "Colonel Sam," as he liked to be known, carried on as President of the subsidiary General Motors of Canada until 1945.[4] Sam McLaughlin made a considerable fortune from establishing motor vehicle manufacturing as a subsidiary of his father's carriage business in 1907. However, he was even more successful at manufacturing myths about himself and his business. Up to the present most people in Oshawa and beyond believe that the McLaughlin Motor Car Company designed and manufactured their own vehicles. In reality, Sam McLaughlin had spent years trying unsuccessfully to find a way into the rapidly expanding industry. Finally, the McLaughlins, facing growing debts and orders they couldn't fulfill, signed a deal with W. C. Durant and Buick that made them little more than assemblers of Buicks in Oshawa. The agreement with Durant specified that the McLaughlin Motor Co. had to duplicate the design of the Buick and use Buick engines, and "were required to purchase all wheels, lamps, radiators, axles, springs, and other parts from Buick suppliers."[5] The only real contribution of the McLaughlins was the branding of the vehicles as McLaughlin-Buick.

Sam McLaughlin was mostly interested in using his wealth for self-aggrandizement and to cement his position as Oshawa's first family. In 1916 he commissioned the building of the most expensive house in Canada. Parkwood, as it was named, was valued at $100,000 at the time, and was a 15,000-square-foot 55-room mansion.[6] Sam also had an estate in Bermuda and spent much of his time there or sailing on his yacht. In later years, McLaughlin used his philanthropy to ensure that his name was featured prominently on such civic features as the McLaughlin Public Library and the Robert McLaughlin Gallery. In 1947 Sam purchased a park that was donated to the Boy Scouts. Named Camp Samac (Sam – Mac), it featured poles dedicated to the Cubs and Scouts, and a forty-foot pole "known as the 'Big Chief' with carvings depicting the life and times of Sam McLaughlin."[7]

Corporate owners are not possible without the existence of workers. The conflict between these classes has shaped and defined historical developments. In order to fully understand the historical developments that made Oshawa a key centre of industry, and eventually the site where industrial unionism made a breakthrough in Canada, examining the role of workers is essential.

Local 222 has played a significant role in the history of the Canadian labour movement. Too many histories begin the story when the United Auto Workers granted Local 222 a charter on March 2, 1937. But workers had been struggling, challenging corporate owners, and building organizations of resistance for decades before the formation of UAW Local 222 and the successful strike it carried out against General Motors.

Oshawa became known as the "Manchester of Canada" in the late 1800s due to a growing manufacturing sector "dominated by the Joseph Hall Works," where, by 1867, 250 workers produced threshing machines, mowers, and ploughs. The Joseph Hall Works also supplied moulded iron to Robert McLaughlin. Other important shops included "the McLaughlin Carriage Works, Mason's seed-drill plant, A. S. Whiting Agricultural Implements, Oshawa Stove Company, W. T. Dingle's

Fanning Mills and Seeders, and the Robson and Lauchland Tanneries."[8] The workers from many of these manufacturing plants featured in a remarkable display of working-class consciousness and pride that took place in downtown Oshawa in 1883.

Workers from this period were usually ignored by the media, and local histories. Their lives attracted less attention than those of the wealthy and politically powerful. But workers had interests and desires, and often the will to act collectively to fight for those interests. Their class interests were opposed to those of their employers, but the conflict did not always manifest in strikes or rebellions. Nevertheless, it was always present beneath the surface, a slowly smoldering ember always ready to burst into flame given the right conditions. "Class happens when some men," wrote E.P. Thompson, "as a result of common experiences (inherited and shared) feel and articulate the identity of their interests as between themselves, and as against other men whose interests are different from (and usually opposed to) theirs."[9]

As manufacturing expanded in Southern Ontario in the middle and late 1880s, workers faced erosion of their traditional craft skills, the use of more unskilled labour, and pressure to work longer hours. Workers responded with major battles across North America for shorter hours, including the Nine Hour Movement in Ontario in the 1870s. By the early 1880s there was a growing demand for the eight-hour day. Championing this demand was a new labour organization—the Knights of Labor.

The Knights of Labor had a growing presence in Canada in the 1880s, particularly in Southern Ontario, and a number of Knights Lodges existed in Oshawa.[10] At the time most unions operated as craft unions—they represented workers with a particular craft skill, such as carpenters, printers, or iron moulders, regardless of their employer. The Knights were one of the earliest labour unions to organize on an industrial basis—including all workers in a workplace in the same union—which had a strong appeal to many workers. The Knights also placed a high value on representing the dignity and honour of work and workers, powerfully represented by their logo of a knight shaking hands with an industrial worker, and prominently promoted their values through the use of union labels and the production, sale, and display of union pins, ribbons, drinking mugs, and even bread plates.[11]

Knights of Labor parade, August 13, 1883, Oshawa. Iron moulders from
the Joseph Hall Works made medallions on their float, quenched them,
and handed them out to the crowd. (Author's collection)

The Knights also addressed the interests of the growing industrial
working class with demands for a more just and democratic society,
including for public education. The Knights of Labor had been founded
in Philadelphia in 1869, and were strongest in the United States, but
had a growing presence in Canada in the 1880s when they were experiencing explosive growth across North America, reaching a peak of
about one million members. The Knights were associated with the
demand for an eight-hour day but were reluctant to endorse the call to
strike on May 1, 1886 that had been issued by the Federation of
Organized Trades and Labor Unions (the precursor of the AFL) to
achieve that goal. Hundreds of thousands of U.S. workers did go on
strike on May 1, including at the McCormick works in Chicago where
two workers were shot and killed by police. The protest rally at
Haymarket Square over the killings led to the Haymarket Massacre,
and the arrest, jailing, and execution of the Haymarket Martyrs. May
Day has become an International Day of Workers' protests in commem-
oration of these events. However, the leaders of the Knights of Labor
condemned the strikes, and the radical labour leaders who led them,
which was a major factor in their rapid decline following 1886.[12]

1883 Oshawa Demonstration

In the early 1880s, Oshawa had become an important centre of both industry and Knights of Labor organizing. This was dramatically illustrated by a major event that took place on August 13, 1883. Although it was termed a "demonstration," it more closely resembled a modern Labour Day parade. Oshawa City Council had declared a civic holiday, and the local Knights assemblies organized a parade and picnic.

Knights' assemblies in Ontario from Bowmanville to London were invited, and "three or four special trains from east and west were required to carry the festive crowd, each one being met at the station by a delegation and band, which led the procession into the city."[13] The parade was estimated to be a mile long, and included municipal, provincial and federal politicians, labour leaders, bands, and floats. "The first exhibit was a printing press churning out hand bills followed by a 'bill-poster' in costume ... all the major local industries had displays, many of them consisting of workers demonstrating the skills and techniques used in the production process. The McLaughlin workers demonstrated how they made wagons."[14] Other workers featured on floats included those from A. S. Whiting, the Oshawa Stove Company, W. T. Dingle's Fanning Mills, and Robson and Lauchland Tanneries.[15] Near the end of the parade, iron moulders from the Joseph Hall Works had constructed sand moulds on their float, were melting cast iron and casting commemorative medals, which were then quenched and thrown out to the crowd.[16]

This event must have been impressive and memorable for workers in the community. Anyone who took part or witnessed it would have remembered it, and some of them undoubtedly later took part in labour organizing.

There was a lull in union organizing after the mid-1880s, partially due to an economic downturn and lost strikes, but probably also because of the precipitous decline of the Knights of Labor in both the United States and Canada.

1902 Strike

However, the underlying conditions of workers and their conflict with the owners of the companies who employed them remained the same, and it was inevitable that the conflict would resurface. The next recorded labour battle at the McLaughlin Carriage Works occurred in February 1902. The Knights of Labor assemblies of carriage workers had led to the formation of an independent union that joined the American Federation of Labor in 1891 as the International Union of Carriage and Wagon Workers.[17] Workers at the McLaughlin works established a local of this union and went on strike on February 18, 1902, for union recognition and a wage increase. The strike involved 263 workers and lasted a month. Robert McLaughlin stuck to his anti-union "open-shop" principle and was able to rely on enough workers staying on the job to eventually defeat the union.[18]

In 1912, the carriage workers union reflected the rapid changes occurring in the vehicle industry and changed its name to the Union of Carriage, Wagon and Automobile Workers (CWAW) and organized on an industrial basis in the new industry. This brought CWAW into conflict with American Federation of Labor (AFL) craft affiliates who claimed jurisdiction over certain workers in auto plants. The AFL conventions in 1915 and 1916 ordered CWAW to drop "Automobile" from its name, and when CWAW refused, it was suspended in 1918 and became an independent union. The union became popularly known as the Auto Workers Union (AWU) and had grown to over 45,000 members by 1919. Then the union was severely battered by an economic downturn and an open-shop campaign by employers in the industry that reduced membership to under 1,000. The AWU leadership was inclined to support socialism, but was hostile to those revolutionary socialists who were establishing a Communist Party in the U.S. in the years following the Russian Revolution. However, given its weakened state by 1922, an alliance was struck with Communists who brought new blood and organizing vigour into the AWU. By the mid-1920s the union was largely under Communist leadership.[19] Initially the AWU had a significant presence in the auto industry in the U.S., particularly in the Detroit area, but none in Canada.

1920s and GM Paternalism

Well before the stock market crash of 1929 and the ensuing Great Depression, Ontario autoworkers were facing hard times. There was pressure to intensify work, combined with repeated wage cuts. On top of this, the work was precarious at best, because most production workers were laid off with no benefits or security in slow periods, as well as for extensive periods every year while plants were retooled for the next year's model. Art Shultz, the first Financial Secretary of Local 222, noted, "We were being laid off in July or August and wondering if we were going to have a pay for Xmas."[20] Skilled workers were somewhat better off, but despite being in demand for the model change periods, many of them faced layoffs the rest of the year. Work was entirely at the discretion of management. Any worker judged to be slower because of age or injury was unlikely to be called back to work after periods of layoff. Supervisors could fire people for any reason (or none). The work in an auto plant was also hot, difficult, and dangerous. Throughout this period workers responded with resistance. Art Shultz remembered that "GM had sit down strikes in the plant on the assembly line. I bet there wasn't a year go by that we didn't have 3 to 5 sit downs in the plant in different areas."[21]

General Motors tried to stave off organized resistance and unionization through a sophisticated approach of what Manley referred to as "welfare capitalism." GM provided workers in Oshawa with some sick pay and medical and dental insurance (although there was a mandatory charge of $6 per year).[22] They also had a savings and investment fund (for qualified workers) and what was termed the "modern dwelling house plan," designed to "encourage thrift." GM funded sports teams, choirs, and a range of leisure activities.[23] GM also had a company union, the Employees' Association, and required all workers to be members. All of these programs had the declared objective "to develop and maintain on a definite and permanent basis, a spirit of mutual confidence and good will between those charged with the responsibility of directing the affairs of the company and employees generally, and so by friendly and sympathetic co-operation one with the other, to bring happiness and prosperity to all members of the General Motors family."[24] There were also less explicit, but clear advantages to management in these programs in increasing their control over workers and making them dependent on the company. The housing scheme, for example, resulted in 75 percent of the workforce having company mortgages.[25] The insurance plan required annual doctor's check-ups, which were then used to ensure workers that were less able because of age or injury did not get recalled to work.

By the late 1920s GM was increasingly turning to efficiency engineers to devise schemes to increase output and profits. In addition to speed-up, this also included group bonus plans that pitted workers against each other and permitted easy management manipulation of bonus calculations.[26]

1928 Strike

A breaking point was reached in early 1928. No labour unions existed in the auto industry in Canada at that time. According to Manley, "Throughout the 1920s the case for industrial unionism as the means of organizing the mass production industries was made most consistently by the CPC (Communist Party of Canada)."[27] Communist Party members worked within the craft union movement (the Trades and Labour Congress) for a number of years with limited success. The Communist-led Trade Union Educational League (TUEL) operated to build support for the Communists' program for workers, and by the end of the 1920s decided to orient itself towards the national union movement that led to the formation of the All-Canadian Congress of Labour (ACCL) in 1927. The Party had a presence in some auto centres, "especially amongst ethnic communities (Ukrainians in Oshawa; Finns, Ukrainians and other Slavs in the Border Cities)."[28] A Communist Party branch had been established in Oshawa in 1925.[29]

Against this backdrop, rebellion broke out again inside the General Motors plant on Monday, March 26, 1928. This time it was sparked by a 30 percent reduction in piece rates on the trim line. This drastic cut was on top of a 45 percent reduction the previous December. Three hundred trim workers walked out. The trimmers, who made and installed such trim items as cushions and upholstery, occupied a strategically important place in the production process. It didn't take long after the trimmers struck before work in the plant came to a halt. It also turned out they had almost universal support from workers in all areas of the plant. By Thursday there were 3,000 strikers enthusiastically taking part in marches and mass meetings out of about 5,000 GM workers. This notably included the women trim line sewing machinists. The *Oshawa Daily Times* reported that "Girls are now taking a prominent part in the strike proceedings. This afternoon about two o'clock another parade filed down King Street and into the New Martin theatre for this afternoon's meeting led by the girls. These girls are from the trimming room, and it is now stated that 100 of them have walked out. With flags and banners, they formed in fours, and it is estimated that there were over 2,000 in the march."[30]

The spontaneous strike showed the capacity for workers to develop democratic and effective organization—they chose a representative committee, arranged picketing, held marches through downtown Oshawa, and made all their decisions at well-attended mass meetings. The strike attracted widespread attention—and offers of help from both the AFL and the ACCL. Members of the Communist Party also were among those supporting the strike and offering advice. A. C. 'Slim' Phillips,[31] chosen by the workers as the committee chairperson, favoured a charter with the ACCL, but was outvoted by workers who were convinced by some leaders of the Toronto Trades and Labor Council that the AFL was better situated to offer concrete support. They were also assured that they would be forming an "industrial union," a dubious promise since it was in complete opposition to the official policy of the AFL, which was to offer provisional federal charters only until workers could be assigned to existing AFL craft unions. Invariably this meant abandoning assembly workers who did not have craft qualifications. It was clear in the mass meetings that were held that the workers put a high priority on establishing a union, and the necessity of it being an industrial union.

During the strike, representatives of the Communist Party, including L. R. Menzies and Jack McDonald, a member of the Toronto Trades and Labour Council, spoke, sold copies of the CPC paper *The Worker*, and distributed leaflets.[32] The leaflets denounced General Motors in language that the *Oshawa Daily Times* described as "of the most violent and 'Red' nature."[33] The positions advocated by the Communists were prescient:

1. Picket the plants and secure 100 percent support for the strikers.
2. Organization of an industrial union.
3. Recognition of the union through direct negotiation with its representatives.
4. Restoration of the rates prevailing before the two wage cuts.
5. No victimization and all workers to be reinstated.
6. No return to work on promises of future arbitration.[34]

The warning against returning to work based on a promise of future arbitration ended up proving far-sighted. Unfortunately, it was ignored.

A mass meeting of workers on Thursday, March 29 rejected a recommendation from their committee to accept the company's offer of reinstatement of the trimmers, a return to work at the prevailing reduced wages, and arbitration by a federal Board of Conciliation.[35] The next day GM agreed to improve their offer by restoring wages to the level prior to the March cuts. Slim Phillips faced opposition from the Friday meeting but convinced the workers to accept this offer and return to work. There was no signed contract, but acceptance hinged on an understanding that a union would be organized, and James Simpson, the TLC Vice-President, arranged an AFL charter for the International Automobile Workers' Federal Labour Union No. 18011. It is important to note that while it was called a "federal labour union," the charter was actually for a local union that was not part of a larger union, but directly under the control of the central AFL. Eventually 3,774 workers signed up, making it "The largest local labour body ever organized in the Dominion at one time." Other AFL federal charters were soon granted to autoworkers in Windsor and Tilbury, but they did not establish any lasting presence.[36]

The new union claimed that they had achieved "Organization of a splendid Industrial Union, affiliated with Trades and Labor Congress of Canada and Chartered by the American Federation of Labor," in the first (and only) edition of their publication, *The Steering Wheel*.[37] However, the policy of the AFL was that "federal" unions "were usually transitory conveniences used to hold workers together until the appropriate craft unions could decide who were to be considered machinists, moulders, sheet metal workers, operating engineers, and so on. This process peeled off the skilled and some of the semiskilled, but left the remainder in limbo."[38] After the strike was settled, and before the conciliation report was completed, an AFL official approached Slim Phillips and asked him to organize the workers into crafts.[39] As the real policy of the AFL became clearer, it caused disquiet among workers who began to see it as a betrayal.

The real nail in the coffin of the federal union, however, was the result of the arbitration panel that the Communists had warned against. A Board of Conciliation and Investigation had been set up

Executive of the Federal Local. Front: R.W. Montgomery, Treasurer;
Robt. Stuart, Vice-President; A.C. 'Slim' Phillips, President; T.E. Maguire,
Financial Secretary. Back: Geo. Lemeu, Recording Secretary; Mary Jarvis,
Entertainment Committee; H.C. Cox, Publicity Committee.
(*Canadian Congress Journal*, Vol. VII, No. 6, June 1928)

consisting of a company representative, a labour representative (James
Simpson), and a chairperson.[40] The results handed down in a report on
May 28, 1928, were shockingly bad. The board ruled against union
recognition. They fully accepted GM's claim that productivity in
Canada was lacking and had to be brought into line with U.S. standards.
Finally, the board ruled that GM could review wage rates in the fall of
1928, prior to the introduction of its 1929 models. There was little doubt
this would mean further wage reductions. The ACCL concluded, "If
the bosses had had three representatives ... instead of one, they could
not have received a report more favourable to their interests."[41]

It would be difficult to dispute the conclusion drawn by the
Communists that the AFL charter was a dead end that had squandered
the militancy and organization of the Oshawa workers. At the inaugural
meeting of a second TLC federal union for auto workers in the Border
Cities, held on May 18, 1928, there were clashes between James Simpson
and Communists. Simpson ended up ranting about "agents of Soviet

Russia who would have the workers gain their ends by civil war, instead of by peaceful appeal to their employers."[42] The Communists responded in a June leaflet addressed "To All Automobile Workers in the Border Cities" that argued, "There are many valuable lessons to be learnt from the actions of the Oshawa workers. You must build a Union, **but it must be a real Industrial Union, under the control of the workers themselves**, if it is to be of real benefit to you."[43] [Emphasis in the original.]

The Communists may have failed to win over the majority of GM workers in Oshawa in March of 1928, but the lessons of that struggle showed that their arguments had merit, and they continued to organize guided by their basic principles.

Chapter 2

1928-1936:
Communists Build a Foundation

Communists were in the forefront of the continuing efforts to unionize auto workers after the collapse of the AFL federal union in Oshawa. Roger Keeran's research into the role of the Communist Party in the auto industry in the United States led him to this conclusion:

> In the 1920s and 1930s Communists in auto were the main voices on behalf of industrial unionism and class struggle. Their ideas—that auto workers needed a single union organized on an industry-wide basis (rather than many unions on a craft basis) and that the auto workers needed strikes (rather than government intervention or employer cooperation) to gain a union—proved apt and progressive. The ideas met the needs of auto workers and pointed to the path that the auto workers eventually took. Moreover, the Communists led the way in putting those ideas into practice. They built local unions. They led strikes. In the auto industry the Communists were not merely legitimate, they were experienced and often outstanding unionists.[1]

There is evidence to show that the same conclusion is warranted in Canada. Similarities between Communist organizing in Canada and the U.S. are to be expected, since the Communist Parties of both countries had close contact with each other, and participated in, and took their lead from, the Communist International (CI) and the Red International of Labor Unions (RILU). Nevertheless, there were also differences, generally due to differences in conditions between the two countries.

The key ideas described by Keeran were part of the broader principles of Communists internationally during this period. A distinction should be made between the underlying **principles** that Communists endeavoured to implement, and the **strategies and tactics** that they adopted in order to reach their objectives. Strategies and tactics are contingent on local, national, and international circumstances, and vary when those circumstances change. There is no doubt that there were significant changes in strategy by the Communist Party of Canada over the period from its founding at the beginning of the 1920s to the 1937 Oshawa strike, but there was also consistency in some basic principles and goals, particularly a class-struggle approach based on shop-floor organizing, militant strikes, and working-class unity.

Keeran notes, "Between the early 1920s and the late 1940s the Communist party went through six periods." The overall line of the Communist movement was determined by the analysis of international events but had implications for organizing carried out in individual countries, including changes in strategies in unions. The first three of those periods are relevant to this study of the Oshawa 1937 strike and the events that led up to it. Keeran describes the first period this way:

> From about 1923 until 1928, was a period that the Comintern viewed as the 'partial stabilization of capitalism.' In this period the Communists, through the Trade Union Educational League (TUEL), headed by William Z. Foster in the United States, attempted to 'bore from within' existing trade unions to support American recognition of the Soviet Union, amalgamate the craft unions into industrial unions, and organize the unorganized workers.[2]

There was a Trade Union Education League in Canada as well, that worked within the existing labour movement from 1923 to 1927.[3] Endicott states that the Sixth Congress of the Communist International or Comintern in the summer of 1928, "foresaw the capitalist world economy entering into a new phase of turbulence and crisis, a sharpening of the danger of war and of the class struggle."[4] During this second period Communists were called on to form independent, revolutionary unions in some industries (but not all). This strategy was implemented earlier in the United States, where the Trade Union Unity League (TUUL) was founded in September 1929.[5] The Canadian Workers' Unity League began on only a provisional basis in November 1929, and its First Congress did not take place until August of 1932.[6]

Then, Keeran notes, "from 1934 until 1939 the Communists followed the Popular Front, a line fully developed at the Seventh Congress of the Comintern in 1935." The focus on unity against rising fascism in this "Third Period" resulted in a decision that Communists in the United States and Canada would enter (or re-enter) AFL unions and join in building the newly established CIO.[7] Again, this new orientation was implemented in the U.S. first. The Communist-led AWU was dissolved in December 1934, after most Communists in the auto industry had shifted their activities to AFL federal unions and Mechanical Educational Society of America (MESA) locals. The TUUL was disbanded by early 1935.[8] In Canada, the Workers' Unity League held its final Convention in November 1935, and was not formally wound up until well into 1936.[9]

Communists themselves certainly believed that these changes in strategy and tactics did not mean changes in their fundamental principles. William Z. Foster, the leading union theorist of the Communist Party of the United States (CPUSA), surveyed "the long struggle of the left-wing and progressive forces for improved trade union organization, policies, and leadership" in his 1947 book *American Trade Unionism: Principles and Organization Strategy and Tactics*.[10] In his conclusion, Foster identifies seven key principles of the left-wing (a term he generally uses to refer to Communists) that he argues were consistent over the preceding twenty-five years, and that were essential to the progress of the union movement in the U.S. These seven principles are industrial unionism, militant unionism, trade union democracy, national trade union unity, international labor unity, independent political action, and the aspiration for socialism.[11] Each of these principles derives from undertaking organizing in the labour movement as part of organizing workers as a class in the struggle against capitalism.

Although there were earlier attempts to establish industrial unionism, the work of Communists in the late 1920s and early 1930s made its success possible. Combined with this was a militant approach of organizing workers to exercise their collective power against employers. Foster defines militant unionism as "unionism based upon the realities of the class struggle," and the rejection of class collaboration, the rejection of the belief in the "harmony-of-interests-between-capital-and-labor."[12] Militant actions, including strikes, sit-down strikes, and the other ways in which workers organized to demonstrate their power at the point of production were essential to the establishment of the UAW in the U.S., and were important in the success in Oshawa as well.

Trade union democracy certainly meant "rank and file expression" and control of unions to Foster. But it also meant the elimination of discrimination and barriers that severely weakened the labour movement, especially prior to the formation of the CIO. Foster rightly points out that "rank discrimination against Negroes regarding membership and employment, refusal to organize women and young workers, persecution and expulsion of left wingers, union election frauds, convention packing, financial corruption, and collusion with employers against opposition elements are only some of the principal undemocratic procedures that sapped and weakened A. F. of L. unions almost from that federation's inception."[13] Combatting discrimination, uniting workers of different ethnic backgrounds, and involving women workers were important to organizing autoworkers in Canada, and in the Oshawa strike. Rank and file democracy, particularly manifested by an extensive network of stewards and regular mass meetings, was absolutely critical to the success of the Oshawa strike.

A working-class outlook also leads to understanding the importance of national labour unity and of international solidarity. In Oshawa, being a part of the UAW-CIO was an expression of that solidarity, and Oshawa GM workers benefitted from it. A class outlook also inspired efforts to organize the unemployed and build working-class solidarity in the communities as well as in the workplace. All of these principles played a part in the efforts to organize auto workers in Canada, as well as the United States.

Communist Strategy for Organizing the Auto Industry – 1921 to 1929

In the 1920s the Communist Party of Canada supported the Red International of Labour Unions (RILU), and aimed to implement RILU strategies, as moderated by Canadian conditions. The *Program of Action* of the RILU was set out in a pamphlet by its General Secretary, Solomon Lozovsky, in July 1921. The program called for:

- Class struggle, not class collaboration
- Industrial unionism

- Factory committees
- Direct, mass action
- Involvement in parliamentary politics
- Establishment of a workers' press
- Equal wages for equal work, and organizing women as active fighters for the social revolution
- Working in unions to win over the masses.[14]

At least one Canadian attended the first RILU Congress—Joseph Knight, representing the Central Council of the One Big Union in Winnipeg.[15]

The Canadian program for carrying out the program of the RILU was laid out in future Communist Party of Canada Secretary General Tim Buck's 1925 pamphlet, *Steps to Power*.[16] The CPC approach was to organize within existing unions, by building workplace fractions, issuing shop papers, and contesting for leadership around a program of class struggle. *Steps to Power* advocated "one union for each industry," nationalization of principal industries, a united union central in Canada, and international solidarity based on class struggle as opposed to class collaboration. It is noteworthy that Buck emphasized organization and education of the "rank and file."

> The real struggle, in fact, is not so much in rallying the rank and file as in overcoming the opposition of the bureaucracy. It is this that makes rank-and-file organization essential. It is only by pressure exerted through rank and file organization that the membership can influence the majority of organisations, and certainly, if amalgamation, nationalization of industry, autonomy, etc., are to become the recognized aims of our labour movement, existing policies will have to be considerably changed.[17]

Fallout from the Oshawa 1928 Strike, Formation of the AWIU

In the wake of the events in Oshawa in 1928, Communist Party activists stepped up their organizing efforts in the auto industry in several centres in Ontario. The Auto Workers Industrial Union (AWIU) of the Border Cities (meaning Windsor and its surrounding area) was founded on June 1, 1928. The All-Canadian Congress of Labour (ACCL) praised the formation of the AWIU-BC, stating that "it offers the workers their only hope—emergence from craft unionism."[18] Meanwhile, there was further turmoil and dissatisfaction in Oshawa when a workers' committee reported that the AFL had not only broken the promise for an industrial union, but that the Local's resources had been squandered—only 75 cents remained in the Local's funds. The workers' committee made this recommendation:

> Whereas it is apparent that the automobile industry in Canada is in great need of a sustained organization campaign and that organization of the industry should be of an industrial nature, and whereas the American Federation of Labor has shown no interest or desire to conduct such a campaign, be it therefore resolved that this local union take steps to become affiliated with a more aggressive body and that the local executive be instructed to take the necessary steps.[19]

The response of James Simpson to *The Evening Telegram* showed the contempt that AFL leaders had for industrial workers. Simpson said "The Oshawa local has proved traitorous to the Federation. They are allowing themselves to be made tools of the Communists. Any troubles they have here are due to themselves and their lack of experience. They are all fools down there anyway ... The majority of the automobile workers in Oshawa are nothing but transplanted farmers, and they behave as such."[20] Simpson also disparaged the ACCL, stating, "I don't call it the All-Canadian Congress of Labor, I call it the All-Canadian Rats. They are nothing better than rats, and they are inspired in everything by Moscow." Simpson also showed his forecasting ability by scoffing at the idea that an organization formed by Canadian auto workers could have any lasting effect on the AFL, saying, "We have gone through that sort of thing before, and we always lick them to a standstill. They'll be crawling back to us within a year." It is noteworthy that Simpson tried to use anti-Communism to justify the AFL's unwillingness to organize auto workers. Simpson told the *Telegram* the next day that he had been misquoted, and somehow, he was able to convince at least some of the leaders of the Oshawa Local to remain in the AFL.[21]

Communist organizers meanwhile had been active in auto plants in Toronto and Oshawa as well as Windsor, resulting in a significant turnout at a national conference in Toronto on November 3, 1928, sponsored by the AWIU of the Border Cities. Delegates in attendance represented Ford, Chrysler, GM, Gotfredson, and Studebaker workers in the Border Cities; GM workers from Oshawa; and Dodge, Durant, Willys-Knight, and Ford workers from Toronto. There were fraternal delegates from the United Automobile, Aircraft and Vehicle Workers' Union of America (UAAVW—the successor to CWAW), including Phil Raymond, the UAAVW Secretary. The ACCL was represented by executive board members S. Sykes, from the OBU, and R. I. Bradley. Tim Buck, secretary of the TUEL, also took part.[22] The conference led to the formation on November 4 of the Auto Workers Industrial Union of Canada, which was immediately recognized as an affiliate of the ACCL.[23] Elected as officers of the new union were James Malcolm, President; Joseph Smith, Vice-President; and Harvey Murphy, Secretary-Treasurer. Tim Buck became General Secretary of the Communist Party of Canada on July 12, 1929. Harvey Murphy was a leading Communist union activist, and later was a key leader of the International Union of Mine Mill and Smelter Workers (Mine Mill).[24]

Meanwhile in Oshawa, workers' opposition to affiliation with the AFL continued to grow. Two membership meetings of the Oshawa local voted unanimously against remaining with the AFL. Another meeting in mid-November held by Simpson and other AFL supporters led to confrontation with members of the new AWIU group in Oshawa so heated that the police were called. Of forty-three people present only eleven stayed to listen to Simpson's appeal to maintain the AFL charter.[25] The AWIU organized in several locations during 1928, and by the end of the year they reported three active chapters with a total of 680 members. On the other hand, the AFL federally chartered locals never became established, and in Windsor and Tilbury they had ceased to function by the end of 1928. The AFL Local in Oshawa also was disbanded in early 1929.[26]

The AWIU advertised a mass meeting for Oshawa workers on Monday, March 4, 1929. The leaflet advertising the meeting focussed on the attacks on workers' living standards by GM through departmental wage cuts, and denounced the company's deceptive, paternalistic policies like the savings scheme designed to garner good publicity while pacifying resistance from workers.

> General Motors is trying to starve the progressive workers into submission by keeping them on the string waiting for work—work which will never come. In this way General Motors is squeezing the oldest workers out of the savings scheme—exposing the whole scheme as a trick and a farce, nothing but a publicity stunt and a means of splitting and dividing your ranks.[27]

Oshawa Workers!

Your Living Standards Are Being Cut from Under Your Feet

The millionaires running the automobile industry in Oshawa have found a new policy of stealing the bread of the thousands of workers employed here. Piecemeal cuts—that is the new policy. The big motor interests are deceiving the men, and keeping the men in each department divided from the rest of the shop, cutting here and cutting there; the General Motors has cut the general average wages by at least 25%. By this piecemeal policy of cutting wages, the company hopes to keep the ranks of the workers divided and thus prevent any effective resistance to the departmental wage-cuts. They are trying to pull the wool over your eyes in this way.

WHAT IS GOING ON?

In this fashion General Motors hope to maintain their enormous rates of profit and drive the fear of victimization and unemployment into the hearts of the workers.

General Motors is trying to starve the progressive workers into submission by keeping them on the string waiting for work—work which will never come. In this way General Motors is squeezing the oldest workers out of the savings scheme—exposing the whole scheme as a trick and a farce, nothing but a publicity stunt and a means of splitting and dividing your ranks. Every intelligent worker knows that General Motors to-day is making many thousands of dollars more out of the piece-meal wage-cuts than the workers have ever got out of the insurance scheme. Hundreds of workers, holding "gold medals" have been crowded out of the plant and are on their last legs to-day. These facts have been covered by a campaign of lies in the daily capitalist press.

YOUR LIVING STANDARDS ARE BEING CUT FROM UNDER YOUR FEET! General Motors are trying to keep your ranks split by their policy of deception, victimization, favoritism, and secrecy. No man can call himself a man and stand for such attacks upon his conditions of life.

WHAT ARE WE GOING TO DO?

As men able to defend your living standards, you cannot allow yourselves to be deceived and divided. Altogether for a struggle of defence against these unscrupulous attacks of the insatiable profiteers! The only weapon for this is organization. Every worker must sooner or later learn this lesson. The Automobile Workers' Industrial Union of Canada is that weapon which alone can defend you from these attacks.

The A.F. of L., which is proving itself to be a servant of the bosses in every industry and which is kow-towing and conspiring with the bosses against the interests of the workers by splitting the ranks of labor all over this continent—this organization must not be allowed to keep us divided. Your place is in the Industrial Union, where you will control and run your own affairs and not be dominated by a crew of highly paid bureaucrats. Here is what the Union stands for:—

1. A basic minimum wage rate (based on government estimates).

2. State unemployed insurance contributed to by employers with rates agreed to by Trade Unions and Trade Union administration.

3. 100% organization of auto workers and recognition of our union.

4. 8-hour day.

5. Time and a half for overtime.

6. Unconditional return of all victimized workers.

7. Time wages for every hour spent on the job.

Above all, we must fight to stop the wage cuts.

The place for every intelligent worker is in the Union. Get behind these demands! Don't wait until you get another slash in your living standards. Don't wait until you find yourself on the street! Don't be deceived by the lies and deceptions of the boss! SOLIDARITY OF THE WORKERS!

COME IN MASSES TO THE
MASS MEETING
MONDAY, MARCH 4th, 8 p.m.
Knights of Pythias Hall

A. R. MOSHER, President All-Canadian Congress of Labor and C.B.R.E., will speak.

Auspices, Executive Committee, Oshawa Local, Automobile Workers' Industrial Union of Canada.

Apply to ALFRED GILES, Secretary, Box 706, Oshawa, Ont.

Auto Workers Industrial Union leaflet calling for a mass meeting of autoworkers in Oshawa, March 4, 1929. (Author's collection)

The Mass Meeting notice repeated the demands for the eight-hour day, time and a half for overtime, and a 100 percent organization of auto workers and "recognition of our union." Added were two new demands for GM—"unconditional return of all victimized workers" and "time wages for every hour spent on the job." Notably, there were also two important political demands put forward—"A basic minimum wage rate (based on government estimates)" and "state unemployed insurance contributed to by employers with rates agreed to by Trade Unions and Trade Union administration." The meeting was held at the Knights of Pythias Hall in Oshawa, and it was advertised that A. R. Mosher, President of the ACCL, would speak. The leaflet was signed "Auspices, Executive Committee, Oshawa Local, Automobile Workers' Industrial Union of Canada. Apply to Alfred Giles, Secretary, Box 706, Oshawa, Ont."[28]

During 1929 the AWIU expanded its reach, establishing several locals in the Border Cities with others in Oshawa and Toronto. The AWIU was involved in a number of brief strikes in early 1929, and one longer, unsuccessful strike of tool and die makers in Oshawa in March.[29] In January, the AWIU began talks with the Detroit-based Auto Workers Union (the new name of the UAAVW) and made plans for international strike assistance and common demands, including plant safety and equal pay for equal work "regardless of age, sex, or race."[30] The AWU had Communist leadership at this time.

Two developments greatly hampered the efforts of the AWIU—aggressive actions by auto company managements to eliminate union organizing, and especially to get rid of radical activists, and a severe economic slump in the auto industry that began five months before the crash of October 1929. First to be fired were any workers associated with union organizing. The auto corporations also hired companies that spied on workers and identified union supporters so they could be fired. One such company, called Corporations' Auxiliary, was able to infiltrate the AWIU executive and provided information that enabled Ford and Chrysler to fire twenty activists in January 1929.[31]

Communist Strategy 1929-1935 – Independent Red Unions

The Communist strategy of primarily working within existing unions was altered after 1929, when the Red International of Labour Unions .

(RILU) advocated the formation of independent revolutionary unions. Lozovsky sent a letter to Toronto in February of 1929 urging the new approach. It was drafted by the Anglo-American Secretariat of the RILU at a time when Canadian Communists Leslie Morris, Sam Carr, and John Weir were prominent members of that body.[32] The new line for union work was consistent with the change in strategic direction of the Communist International (Comintern) that is popularly described as "the Third Period." The Third Period was marked by an emphasis on organizing workers on a class-struggle basis to challenge capitalism. Due to the devastating impact of the Depression on workers in western countries, including the United States and Canada, this strategy resonated with many workers. Many were also influenced by the example of the Soviet Union, which had avoided the severe effects of the Depression, and in fact carried out substantial industrialization during this period. Many union activists visited the Soviet Union during these years, and Canadian unionists continued to play a significant role in the activities of the RILU. The delegation of Canadians to the Fifth Congress of the RILU in late summer 1930 included five women, led by Rebecca (Becky) Buhay, and six male unionists, led by Tom McEwen.[33]

In the United States, the CPUSA adapted to the Third Period by relaunching the TUEL as the Trade Union Unity League (TUUL) at a Convention in Cleveland from August 31 to September 1, 1929. The 690 delegates approved a constitution that provided for three types of industrial organization—industrial unions, industrial leagues, and trade union minority groups. The minority groups worked within existing AFL unions. While the program of the TUUL proposed to form new unions "only where the A. F. of L. unions were decrepit or non-existent," it was clear that in the major industries that were mostly unorganized there would be attempts to launch militant, left-led industrial unions.[34] In Canada, the TUEL was relaunched under the name of The Workers' Unity League (WUL) only in January of 1930, and with less fanfare than the formation of the TUUL several months earlier. Although the WUL put more emphasis on founding left-led unions to organize in several basic industries, instead of working within existing unions, the principles advocated were still consistent with what was laid out in *Steps to Power*. The WUL Charter proclaimed:

Workers' Unity League Charter for the British Columbia
Relief Camp Workers' Union. (Commons.wikipedia.org)

The Workers' Unity League of Canada stands for the unity and organization of the Canadian workers in daily struggle to defend and advance
their economic interests. For this reason, the Workers' Unity League and
its affiliated unions pursue a firm class policy and fight for the united
front of the working class against the class of capitalist employers.

The workers must rely upon their own solidarity, unity and organized
strength to resist the attacks of capital and to defend and advance the
interests of the working people. The W. U. L. is therefore against all
schemes of class collaboration, compulsory arbitration and company
unionism which always serve only the interests of capital and are the
main line and policy of the agents of the capitalist class in the working
class movement.[35]

The Workers' Unity League was to be composed of 1) National
Industrial Unions, 2) National Rank and File Movements, 3) Local
Industrial Unions (where no National Industrial Union exists) and
Militant Rank and File groups (where no National Rank and File
Movement exists).[36] The WUL Constitution included this on "Fraternal
Relations":

The Workers Unity League of Canada shall strive to strengthen and improve its existing fraternal relationships with the Red International of Labor Unions, the Minority Movement of Great Britain and the Trade Union Unity League of the U.S.A. (without entering into any organic relations or connections with any of these organizations) and will seek to achieve fraternal co-operation with these organizations in the various trade union campaigns in the course of WUL activities.[37]

The WUL expanded to include a number of affiliated unions in major industries where the craft-centred TLC had no presence and no desire to organize. This included the Lumber Workers Industrial Union, the Industrial Union of Needle Trades Workers, the Shoe and Leather Workers Industrial Union, and the Fishermen and Cannery Workers Industrial Union. The WUL also had dual unions that contested with AFL-TLC affiliates, such as the Mine Workers' Union of Canada. The WUL founded the National Unemployed Workers' Association (NUWA) in 1930, and in 1932 chartered the BC Relief Camp Workers' Union that organized workers in relief camps (a Depression-era response of the Canadian government that put single able-bodied men to work for 10 cents per day).[38] A strike by the Relief Camp Workers' Union in April 1935 developed into the historic On-to-Ottawa Trek that ended with RCMP armed suppression of the trekkers and their supporters in Regina on July 1.[39]

The change in strategy of Communist organizers from working within TLC unions to founding independent, class-struggle unions had very little practical impact on workers at GM in Oshawa. By the time the WUL was founded, the AWIU had already left the ACCL, and there was no TLC presence at GM anymore, because the AFL federal local had disappeared. Organizing around the AWIU was all that was left in Oshawa, regardless of the broader national and international orientation. What *did* make a difference in Oshawa was the determined and courageous organizing that was done under Communist leadership amongst the unemployed, in ethnic organizations, and in maintaining a clandestine organizing presence in GM and other auto industry plants in the Oshawa area, all of which provided a significant base for later advances. These important building blocks were only possible because of the role of Communist activists guided by the principles and strategies of the CPC, RILU, and Comintern.

Economic Depression, Political Repression

The economic downturn in the auto industry was exacerbated by a disastrous drop in auto exports to Commonwealth countries that had accounted for around 30 percent of total Canadian production. The Depression followed, and from 1930 to 1933 some 50 percent of jobs in the auto industry disappeared. There were drastic wage cuts for the workers still working—the daily wage at Ford, for example, had been cut from $7 to $4 by 1933.[40]

This was also a time of heightened surveillance of activity by Communists, aggressive action by police in trying to prevent or disrupt meetings and organizing, and legal and political repression at the municipal, provincial, and federal levels, including deportations, and even the jailing of eight leaders of the Communist Party arrested in 1931 under Section 98 of the Criminal Code, including Tom McEwen of the WUL, who was given a prison sentence of five years.

The immediate impact of the economic downturn on the AWIU was that it made it difficult to collect dues from the members who were left. By mid-1929 the AWIU had been expelled from the ACCL for non-payment of per capita dues.[41] While the combination of adverse conditions led to the AWIU not functioning as an official organization, Communists continued to organize in factories and particularly among the unemployed. In the plants, Communists kept shop groups going, and produced and distributed "shop papers" that highlighted local grievances. The papers were mostly clandestine. Many were issued in the name of the Communist Party with names like *The Ford Worker* and *The Chrysler Worker*.[42] Frank Marquart, a tool grinder in a small auto industry shop in Detroit, helped AWU organizers by surreptitiously putting leaflets near the time clock. He describes the shop papers this way:

> They fairly bristled with live, on-the-spot shop reports, exposing flagrant health hazards in the paint shop, describing brutal acts of this or that foreman toward the men under him, citing facts and figures about speedup on specific job operations, revealing how workers got shortchanged by a bonus system no one could figure out …Those papers played a significant role in preparing auto workers' minds for the union thrust that was to come in the days ahead.[43]

In early 1930, there was an effort to revive the AWIU in Canada, and it became a WUL affiliate. George Wanden visited auto centres in

Shop papers issued by Communist Party of the U.S. factory and shop branches or nuclei in the late 1920s. (Robert Dunn, *Labor and Automobiles*, p. 203.)

an attempt to reorganize the old AWIU locals on a shop basis.[44] During the early '30s the Communists developed more clandestine organizing methods—individual discussions leading to home visits and the formation of shop groups. The shop groups discussed grievances as well as political theory. By the spring of 1933 there were fourteen shop groups in eight Border Cities' plants, as well as a central "shop council" with delegates from each shop group.[45]

Similar clandestine organizing was also taking place in Oshawa. In a 1982 interview, J. B. Salsberg, one of the CPC's leading union organizers in Southern Ontario, remembered that "the left wing concentrated certain talented people on Oshawa in the hope that they would succeed in breaking through the resistance." Salsberg mentioned Becky Buhay (in a rather condescending way) and Harvey Murphy,[46] who later were quite prominent in the CPC.

> Poor Becky trying to break through; very difficult; forming little groups and then something would happen and somebody would be fired or then there would be no work, it was quite seasonal in those days, and you felt she was doing yeoman work but there was little to show for it … very occasionally there would be a bit of fire break out from this smoke that these tried to build up and then it would collapse. While Becky and Murphy were there, they did win individuals, some of them they took into the Party, some formed little groups, but never really a breakthrough.[47]

In this very difficult period, there were still a number of department strikes in Oshawa. Strikes against wage cuts in April of 1930 and January of 1932 were listed by the Federal Department of Labour. In November 1932, a strike of polishers and buffers at Coulter Manufacturing in Oshawa, a GM supplier company, successfully won the reinstatement of workers who had been fired for asking for a wage increase.[48]

Communist organizing of the unemployed was vigorous and successful, particularly in Windsor, but in Oshawa as well. Local Unemployed Councils, as well as the National Unemployed Workers' Association (NUWA), coordinated activities. In Windsor, in addition to fighting evictions and advocating for relief, organizers also elected three progressive councillors in East Windsor in 1933.[49]

In July 1930, there was a rally in Memorial Park in central Oshawa against unemployment led by the CPC that attracted 250 people.[50] A larger rally and march were held in September of 1930, and as this organization continued, there was conflict over the political direction it should take. A local leader, Eddy McDonald, clashed physically with Communist activist John Farkas at one public event in Memorial Park.[51] McDonald and his supporters made charges, reported in the press, that the CPC had eight paid operators in Oshawa, as well as "four female teachers who taught communism to many of the children of foreign birth at the 'Red' school."[52] The *Oshawa Daily Times* applauded when McDonald expelled Harry Jack Grey from the unemployed association on the grounds that he was a "Red sympathizer."[53] McDonald was a one-time GM worker who exhibited an "eccentric and confused radicalism" in the words of researcher James Pendergest.[54] McDonald ran for Oshawa mayor twice, clashed with Communists within the unemployed workers organization, and also was charged with the theft of some railroad ties.[55] McDonald was later arrested for breaking the terms of his probation on the previous theft charge, and then deported.[56]

By 1932, McDonald's erratic leadership of the unemployed had been supplanted by steadier efforts by Communists under the auspices of the NUWA. In April, Sam Elliot led an unemployed rally in Memorial Park followed by a street parade. Elliot also led the May Day march in Oshawa, whose main demand was against the plan for a "food depot" for the unemployed.[57]

The level of unemployed organizing by the Communists was quite remarkable. By early 1933, the CPC was able to organize a Provisional Central Committee of Unemployed Councils. Oshawa was divided into sections and block committees were organized. A hall was rented downtown to serve as headquarters for the Unemployed Councils, and it was open to all workers daily from 10 a.m. to 10 p.m.[58] The Unemployed Councils opposed the attempt to force unemployed single men who ate in Oshawa's soup kitchen to sign statements that they were willing to work on a farm for five dollars a month. A successful united effort by the Unemployed Council, the Fathers' and Mothers' Associations, and the Women's Industrial League forced the Welfare Board to continue to provide relief to single unemployed men who refused to go to the government airport at Trenton to work for twenty cents per day. The victory was temporary, however, as eventually hundreds of men were forced to go to work camps at Trenton and Barriefield. *The Worker* reported that 200 men were cut off relief for refusing, and family relief was reduced from 70 cents per week to 40 cents.

Militancy grew, and eventually even married men on relief work went on strike in support of the single unemployed. A petition was circulated with the following demands:

1. That the Welfare Board open the hostel for all single men immediately.
2. That the Welfare Board cancel the contract with the Dominion Stores for bread, and that the unemployed be allowed to obtain their bread from whatever store they wish.

3. That the continual rise of prices of goods in the relief store be stopped, and that prices be stabilized on the basis of the lowest price during the last ten weeks.

It is notable that the bakers and bakery drivers supported this petition, since previously local bakeries supplied the bread to workers on relief and delivered it.[59]

Another important arena of Communist organizing was in various ethnic organizations. Manley notes that much of the core of Communist organizing in the auto centres was in ethnic communities, "Ukrainians in Oshawa, Finns, Ukrainians, and other Slavs in the Border Cities."[60] In Oshawa, left-wing Ukrainians were represented by the Ukrainian Labor Temple Association (ULTA), and meetings were held in what the local press termed the "Communist Hall."[61] Salsberg also mentioned Party work in Oshawa within "minority groups in Oshawa who had their national halls. Ukrainians and such. They would carry on amongst their people. So it began to spread and extend outside."[62] John Farkas, who had clashed with Eddy McDonald, was one of a number of workers of Hungarian heritage who played a role in Communist organizing in Oshawa. Ukrainian "Big Bill Gelech" is mentioned by Salsberg, and his name ended up on the UAW Local 222 founding charter.[63]

In addition to being subject to firing and arrests, foreign-born Communists and allied activists were faced with virulent prejudice, such as that exhibited by the *Oshawa Daily Times* against John Farkas, and more seriously, deportation for the "crime" of radicalism. There was a widespread targeting of Communists and people associated with them in the 1930s. This included the use of Section 98 of the Criminal Code to justify "raiding the offices of the Party and the homes of three of its leaders, and the offices of the Workers Unity League and the official paper, *The Worker*, on 11 and 12 August 1931." Eight leaders of the CPC were arrested and convicted.

> On appeal, the seditious conspiracy charges were dropped, but the Section 98 charges stood. Thus, after February 1932, the Communist Party's status as an illegal organization was confirmed; all of its members were chargeable under Section 98.[64]

After this decision, according to Barbara Ann Roberts, "the only evidence needed for deportation on political grounds was to prove that the immigrant was a member of some communist organization."[65] On May Day, 1932 raids were carried out in six cities, and eleven radicals were arrested, including John Farkas in Oshawa. They were kept incommunicado and sent to Halifax for deportation hearings. *The Canadian Labor Defender* described the raids in a June 1932 article:

> Workers were awakened in the early hours of the morning ... snatched away from their families, loaded into automobiles, taken miles from their homes, shipped aboard a train, bound for somewhere unknown to their families, friends or themselves. Once aboard a train, they were kept handcuffed and guarded by a heavily-armed escort of 'Mounties' ... On arrival in Halifax, these militant workers were placed in a huge dormitory at the Immigration Headquarters on the pier. For two days they were not allowed to communicate with their friends or to obtain defence counsel.[66]

Farkas had been active in the Unemployed Workers Association, ethnic organizations, and the Canadian Labour Defence League (CLDL). It was alleged that when arrested he had in his possession literature of an "extremely radical nature, revolutionary in its teachings and distinctly Communistic in its expression," and that he had "caused considerable trouble in Oshawa due to his radical tendencies and his active participation in demonstrations." Farkas was deported in December 1932.[67]

The Canadian Labour Defence League

The defence of workers or radicals targeted for arrests, deportations, or other legal victimization was a key facet of Communist organizing in the late '20s and throughout the '30s. The Canadian Labour Defence League (CLDL) was founded in 1925 to:

> unite all forces willing to co-operate in the work of labour defense ... that will stand as an ever willing and ever ready champion ... of the industrial and agricultural workers, regardless of their political or industrial affiliations ... who were persecuted on account of their activity in the struggle for the class interests of the industrial and agricultural workers.[68]

The CLDL began with a defence campaign for over seventy-five members of the Mine Workers Union of Canada awaiting trial in Calgary.[69] The CLDL defended some 6,000 people over the fifteen years of its existence and was successful in building broad support for a number of the causes it took on. The CLDL campaign against Section 98 and in defence of the eight jailed CPC leaders raised hundreds of thousands of dollars and generated broad public support, including massive petitions against prison conditions—one signed by 459,000 people, another by 200,000.[70] By the end of 1932, Petryshyn says, "the CLDL had managed to build up a huge protest movement with even the churches committing themselves against Section 98."[71] A local section of the CLDL was formed in Oshawa in January 1932, and called for the repeal of Section 98 and the release of political prisoners. The *Oshawa Daily Times* reported that there was a call to:

> Organize campaigns of protest against the "white terror" in other capitalist countries and to give moral and financial aid whenever possible to the victims of such terror; to collect materials and give publicity to facts regarding the persecution of workers and to expose anti-labor activities, labor spy systems, etc.[72]

The CLDL was affiliated to International Red Aid, as was the International Labor Defense (ILD) in the United States. There was considerable overlap and mutual benefit between the CLDL, the Communists, ethnic organizations facing discrimination and deportations, labour organizers, and many people who supported civil liberties and free speech and were appalled by police overreach—such as efforts to make it illegal to speak any language other than English at public meetings in Toronto. There was an infamous incident at the Strand Theatre in Toronto on January 22, 1929, when Toronto police threw a tear gas canister and arrested Philip Halperin for speaking in Yiddish at a memorial meeting marking the anniversary of Lenin's death.[73]

There was a noticeable shift in 1933. Economic conditions improved somewhat, and union organizing picked up. The auto industry in the U.S. was "riddled with strikes," and in contemplating one of the major battles, at Briggs Auto Body in Detroit in February 1933, Windsor Mayor David Croll noted "a change of temper which is very significant."[74] By 1934, worker militancy in the United States reached new peaks. The year was marked with three significant strike battles that lasted for months. A strike by an AFL Federal Labour Union at Auto-Lite, an automotive supplier in Toledo, began on April 12. Near the end of the seven-week strike, there was a five-day running battle between nearly 10,000 strikers and 1,300 members of the Ohio National Guard.[75] On May 9, 1934, the longshore workers in every U.S. West Coast port walked out. The strike by the International Longshoremen's Association lasted eighty-three days, and culminated with a general strike in San Francisco that won recognition for the union. The third strike was by Teamsters in Minneapolis and started on May 16, 1934. The strike by the International Brotherhood of Teamsters Local 584 lasted until August 22, featured some violent battles with the National Guard, gained support and sympathy strikes from other workers, and won a collective agreement. Remarkably, from May 16 to June 3, all three strikes were in progress at the same time. Communists or other left activists played a role in all of these epic battles. The 1934 worker militancy in the U.S. was not matched in Canada, but it provided inspiration and encouragement on both sides of the border.

In both the U.S. and Canada, organizing of unorganized workers was still being carried out almost exclusively by left-led organizations (the TUUL in the U.S., the WUL in Canada). The WUL was the most active labour body in Canada during the 1930s, expanding its membership to a peak of 40,000. In 1933 and 1934, the WUL "led a majority of all strikes and established union bases in a host of hitherto unorganized or weakly organized industries."[76] The WUL led a number of strikes in Southern Ontario shoe and furniture plants in 1933. During the Stratford furniture strike, Communists brought a delegation of strikers to a Windsor rally calling for the release of the CPC leaders jailed in 1931. The October 1933 event became a Stratford solidarity rally.[77]

WUL organizers such as Sam Scarlett and Fred Collins continued to organize in Windsor auto plants, and a major breakthrough took place in March, when 250 workers struck at Auto Specialties. The battle at Auto Specialties demonstrates the depth and effectiveness of the CPC/WUL organizing and preparation. The exciting events are described well in Manley's article "Communists and Autoworkers."[78] The strike began when fifteen workers presented a carefully prepared list of demands that included recognition of the AWU and a union shop committee, increased wages and pay per hour instead of piece rates, and an eight-hour day with time and a half for overtime. The demands were rejected, and several of the workers were fired. Within hours the strikers had functioning committees raising relief, organizing picketing, and handling publicity. A negotiating committee was selected. Workers picketed the plant and the Federal Employment office (suspected of recruiting scabs) and distributed leaflets. The round-the-clock picketing was sustained by coffee and hot meals from a permanent strike kitchen led by Georgia Ketcheson, a prominent Windsor Communist.

The importance of the Communists' prior work and strategies is clear in a number of telling details. The strike kitchen was set up in the Hungarian Hall, underlining the value of the Party's work with ethnic organizations. CPC organizing with the unemployed meant that when a call went out for unemployed workers to support the strike, "Hundreds of picketers crowded the sidewalk in front of the plant, forming an impenetrable chain of moving humanity that stretched for several city blocks."[79] Within a few days the strikers achieved notable success, including overtime after ten hours and recognition of a shop committee (but not formal recognition of the union).

The victory at Auto Specialties was followed by a successful strike at Windsor Bedding, but the WUL suffered a painful defeat in a strike at Canadian Motor Lamp, and other organizing efforts fell short. Auto companies used layoffs and firings to eliminate union activists. By the end of 1934 open AWU organizing was not being sustained, although the Party kept its shop groups going, mostly in an underground way.[80]

Manley points out that in the wake of setbacks in 1934, the CPC engaged in a review of the failures, and assessed the lessons learned. This was also at the same time that the position of the Comintern and RILU was shifting towards a united front policy. In the United States Communists were operating in the newly chartered AFL federal unions, as well as continuing to lead the AWU. Over the course of 1934, the emphasis shifted strongly to working in the AFL, because the federal unions were demonstrating a greater capacity to attract auto workers, and moreover, "Communists like Mortimer found it possible to do effective organizing without facing expulsion for their political or dissident ideas." The AWU in the U.S. was dissolved in December 1934, at which time most of the 630 Communist Party members in the industry were already working in the AFL, or the Mechanics Educational Society of America (MESA— which centred its organizing on skilled workers).[81] The Communists in Canada were following a similar path, and the Canadian AWU quietly disappeared at the end of 1934.[82]

Chapter 3

Setting the Stage

At the end of 1934, active organizing in the auto industry in Canada was at a low point, and consisted mostly of clandestine work by Communists and their allies. Yet, barely two years later, a massive strike broke out at the General Motors vehicle assembly plant in Oshawa. The strike was not only a success for the workers in Oshawa, but it finally breached the determined opposition of corporate owners and governments to industrial unions. What factors lay behind this dramatic change?

International economic and political developments were important, as were the policies and activities of the international Communist movement. The rise in labour militancy around the world, and particularly in the United States, often led by Communists or socialists, was critical. There can be no doubt that the patient and courageous organizing in the workplaces and community of Oshawa in the preceding ten years was also essential—the 1937 strike could not have succeeded without it. In the conduct of the strike itself, the strategies and tactics of the strike leaders were crucially important. This includes the organization and active participation of rank-and-file workers, successful efforts to build labour and community solidarity, and tough resistance to the extraordinary efforts of Ontario Premier Mitch Hepburn to interfere in the strike and prevent a settlement. Hepburn put pressure on GM of Canada management, attacked union organizers and their supporters, and used the media to try to whip up hysteria about the CIO, claiming Oshawa was "the first open attempt on the part of [John L.] Lewis and his CIO henchmen to assume the position of dominating and dictating to Canadian industry."[1] At one point, Hepburn told the press that it was necessary to have more police in Oshawa because he had a secret report that the CIO was working "hand-in-glove with international communism."[2] At crucial points there were attempts to derail or undermine the strike or compromise its goals that had to be defeated. It is evident that the ideological, strategic and tactical leadership provided by seasoned Communist activists and their supporters over the preceding years, particularly their commitment to a class struggle approach, provided lessons that made it more likely that the strike leadership stayed on track, or that the membership could correct them if they got off track.

The International Context

By 1937, the capitalist world was in the seventh year of the widest, deepest, and longest depression in perhaps a century. In North America, unemployment rates peaked at over 25 percent, and both urban and rural workers faced devastating poverty and losses, made all the worse by the fact that neither unemployment insurance nor medical care was available to most workers. The situation was similar in Europe and many capitalist countries around the world. Capitalism as an economic/political system was increasingly called into question. Communist movements gained in strength and influence as workers looked for alternatives to improve their conditions of work and life.

Labour militancy was on the rise in Europe, especially in France and Italy where there was a wave of workers carrying out sit-down strikes. Long militant strikes in the U.S. in 1934, especially the West Coast waterfront strike that led to the San Francisco General Strike, were shaking up relations between workers and capitalist corporate owners in the United States, and their success emboldened other North American workers. At the same time there was a growing movement to unionize the unorganized mass industries, such as auto and steel, that led to the formation of the Committee for Industrial Organization (CIO) within the American Federation of Labor (AFL), led by John L. Lewis and the United Mineworkers. This movement forced the AFL to charter the United Auto Workers in 1935 as a body to represent autoworkers in North America.[3]

The existence of the Soviet Union was a counter example of the possibilities of a society operated on a socialist basis. This was

Undated picture. Back: Lloyd Peel, Dick Steele, Bill Walsh. Front: Harry Binder, Karl Motkaluk, Joe Levitt. Lloyd Peel later played an important role in the 1949 wildcat strike at GM Oshawa. Steele, Walsh, Binder and Levitt were all prominent in the Canadian Communist movement. (Ontario Jewish Archives, Steele and Walsh family collection, 2017_2_12_1031)

particularly powerful when most of the capitalist world was engulfed in a seemingly unsolvable economic crisis. It was more powerful because there was an international Communist movement that developed collective strategies and provided leadership for the labour movement and other mass movements. Many U.S. and Canadian unionists, or workers who later became union activists and leaders, visited the Soviet Union during the 1930s. For example, Dick Steele and Bill Walsh were young travellers who ended up working in an industrial plant in Minsk and later in a plant in Moscow. They spent over two years in the Soviet Union from 1931 to 1933 and became committed Communists there.[4] On their return to Canada, both became active in the union movement, and Dick Steele spent some time in Oshawa organizing steel workers and cooperating with auto worker organizers.[5] Walter Reuther, who had been a member of the Auto Workers Union in Detroit in 1930,[6] visited and worked in the Soviet Union with his

Canadian Soldiers Tops Says Cpl. Lloyd Peel

One of the members of Local 222, in receipt of a letter from Bro. Lloyd Peel, now a tank Corporal with the invasion forces in France and Belgium, has turned it over to the Oshaworker for publication. Eliminating the few personal remarks of Cpl. Peel to his friend, the main body of the letter is quoted here below.

"As you know Paul K. (Paul Krawchuk who was killed in France was the first president of the Fur Workers at Robson Leather here.—Ed.) was in my squadron, in fact in my troop. We had both been "knocked out" of our tanks once. It was in the battle to close the gap that he got it for the second time and he failed to get out of the tank. It was a drive a la Russe and could have happened to anyone. He was a great guy and showed no lack of courage.

"The same day I had a few minutes' talk with Dick Steele after the attack was over. He was full of enthusiasm and very pleased he had the opportunity to kill so many Germans. A week later I heard he had been killed the next day. I guess you knew Dick as well as I did—no you couldn't have as we were together continuously while we were in England. He is my greatest loss of the war. I could never hope to have a better friend. It is impossible to believe this could happen to Dick, he was so full of life, never once did I see him depressed. His loss to us is tremendous. The first thing you know there will be tear drops all over this damn letter.

"The people of France seem to be very tired and dirty, while the opposite is true of Belgium. The children of Belgium are the handsomest in the world, really nice. We have had a terrific welcome in both countries. If your brother could be with the army now, he would be very proud of the Canadians. We think we are good.

"The boys don't need any propaganda to make them hate the enemy, especially the S.S. and the snipers. We captured a Russian boy from Moscow fighting with the Germans the other day. I don't know what to think of them. He was quite intelligent, age 21, captured at Smolensk in 1941, spent a dog's life in Germany, was told Russia was finished and that he would get good food, etc., if he joined the army.

"By the way our main course now is eggs, we exchange our cans for them."

As always,

Lloyd.

Letter from Lloyd Peel printed in the October 18, 1944, *Oshaworker* mentions the death in combat of Dick Steele. (*The Oshaworker*) brother Victor from November 1933 to June 1935. Both Walter and Victor Reuther (along with a third brother Roy) joined the early UAW organizing effort on their return. Walter Reuther was on the UAW International Executive Board at the time of the Oshawa strike.[7]

One of the most prominent unionists to visit the Soviet Union was J. B. McLachlan, a fiery Nova Scotia mine worker leader, who had led several major miners' strikes in the 1920s and who was jailed for seditious libel in 1923. McLachlan visited the Soviet Union in late 1931 including three weeks touring the coal-mining centre of the Donbas. On his return, McLachlan addressed public meetings of miners contrasting conditions they were facing with what he had observed in the Soviet Union. Whereas in Canada coal mines were noted for bad ventilation, unsafe work, and out-of-date machinery, McLachlan reported that in Soviet mines "the machinery is the last word in modern efficiency and the mines are absolutely safe. The timbers are of a quality never used over here and they are placed side by side to avoid down falls. In all the time I visited, I did not see one hang-over or rotting and broken timber." Beyond working conditions, McLachlan noted that miners earned high salaries—higher than office workers and even doctors—and at production meetings "the workers had all the say." Further, "in Canada there were 600,000 unemployed. In Russia none." David Frank reported that "each example was driven home with effect. 'Can you imagine that being done here?' McLachlan asked, and the answers came back in ripples of laughter throughout the audience."[8] McLachlan was President of the Workers' Unity League from its founding in 1930 to its dissolution in 1936.[9]

United Front Against Fascism

The coming to power of Hitler in Germany in 1933 and his alliance with fascist Italy and Japan marked another significant international development that had strong repercussions in North America. Unions were being crushed by fascist governments in Germany and Italy, and fascist organizations were gaining support, not only in Eastern Europe and France, but also in Britain, the United States, and Canada. There were also strong signals that the ruling class in Western countries were happy to acquiesce to Hitler's expansionism or even encourage it, especially if they felt that it would be primarily directed against the

Ford workers and their children picket during the April 1941 strike
at Ford's Rouge complex. Their signs point out that Henry Ford had
received a medal from Hitler. (The Henry Ford Museum)

Soviet Union. Elites from members of the British royal family to Henry
Ford showed their fascist sympathies.[10]

Ford's friendly relations with Hitler figured in UAW organizing
campaigns from 1937 to 1941. The UAW published Upton Sinclair's novel,
The Flivver King, in 1937. The novel depicts Henry Ford as the title char-
acter, a right-wing antisemite and virulent anti-Communist.[11] There is
also a widely reprinted photo of children picketing during the April 1941
Ford Strike carrying signs that say, "Why did Ford get a Nazi medal?"
and "Ford Hitler" with a large swastika in between those two words.[12]

In light of the growing threat of fascism internationally, the
Comintern began to advocate for a broadly based United Front against
Fascism that included social democrats and others. In Canada, as
within the broader Comintern, this shift was the result of a period of
debate between supporters of the new approach and those who argued
for maintaining the previous strategy. Stephen Endicott, in *Raising the
Workers' Flag*, notes that this debate took place beginning in early 1933
and was not resolved until 1935. Endicott quotes E. H. Carr's view that
"it was the pressure of external events rather than 'pressure from
Moscow' which drove the Third International 'along the path of a
united, and later the popular, front.'"[13]

By March of 1935 the Red International of Labor Unions declared that conditions "were extremely favourable for a broad fight for trade-union unity."[14] The Third (and as it turns out, the final) Convention of the Workers' Unity League, in November 1935, endorsed a resolution calling for "One Union—One Industry."[15] Following this resolution, WUL unions negotiated unity with AFL unions in their industries. At this time the unions that made up the Committee for Industrial Organization (CIO) were still part of the American Federation of Labor, and so it is the AFL that WUL militants entered – in most cases with their Local Unions and Local Union leadership intact.[16] The formal decision to disband the WUL came in April 1936.[17]

While this was happening, the WUL union for autoworkers, the Auto Workers Industrial Union (AIWU) did not have functioning local unions, and so there was no formal process of merger negotiations with an AFL union in the auto industry. In the United States the AFL had chartered "federal unions" for workers in auto assembly and parts plants for a few years, and finally agreed to bring them together at a convention to found the United Auto Workers in 1935. Initially the UAW was directly administered by the AFL and had no democratically elected leadership. But rank-and-file pressure and the organizing of determined left leaders like Wyndham Mortimer forced the AFL to allow the UAW to become an independently functioning union at its 1936 convention. By the end of 1936, organizers and militant workers in Canada were working to establish UAW locals on this side of the border.

In both the United States and Canada, the new Communist policy led to the decision to call for unity of the labour movement and the dissolution of the left-led labour centrals, the Trade Union Unity League in the U.S., and the Workers' Unity League in Canada. Because this was happening at the same time as the creation and explosive growth of the CIO, the result was that thousands of experienced and competent Communist union organizers became part of the CIO organizing efforts. The call for a united movement against fascism gained support in Canada, including amongst workers. There were anti-fascist protests, including demonstrations against German warships visiting Montreal and Vancouver.[18] The Committee to Aid Spanish Democracy was sponsored by prominent unionists and CCF leaders, and 1,200 Canadian volunteers fought in Spain as the Mackenzie-Papineau Battalion defending the Popular Front government against Franco's military coup.[19]

Formation of the UAW, Flint Sit-Down Strike

Labour militancy picked up in the United States sooner and more broadly than in Canada, particularly in the auto industry. The Communist-led Auto Workers Union played a leading role, but there was organizing activity by other unions as well. The Industrial Workers of the World (IWW) in Detroit held shop gate meetings, distributed literature, and had a six-day-a-week radio program.[20] The very militant Mechanics' Educational Society of America (MESA), which mainly represented tool and die makers and other tooling trades in Michigan, was founded in 1933. In September 1933, MESA struck for a single contract that would cover workers at tooling shops owned by the auto companies, and also workers at independent tool shop contractors. The strike occurred in the three major auto centres of Detroit, Pontiac, and Flint. When scabs were employed in several shops to try to break the strike, a roving group of strikers drove from one strike-breaking shop to another storming the gates, breaking windows, and making bonfires of blueprints to prevent work continuing. The action was dubbed "the riotcade" by the press.[21] The Associated Auto Workers of America (AAWA) and the Automotive Industrial Workers Association (AIWA) were other independent unions of auto workers that functioned at that time.[22]

The growing demand for unionization in auto and auto parts shops had led the AFL to issue direct federal charters to several Locals in the U.S. Unlike the federal charter issued to Oshawa GM workers in 1928, the federal unions in the States had more staying power. Several of them were led by Communists or other leftists, notably the White Motor Local in Cleveland led by Wyndham Mortimer. Mortimer had organized a Local of the AWU in 1933, but when the AFL offered a federal union charter, and faced with an onslaught of anti-Communism, the AWU Local decided to dissolve and have all their members join the federal union. Keeran notes, "Soon Mortimer and his supporters had distinguished the union as one of the most militant, independent, and successful locals in the industry."[23]

The White Motor Local, along with several other federal unions, began a strong push for an AFL charter for an industrial union covering the auto industry. MESA and the AWU supported the same position. The AFL responded to the growing pressure by calling a National Conference of United Automobile Workers Federated Labor Unions on June 23 and 24, 1934. The AWU issued an "Open Letter" to the Conference calling for "a united industrial union of all auto workers, including the member[s] of all unions and crafts in the auto industry, with control lodged in the hands of the workers in the shops."[24] Despite vigorous opposition, the Conference voted to form a National Council, rather than establishing an industrial union. Wyndham Mortimer's White Motor local then set up the Cleveland District Auto Council (CDAC), which became the centre of dissident forces. The CDAC published the first UAW newspaper, *The United Auto Worker*, edited by Henry Kraus (who was close to the Communist Party). Before long the paper had a circulation of 65,000 being distributed to autoworkers through contacts Mortimer made at the Conference.[25] An August 1934 conference held by the CDAC issued a manifesto that urged "a policy of aggressive struggle against the employers, the establishment of militant leadership in the unions, and the unification of the federal local[s] into an International Union within the AFL based on the principle of industrial unionism and rank and file control."[26]

The AFL leadership eventually gave in to the sustained pressure and called a Convention to found the United Automobile Workers in August 1935. However, the AFL maintained control of the new union—including appointing the president and executive. Two months later, the 1935 Convention of the AFL again debated the need to organize the unorganized and unionize the growing mass industries of rubber, steel, and auto. John L. Lewis of the United Mine Workers (UMW) became a leading spokesperson for this demand. When it was voted down, Lewis convened a group of supportive unions who formed the Committee for Industrial Organizations (CIO) within the AFL.[27]

Communist policy in the U.S. had already started to shift away from a focus on the Communist-led unions of the TUUL. In January 1934, the CPUSA Political Bureau issued a directive to Communist organizers to strengthen opposition work within the AFL and independent unions.[28] When the AWU was dissolved in December 1934, it was down to 21 locals and 450 members. Keeran noted, "Most of the 630 Communist party members in the industry were already functioning in the AFL and MESA unions."[29]

Mortimer and other reformers continued to organize, and by the time of the second UAW Convention in April of 1936, they had an unstoppable majority. The UAW convention that opened in South Bend, Indiana, on April 27, 1936, "represented the triumph of the Communist-initiated Progressive movement for an international, industrial union that was controlled by the rank and file and was geared to militant organizing and strike action."[30] Once the UAW had control of its own affairs, the AAWA and AIWA joined, as did many members of MESA.

The newly independent union made the bold decision to take on the task of organizing the hundreds of thousands of unorganized auto workers by starting with General Motors, the largest and wealthiest corporation in the world. The UAW had only $25,000 in the treasury at the time. Wyndham Mortimer, by then the UAW First Vice-President described it this way:

> We had however, something that money could not buy. We had confidence and a spirit of sacrifice that eventually enabled us to accomplish what many had thought was impossible. We spent the first month after the convention in surveying the situation in the industry … we decided that our main effort must be to strike General Motors after the Christmas holidays. We set January 1, 1937, as the deadline.[31]

The UAW strategy centred on two GM plants, Fisher Body #1 in Flint, Michigan, which stamped body components for all Buicks, Pontiacs, and Oldsmobiles, and the Fisher Body plant in Cleveland, Ohio, which made all the stampings for Chevrolet. Striking both plants would paralyze virtually all GM operations.[32] The Cleveland plant was well-organized (Cleveland was Mortimer's home base), but Flint was not. The five Locals in Flint originally chartered by the AFL were down to only 122 members, and these were regarded by most auto workers in Flint as paid agents of GM. Mortimer, later assisted by Bob Travis and Henry Kraus, carried out a careful organizing campaign over the next several months, carefully side stepping the 122 untrustworthy members.

On December 28, a strike broke out in the Cleveland Fisher Body plant sparked by some firings, and the workers occupied the factory.

NEW MASSES
FEBRUARY 1937

Behind the Auto Strike

New Masses, February 1937

Mortimer promised the workers the full support of the International Union and issued a press release stating that the strike would only be settled as part of a national agreement with GM. At this point, GM management must have realized their vulnerability and quietly began to remove the crucial dies from Fisher #1. A worker notified Travis who immediately called a lunchtime meeting in the union hall across the street. The decision was made that only a sit-in could stop the dies from being removed and protect the workers' jobs. The workers left the meeting, returned to the plant, and took it over. Thus started the incredible forty-four-day Flint sit-down strike.[33]

Over the next several weeks, the strikers withstood attacks by the Flint police, injunctions, efforts to freeze them out by cutting off the heat and water, and furious attacks by media. They set up their own council with a mayor and their own police force. The company police were asked to leave, and the union patrolled the plant, keeping everything clean and orderly. A nearby restaurant was turned over to the strikers, and volunteers prepared food under the supervision of a professional cook from the Detroit Cooks Union employed by the union and delivered it daily to the sit-downers.[34] The rank-and-file democracy and engagement of workers were remarkable, and key factors in the sit-downers being able to maintain their occupation for the long haul. Walter Linder, a former CPUSA union organizer, wrote a history of the Flint Sit-Down Strike. He described the internal organization of the sit-down this way:

> Once inside they set about organizing one of the most effective strike apparatuses ever seen in the United States. Immediately after securing the plant, they held a mass meeting and elected a committee of stewards and a strike strategy committee of five to govern the strike. Bud Simons was elected chairman, and Walter Moore and Joe Devitt, all leaders of the original sit-down on November 13, had central roles on this body. Then committees were organized: food, police, information, sanitation and health, safety, "kangaroo court," entertainment, education and athletics. Since all committees were democratically elected, their authority was unquestioned. The supreme body remained the 1,200 who stayed to hold the plant, the rest being sent outside to perform other tasks. Two meetings of the entire plant were held daily at which any change could be made in the administration.[35]

The Flint sit-down strike was also notable for the engagement of women in strike support activities. A women's auxiliary organized everything from meal preparation to visiting committees to strikers' wives (the "Goodwill Committee"). The famous Women's Emergency Brigade played a critical role in battles with police and GM security.[36]

The sit-down strike attracted immediate and worldwide attention. It was the major news story of the day and dominated news reels, newspapers, and radio. Even *Life* magazine had a cover story and seven-page photo spread of scenes from inside and outside the struck plants, including pictures of Joe Devitt, Bud Simons, and Simons' family.[37] The *Life* article begins:

> One of the least influential labor unions in any major U. S. industry, up to the end of 1936, was the United Automobile Workers of America. Within ten days after 1937 began, the members of this hitherto puny union had effectively tied up great General Motors Corp. They had done it by the simple process of sitting down in a few strategic plants, refusing to budge. Sit-down is a new word in Labor's vocabulary, a new tactic in its battle. U. A. W. imported it from France, tried it out in parts-making industries before using it for a frontal attack on General Motors. [There were] 89,000 workers who were sitting down on Jan.8.

The Flint sit-down strike received prominent coverage in Canadian media, with the *Toronto Daily Star* featuring photos of the sit-downers

The Women's Emergency Brigade played a crucial role during the forty-four-day Flint Sit-Down Strike. Dorothy Kraus is sixth from the right. (Walter P. Reuther Library)

Life magazine January 18, 1937, featured the Flint Sit-Down. The caption is, "A mass meeting of 1,200 strikers is held in Fisher No. 1 with Bud Simons (left on platform) presiding, an organizer speaking."

and Michigan National Guard emplacements during the strike, and a banner headline on page 1 when the strike was settled (displacing coverage of the Dionne quintuplets).[38]

On January 11, 1937, the heat was turned off to the occupied plant and the Flint police gathered outside. They attacked the plant, using teargas to try to force the workers out, but they were repelled by streams of water from hoses and car door hinges and other projectiles. The police opened fire, wounding fourteen workers, but they were forced to retreat from what the strikers called "The Battle of Bulls Run." GM was granted an injunction, but it collapsed when it was revealed that Judge Black, who had issued it, owned 3,665 shares of GM stock. When another injunction was issued and the sit-downers refused to leave, Governor Murphy called in the Michigan National Guard, and they set up machine gun placements overlooking the plants. To regain the initiative, the union organizers came up with a daring plan. They discussed plans to seize Chevy Plant 9 at a clandestine meeting with selected trusted members, knowing that a few of them were company spies. When a battle broke out the next day at Chevy 9, GM was prepared and rushed all of their security forces there, brutally attacking workers inside while members of the Women's Emergency Brigade smashed windows to allow fresh air to blow away some of the tear gas being deployed. Meanwhile the crucial Chevy Engine Plant 4 was left unguarded, and the union forces were able to seize and barricade it. This forced GM back to the bargaining table.[39]

After forty-four days, the sit-downers achieved the seemingly impossible—an agreement by GM to recognize the UAW and bargain a contract with them. It would be difficult to exaggerate the importance of the victory and its impact on workers in the United States, Canada, and internationally. Roger Keeran judged it, "the most significant triumph ever for the UAW, the CIO, and mass production workers generally." Keeran continued:

> The GM victory stimulated a massive wave of sit-down strikes. One day, shortly after the GM settlement, Detroit experienced 18 sit-down strikes, and Detroit Superintendent of Police Fred M. Frahm, claimed that Communists were active in 'practically all' of them. With or without Communists, sit-downs, conventional strikes, and strike threats soon produced UAW contracts with Chrysler, Hudson, Packard, Studebaker,

TORONTO, SATURDAY, FEBRUARY 6, 1937

MACHINE GUNS TRAINED ON STRIKE PLANTS IN FLINT

With their machine-gun mounted and trained on General Motors plants in Flint, Mich., these national guardsmen stand guard as Governor Frank Murphy of Michigan works to bring about a peaceful conciliation between plant officials and leaders of the automobile workers sit-down strike. A court order demanding sit-down strikers leave the plants was granted but strikers have refused to leave in spit of the threat of force.

On February 6, 1937, the *Toronto Daily Star* ran this photo, with the caption "Machine Guns Trained on Strike Plants in Flint."

The UAW forced GM to recognize the union on February 11, 1937,
after the forty-four-day sit-down strike in Flint. (UAW)

Briggs, Murray Body, Motor Products, Timken Detroit Axle, L.A. Young
Spring and Wire, Bohn Aluminum, and most other major auto firms except
Ford. UAW membership jumped from 88,000 in February to 400,000 in
October. The impact of the GM strike spread well beyond auto. In 1937,
some 477 sit-downs occurred, affecting 400,000 workers.[40]

The Flint sit-down strike was certainly judged to be a significant
victory by the Communists. William Weinstone, Secretary of the
Michigan District of the CPUSA, wrote that the victory consisted of
several things, starting with "the fact that the union was able completely to paralyze production for forty-four days" thereby forcing GM
to grant collective bargaining rights. Weinstone also heralded the
ability of the union to withstand violent attacks on the occupied plants
and to defeat injunctions. Weinstone stated that the last indicator of
the union's victory:

Consists finally in the fact that the policy of industrial unionism and progressive leadership, based upon rank-and-file democracy, has proven to be

the only correct form of organization which can effectively meet and defeat the corporations of big capital.[41]

The emphasis on rank-and-file democracy, progressive leadership (by which Weinstone certainly meant leadership by people with a Communist outlook and their allies), and industrial unionism brings us back to three key principles of working class organizing advocated by Communists that were of significance before and during the upsurge of working-class battles in the 1930s.

In particular, Weinstone pointed out that Communists played a vital role in the Flint sit-down through preparation for the strike, and in mobilizing support during the strike. "At the most decisive points of the struggle," noted Weinstone, "the Communist workers combated any tendency to waver in the face of the sharp blows of the enemy and helped keep the ranks as firm as possible."[42]

Weinstone highlighted the distribution of the *Daily Worker* during the strike, which he says was generally welcomed by the workers, and was of value, because, "where democratic policies prevail and the opinion of all groups is allowed, there the consciousness of the workers is highest and the greatest unity and militancy obtain."[43] The CPUSA was not without self-criticism in this review, however. Weinstone commented on "the necessity of showing to the workers the face of the Party," and said, "This was by no means done to any sufficient extent during the strike."[44]

One of the first major battles following the Flint victory occurred on March 8, 1937 when over 60,000 Chrysler workers occupied every Chrysler plant in Detroit. The sit-down featured much the same inspiring scenes of worker control as Flint, and lasted seventeen days, until Chrysler agreed to negotiate and promised that the plants would remain shut down and no scabs would be brought in. A contract was signed a week later.

On February 16, 1937, the UAW began the negotiations called for by the February 11 agreement. The top UAW leaders faced a very intransigent management, but finally reached an agreement on March 12 that "covered grievance procedure, recognition of shop committees (stewards), wage adjustments, six-month probationary period, lay-offs and rehires by seniority, seniority retained in transfers, and posting of seniority lists."[45]

North of the Border: 1935 and 1936

At the beginning of 1935, conditions in the auto industry in Canada were dramatically different than in the U.S. where burgeoning organizing was taking place. Where 137 delegates from 77 federal labour unions had taken part in the June 1934 National Conference in the U.S., in Canada no federal labour unions had existed since 1929. The auto sector in Canada was significantly smaller than the U.S. industry, and dominated by U.S. companies motivated by high tariffs to assemble vehicles in Canada for the domestic and (duty-free) Commonwealth export markets.[46] Robert Dunn's survey of conditions in the auto industry in 1929 noted this about Canada:

> Automobile companies from this country [the U.S.] have secured such a hold on the Canadian industry that the Canadian production of cars is now usually included in figures dealing with U.S. production ... Of the 14 makes of cars produced today in Canadian plants only one (the Brooks Steamer, in a factory that turns out one a day!) is not produced in the United States.[47]

In 1928 Ford had 170,000 workers in the U.S. (120,000 in Detroit), and although it was the largest auto employer in Canada, it had only 10,000 workers on this side of the border. GM had 209,500 workers in the U.S., and under 10,000 in Canada.[48]

The AFL-affiliated union centre in Canada, the TLC, was showing no signs of making any efforts to organize any mass production industries. In fact, "the TLC showed little appreciation of the union-building possibilities presented by the rising level of class struggle in 1933-34. Instead, it provided plenty of evidence that its anti-communism was as strong as ever."[49]

With no real alternatives, Canadian Communists continued their work with the WUL. In 1933 and 1934, there had been an upsurge in strike activity, and the WUL led over 50 percent of the non-coal mining industry strikes, encompassing 50 percent of striking workers and 71 percent of striker days.[50] Improvements in wages and/or working conditions were achieved in three quarters of those strikes. However, by the end of 1934 progress was ended by some painful defeats. In 1935, the Communist position internationally and in Canada was shifting towards the united front approach and greater unity with established union centres, but there was less room for that to happen in Canada than in the U.S. In February 1935 the WUL President, J. B. McLachlan, and General Secretary, Tom McEwen, issued an open letter proposing the amalgamation of all existing trade unions on a basis of common resistance to the attacks of capital and a program of 100 percent unionism based on full trade-union democracy.[51] The TLC and ACCL declined to reply to McLachlan's letter offering to discuss restoration of unity through a merger.[52]

The Third Convention of the WUL in November 1935 turned out to be its last. The central policy resolution presented called for "One Union—One Industry" and cooperation with the TLC, ACCL, and the Catholic and independent unions. "We are prepared to agree that WUL unions shall merge with other unions, even if this means that the WUL unions would sever their affiliation with us and affiliate to the AFL," said McEwen.[53] Endicott notes that this implied that "the WUL was prepared to go as far as ending its separate existence as a trade union centre ... and to lead its 35,000 members, including 6,000 to 7,000 communists, back into the AFL and the Trades and Labour Congress of Canada."[54]

By the end of 1935, the CPC was urging the WUL unions to join the TLC under whatever terms could be arranged. Many WUL locals simply changed their names and continued to operate with their existing leadership. Endicott noted that in this process "many left wingers gained executive or organizers' posts."[55] Thus, by 1936, the main strategy of the Communists in the labour movement in Canada is described by Manley as building a left caucus in the international movement that "coaxed the CIO north while pursuing its main objective of winning over the TLC to industrial unionism."[56]

Underground Work

Since the defeats and difficulties at the end of 1934, the AWU in Canada had mainly operated on an underground basis. Nevertheless, organizing by Communists continued in auto assembly and parts plants. In Oshawa, a union presence was also maintained by the Moulders Social Club, which represented skilled iron moulders. Meanwhile activists at the Toronto Ford assembly plant produced and distributed the *Ford Auto Worker* on a bi-weekly basis, a rather ambitious achievement for a clandestine operation.[57] The Fittings Foundry in Oshawa was the site of one of only two auto strikes in 1935, and Communists played an active role.[58] The strike was led by the Moulders Social Club. The *Oshawa Daily Times* noted that "the strikers are being supported in their efforts by the Oshawa Protective Workers Association, which was active in the attempted relief strike about a month ago."[59]

One example of the informal workplace rank-and-file actions being undertaken was in the axle department in the McKinnon plant in St. Catharines, and was written about in *The Worker* in April 1936. When management tried to relocate a group leader who was considered to be fair and reasonable in the distribution of the group bonus, all the workers in the shop signed a "round robin" threatening to strike unless the transfer was rescinded. The company granted their demand.[60] The Communist *Daily Clarion* reported on relatively successful short work stoppages in the Oshawa GM plant, notably a one-hour strike by trim line sewing machinists.[61] George Burt remembered that "by 1936 we were ripe for the union. You could see it coming in the increasing number of stoppages, particularly in the body shop."[62]

Tim Buck was leader of the Communist Party of Canada at the time and had been involved in the formation of the AWIU in 1929. Buck notes that:

> We had been forced to organize the union in an underground way because General Motors in Oshawa and the Ford Company in Windsor had both adopted the practice of eliminating any man who was even suspected of working to build a union. The result is that we had rather small local unions operating as completely underground organizations in these plants and in the McKinnon plant in St. Catharines. These organizations were well-known to the workers in the plant, but their officers and the number of members were not known. The union was fairly strong and influential in the body department at General Motors, particularly among the upholsterers.[63]

Communist activists operating within the AWU (formerly the AWIU) or WUL were still the only ones working to organize the auto industry in Canada in 1935 and 1936. The number involved is hard to know for certain, given the clandestine nature of the organizations, but it is likely that there were hundreds of workers involved in the auto plants. This is substantiated by the recollections of early union activists who had direct or indirect knowledge of this work. Bill Rutherford is one. Rutherford later became a leading figure in Local 222 as a leader

These Men Lead Local 222 During 1945

Edwin Nicholls, back row centre, towers over the rest
of the 1945 Local 222 Executive Board. (Local 222)

of the Skinner plant unit (later Houdaille) and was vice president of the
Local for a time. Rutherford remembers that, "really the UAW started
through the Workers Unity League before Schultz or Millard or those
guys ever joined the union. There were 600 or 700 members there …
It's the All Workers Unity League. Actually, it was a Communist Party
organization."[64] Rutherford's recollection has added weight because
according to Don Nicholls, "the secretary of that union [AWIU] at that
time was Bill Rutherford Senior, not the guy from Houdaille, but his
dad."[65] Don Nicholls' account of his own father's experience underlines
the secretive methods of organizing that were necessary, but also the
extent of it:

> He happened to know the secretary [of the AWIU], but other than that, he
> only knew the person who handed him the literature and the person to
> who he handed it off to afterwards. So that way, if somebody was caught
> or whatever, they could only squeal on two other people. And there was
> over 300 members of that Auto Workers Industrial Union in 1937 when the
> UAW came in. So they had a pretty good base to organize from. That was
> a left-wing union, of course.[66]

Don Nicholls' father had worked at a supplier company that made
plush for the seats for GM, and left there to work at GM in 1929. "He

joined the Auto Workers Industrial Union and that was part of the Workers' Unity League." Don's father, Edwin Nicholls, was later an activist member of Local 222 and held elected positions including being a member of the Local Executive Board.

Joe Salsberg, at the time a leading union organizer for the CPC, confirms the presence of WUL organizers, but reports a smaller number. "I don't know how many would be in the WUL in Oshawa. We never really kept books, but I would say that there were always a couple of dozen who would be looked upon as stable contacts and people who dare occasionally to come out."[67] Memory is tricky, and Rutherford and Nicholls may be reporting optimistic numbers, but on the other hand, Salsberg may well have played down the numbers because this interview was done in 1982, more than twenty years after he had left the CPC when he had become pointedly anti-communist.[68] There are other sections in the interview where it is clear Salsberg downplays the role of others, making disparaging remarks such as referring to Becky Buhay as "poor Becky," and calling a member of the Young Communist League who introduced him at a 1936 rally against fascism in Oshawa, "the little girl." Whatever the actual number of members, it is clear that the WUL had built a substantial network of activists and supporters with influence in the workplace. This strong base of WUL activists in key auto plants, meant that the second major effort to organize Oshawa took place on a far stronger foundation than in 1928—there was now a base of experienced activists who were committed to a working-class perspective.

Company Union

In 1935, GM of Canada President R. S. McLaughlin started an employee association, or "company union," a scheme the company had used before 1928. The employee association had thirty-nine elected representatives from different departments and could present suggestions or grievances to management but had no power to enforce any rights in the absence of a collective agreement.[69] While this was clearly designed to coopt any efforts at unionization, it had an unintended consequence— it provided workers with the opportunity to collectively discuss problems and explore avenues for putting pressure on management. Pendergest notes that the "organization was a sham but it did provide a vehicle through which militant workers could demonstrate leadership by example."[70]

One such developing militant was George Burt, a journeyworker plumber with some previous union experience who had been hired by GM in 1929 as a torch solderer. Burt worked in the strategically import-ant body shop, which became a centre of work stoppages. He became one of the workers chosen to discuss issues with management and later provided an insightful account of the process in a UAW Education Department pamphlet, *Where Was George Burt?* Burt describes it as "a wonderful experience to complete my education":

> We were learning. Some other guys and I agreed that a certain time, all at once, so there would be no discrimination, we would shut the line down. The button was right beside me. The signal for my guys, there were about 40 in my group, was that I would take off my overalls.
>
> I took my overalls off, gave the signal ... only my group went out, the others did not go, but that was enough to shut her down ...
>
> By late 1936 we had moved along so that the company was meeting our committee in the presence of Chief Conciliation Officer of the Department of Labour, Louis Fine. This way we did manage to get our prices increased a little and our working conditions somewhat rectified.
>
> All these things were planned downtown in a beer parlour, sometimes in each other's homes. There was no union but we were conscious in thirty-six that there was a union. We knew what was taking place in Detroit.[71]

This description provides some remarkable details. It is clear that the employee association allowed militant workers to create networks, identify strategic work locations, and try out tactics that became as advanced and militant as repeated work stoppages. The organization and unity of the workers was strong enough that management agreed to government mediation and made some concessions, rather than firing the ringleaders as they would have done in earlier years. H. A. Logan suggests that there was a deliberate strategy by Communists "for the capture of company unions in these industries by having tried men accept nominations and stand for office."[72] That strategy also seems to have been followed by Communist organizers working with a company union at the International Harvester Tractor Works in Chicago. Toni Gilpin states that "the Tractor Works Council—designed by International Harvester's management to serve its interests—had

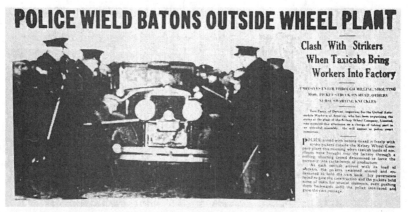

Local 195 was the first Local of the UAW chartered in Canada.
The Local went on strike against the Kelsey Wheel plant in Windsor,
and faced police violence and arrests. (*Windsor Star*)

become, in practice, a Communist Party-affiliated labor organization"
as a result of the work of Communist organizers.[73]

Kelsey Wheel and Local 195

Even before the Flint sit-down, Canadian workers were influenced by
growing labour militancy and organization across the border, especially
by the newly fledged UAW. By the end of 1935, the CPC was wholeheart-
edly urging auto workers in Canada to join the UAW.[74] The first
Canadian local, Local 195, was chartered on December 11, 1936, by
workers at Kelsey Wheel in Windsor, Ontario. A Scottish immigrant,
James Napier, took the lead. Napier was assisted by CPC and WUL
activists in the plant, and in the community. They crossed the border
to meet with UAW leaders of the Detroit West Side Local 174, and
discovered the U.S. local was in the midst of organizing the Kelsey
Wheel parent plant in Detroit. However, even before the Canadians
had secured a UAW charter, five of the leaders, including Napier, were
fired. According to Napier, the five had met with a business agent for
the Bricklayer's Union who had urged them to join the AFL-affiliated
Machinists instead of the "communist controlled" UAW. They declined
to sign Machinists cards, and all ended up being fired by Kelsey
Wheel— presumably they had been informed on.[75] Despite the firings,
the Windsor workers proceeded to secure a UAW charter. They were

promised by Walter Reuther, then the President of Local 174, that if they could get their plant to go on strike as well, "no settlement would be made that did not cover both plants."[76] The U.S. Kelsey Wheel workers began a sit-down strike on December 14, and workers in Windsor joined them on strike on December 16, assisted by UAW organizer Tom Parry. There were several pitched battles between police and picketers during the strike in Windsor, and Parry and others were arrested. The *Windsor Star* headline on December 20 was "Police Wield Batons Outside Wheel Plant: Clash With Strikers When Taxicabs Bring Workers Into Factory."[77]

Despite Reuther's promise, the U.S. workers settled on December 24 without including the Windsor plant. The Windsor strikers felt betrayed, and Local 195 was forced to agree to settle with Kelsey Wheel on December 30 without a written contract or recognition of the UAW. Manley suggests that Napier's conclusion that Reuther had sold them out "seems to lend support to Irving Abella's contention that UAW affiliation was of doubtful value to Canadian workers."[78] Napier himself explicitly disagreed, and Manley later in his article concludes that for the Oshawa workers, the UAW "was an unambiguously industrial union; it had humbled one of the giants of the industry; it was ready to recruit Canadian members; and there was no alternative to it."[79]

Despite the firings, Napier did not give up. He went to the UAW headquarters where he had a discussion with Wyndham Mortimer and Bob Travis, then in the midst of the Flint Sit-down battle. Napier recounts that, "I told them of the verbal agreement with Reuther and how he sold us out. They hadn't heard the story before, but they weren't surprised." Mortimer told Napier to contact him as soon as the GM strike was won, and he would arrange for a meeting of Local 174 "to right the wrong."[80] Napier relates that shortly after the victory against GM was secured, "I did meet Mortimer and Travis again and they did cause to be called a meeting of the shop stewards of Reuther's own west side Local 174." Napier and three other Windsor workers were able to explain that the Windsor workers had not been included in the Kelsey Wheel settlement, although they had been promised they would by Reuther, and that five of them were still fired. The stewards passed a motion pledging job actions in Detroit if the five were not rehired. The end result was that "Kennedy, the general manager of all Kelsey operations" contacted the head of the Windsor Kelsey Wheel plant. "With the bargaining committee of Local 174 present, he told Campbell to reinstate the five of us at once. He did not want operations closed down again because of a 'two-bit plant in Canada.' Campbell did what he was told."[81] Once Napier and the others were returned to work, they were able to establish a steward system with enough support from the work force to win concessions from management consistently over the next several years, even without a written contract.[82]

Napier drew two lessons from his experience at Kelsey Wheel—the need for international unions, but also the need for principled leadership. "Our experience at Kelsey Wheel showed how far we would have got had we not chosen to organize ourselves into an international union. Needless to say, we would have been smothered in our infancy. However, even though we did join an international union, our strike was nearly scuttled by unprincipled leadership —by Reuther." Napier credits Communists and their supporters, particularly Mortimer and Travis, with being able to provide the leadership that was needed for success.[83]

UAW Local 199, representing workers at McKinnon Industries in St. Catharines (a GM subsidiary), was chartered only days after Local 195, on December 15, 1936. Communists played a leading role in organizing Local 199 as well. Both Locals 195 and 199 were significant players in the battle to organize General Motors of Canada just a few months later.

Preparatory organizing was already happening in Oshawa in December 1936. The *Oshawa Daily Times* ran a story on December 30 with the provocative headline "Labour Agitators Distribute Insidious Literature Here":

> Echoes of trouble with workers in automobile plants in Windsor, Detroit and Flint, Michigan, were heard in Oshawa yesterday. Hundreds of pamphlet letters were distributed throughout the city yesterday announcing that an attempt would be made here towards the "unionization of labor", and that an organizer was to come to Oshawa for this purpose. Accompanying the letters was a four page newspaper published at Flint, Michigan, claiming success of strikers in that city.[84]

The story went on to say that "five labor agitators" from Flint had been arrested in Windsor the previous week for organizing at auto plants there. The five were alleged to be responsible for bringing literature to Oshawa that was distributed "by local communists and labor union sympathizers."

The underground organizing in Oshawa, the beginnings of UAW organizing in Canada in Windsor and St. Catharines, and the inspiring battles in Flint and Detroit all set the stage for the coming showdown in Oshawa.

Chapter 4

Organizing for the Strike – Leadership and Engagement

The stage had been set for the battle to unionize GM in Oshawa by developments locally, nationally, in the United States, and on the world scale. But the results of the battle would be largely determined by the actors who set foot on that stage; the strategies and tactics they employed; the balance of forces—workers, corporate owners, government and media—and crucially, by the leadership exercised.

Objective factors may create the possibility for change, but subjective factors determine whether or not change is achieved, and more importantly, the direction of the change. This is where leadership is critical. Strategies and tactics have to be based on objective reality, but they must also be guided by the goal that is sought, and the appropriate actions that will be most likely to achieve success. In most cases, directions, strategy, and tactics will be contested. Also important in labour struggles, but not always examined closely, is the relationship between leaders and rank and file workers. Have leaders built support for their principles and objectives? Have they engaged active participation from rank-and-file workers? How do they react if their proposals are rejected at any point?

The immediate success and lasting significance of the Oshawa 1937 strike was largely possible due to two important strategic directions. First was the emphasis on engagement of rank-and-file workers, and workers in the community. This reliance on a working-class struggle approach had been consistently advocated by Communists since the program of the RILU. The implementation of this strategic outlook in

Oshawa included the creation of a huge stewards' body in the GM workforce and democratic engagement of rank-and-file workers in every step of the organizing effort and strike, including regular mass meetings. There was an impressive mobilization of support from other workers in the community and from labour and progressive organizations across Ontario and beyond. The organizing also built support from women strikers, and women family members of strikers.

Another key strategic direction was to recognize the importance of joining with the industrial union effort spearheaded by the CIO and carrying out the Oshawa campaign as part of the UAW. This was also consistent with two key planks of the Communist platform for union organizing—the necessity of industrial unionism and international solidarity.

Communists did not play an open role in the leadership during the course of the strike. They kept a low profile because of their assessment that it was necessary to ensure a broader united front effort. Despite this, there were ferocious attacks on the strike, and on the UAW and CIO, as being directed by foreign agitators and Communists. These attacks were led by Premier Hepburn, and were amplified by most of the media. It is an open question whether or not the Communists and their allies could have played a stronger, more visible role during the Oshawa strike, and during the broader campaign for industrial unionism, and what that would have meant for future developments in the Canadian labour movement. However, even without open CPC members putting them forward, the policies and strategies that they had been championing were decisively important to the strike.

Over the course of the strike, leadership also had to show an agile response to changing circumstances and different efforts to undermine, crush, subvert, or split the ranks of the strikers, including from within. There were conflicts over key strategic/tactical decisions during the course of the strike, both with political actors from outside the union, and from within the union leadership. Oshawa Mayor Alex C. Hall, for example, tried to portray himself as a supporter of the strike despite being a member of the Conservative Party. Yet, at a critical juncture, Mayor Hall made a serious effort to undermine the strike. An example of an internal union conflict occurred early in the strike between Local 222 President Charlie Millard and other leaders, including UAW organizer Hugh Thompson. This may well have reflected underlying ideological differences. In both cases, smart tactics and relying on rank-and-file decision making prevented the strike from being side-tracked and possibly defeated.

Objective Conditions

General Motors workers in Oshawa knew that their work was contributing to record profits for the corporation—GM's consolidated after-tax profits in 1936 were almost $240 million.[1] Despite this, GM continued their efforts to drive down wages and intensify work.

"The Oshawa Assembly workers at that time were earning approximately $600 per year, working only six or seven months a year and some months working only two or three days a week."[2] Production workers suffered long layoffs while the plant was retooled annually for the next year's production model. Many tradespeople suffered the reverse—long hours during the change-over period and layoffs afterwards. When the plant was in production, the hours were excessive, as George Burt recalled:

> Hours were brutal. When the plant was going we worked 59 hours a week, five ten-hour days and on Saturday we got off an hour earlier. During the busy season, starting about January, we went on twelve hours a day—all straight time. Twelve hours three days a week, ten hours two days, and nine hours on Saturday, our short work day. That is the way we used to work, when we worked, in the busy season.[3]

While they were working, they were subject to relentless efforts to intensify their work and were under constant observation by supervisors who had total power to fire workers on the spot for any reason. Workers also knew that when they were laid off and when they were called back was totally at the discretion of management, and favouritism was rife.

In addition, as George Burt noted, workers "were paid through a bonus efficiency plan (piece work) which was tailor-made for a company that desired to make us work progressively harder for less money."[4] In 1937, the piece work rate required workers to produce hourly "27 jobs at a base rate of 52 cents an hour on a 140 percent efficiency basis."[5] Sam Gindin notes that, "In early 1937, GM announced wage cuts for the fifth time in five years ... actual wages were twenty per cent below where they were in the twenties."[6]

Just prior to the strike, General Motors had released a statement to the press that they thought would demonstrate workers had no need to strike. GM bragged that their total payroll for March 16 to 31, which was being issued on April 7, was to be $323,152—"the largest amount of money to be handed out in the history of the Oshawa plant."[7] However, for the 3,700 employees that meant they earned an average of $87.34 while working an average of 118 hours during that period— which works out to about 74 cents per hour.[8] A statement issued a week later provided a more detailed breakdown, and highlighted the precarious nature of work at GM. The statement showed that in the previous year "male employees engaged in productive work in the General Motors Oshawa plant worked 39 weeks at an average of 45 hours each week and received an hourly rate of pay 63.5 cents, while female employees engaged in productive work averaged 32.6 cents per hour for 33.5 weeks of 45 hours each week."[9] Workers, of course, received no pay during the weeks they were not needed.

Most GM Oshawa workers were on the "group bonus" scheme, which varied wages according to groups reaching productive targets. Others were classified as day-workers. GM provided this breakdown of the workforce in March of 1937:[10]

	Classification	No. of Workers	Hourly Pay
Men	Group Bonus	2256	$0.55 to $1.04
Men	Day-worker	1201	$0.45 to $0.89
Women	Group Bonus	249	$0.34 to $0.52
Women	Day-worker	56	$0.27 to $0.75

Figure 1. GM Workforce classifications and hourly pay, March 1937.

Resistance to wage cuts and speedup had already generated the beginnings of organized resistance, including sporadic work stoppages. Events in Detroit and Flint were on everyone's mind. In early 1937, everything was ready and waiting for the spark.

First Steps – The Charter
Organization to form a UAW Local in Oshawa had begun even before the Flint sit-down started on December 30, 1936. Pendergest reports

The UAW issued a charter to Local 222 on March 2, 1937. Among
the 15 names on the charter is that of William Gelech, who had originally
contacted the UAW to send an organizer to Oshawa. (Local 222)

that a meeting was held on November 11, 1936, in the home of Malcolm Smith with only three other people present. "In order to avoid people who could not be trusted, they decided to sign only fifteen members, the number necessary to apply to Detroit for a charter."[11] This is a clear indication that the goal was to affiliate with the UAW, which required fifteen members to apply for a local union charter. Logan cites Malcolm Smith, his brother James, and Robert Stacey as members of the WUL, although by the time of the meeting the WUL had been dissolved.[12]

Bill Rutherford describes the initial group as a "unity group" that included Communists and others, including U.K. immigrant supporters of the Independent Labour Party, like the Smiths. According to Rutherford, "I've got the list somewhere in my house of the original 15 guys who paid the dollar for the Charter; their names are not on that Charter, only half of them."[13] Salsberg confirmed that the names on the charter were revised "for the sake of unity," leaving out some "wonderful auto workers" and including others who had contributed "little or nothing."[14] The final version did include James Smith, Malcolm Smith, and Bill Gelech, who was publicly known as a Communist.[15] Bill Rutherford supplied Dan Benedict, then on staff with the CAW, with a list of the original fifteen names on the charter, at the Retirees Council meeting on August 24, 1990. Five of the names have the notation "CP" beside them, presumably identifying them as members of the Communist Party. Bill Gelech and James Smith are on the original list, but C. H. Millard and Art Shultz are not.[16] Abella was particularly dismissive of the Unity Group and their left politics:

> By the beginning of 1937 there existed in the plant only a clandestine committee, known as the Unity Group, of some few dozen men who met secretly and regularly to discuss ways of improving working conditions. Though they probably would have achieved little in any case, they spent most of their time debating the virtues of socialism and communism; understandably, they achieved nothing.[17]

One might suggest "they achieved nothing"—except the unionization of GM Oshawa and the triumph of industrial unionism in Canada. At the very least, they made a significant contribution to that triumph. Abella cites no source for his disparaging remarks. Many sources, including Pendergest, Rutherford, and workers who were involved at the time like Ethel Thomson, acknowledge that the group played a significant, and likely a leading role in unionizing GM Oshawa.[18]

February 15, 1937 – Speedup Triggers Walkout

Abella minimizes the role of the activists even further by stating, "What the men in the plant could not do for themselves—organize a union—the company helped them to do."[19] There is no doubt that the management announcement of an increase to the line speed on February 15, 1937, was a triggering event. But there is also no doubt that the workers who had been actively organizing inside the plant for a decade under the leadership of Communist-affiliated organizations (the AWIU, WUL, and the Unity Group) were in a position to mobilize an effective response because of the groundwork they had done. It is telling that the resistance was centred in the body shop, where the WUL had built up a base of support. George Burt's organizing efforts with the employee association had also been centred on the body shop. George Burt stated, "In Oshawa there was a group of people who had been debating how they would get in touch with the CIO. I was not part of that group ... but I knew these people and some of them worked with us in the body shop, especially in the body shop, because in the beginning that was the only place there was any union activity."[20]

Pendergest explained GM's imposition of what he termed a "speed-up-wage-cut":

> General Motors sent industrial engineers to Oshawa to speed up production ... The workers had been turning out 27 jobs at a base rate of 52 cents an hour on a 140 percent efficiency basis and were told to increase production to 32 jobs at a rate of 57 cents an hour on the same efficiency basis. The men claimed they could not do this and that it would mean a net decrease in the wage scale by 13 percent.[21]

The body shop workers were in a key part of the assembly process, and had the ability to shut down the rest of the plant if they stopped work. Pendergest states that opposition to the speed-up started with "about 800 men in the two body shops." They rented the CCF hall in Oshawa and held a meeting on Wednesday, February 17 at which they elected a committee to meet with management. When the discussion with management was unsuccessful, they held another meeting of about one hundred workers on Thursday night and voted to strike the next day.[22] This shows a significant degree of organization that would have been difficult to achieve without the solid foundation of the previous organizing efforts. Abella doesn't mention the two meetings at the CCF hall, leaving the impression the February 19 strike was spontaneous.

The overall strategic decision to organize Oshawa under the leadership of the UAW was a consequence of the Communists' decision to work for "one industry—one union" after 1935. The call for an organizer in February of 1937 was a response to the immediate situation, which was about to boil over. Whoever made the actual phone call (or phone calls), the decision was based on an analysis that a united front strategy had the best chance of success and could lead to very significant advances for workers across Canada, not just in Oshawa. In the words of Communist Party leader Tim Buck:

> We saw in this strike a possibility of establishing the right of the automobile workers to have a union. We knew that if we established it in Oshawa, it wouldn't be long before it could be established in all the other automobile centres. So we conceived the idea of transforming the strike from an isolated activity to a part of the general automobile workers' movement of North America. There was some opposition because many of our members knew that if the United Automobile Workers of America (UAW) secured control of the strike, it would mean an entirely different type of leadership, and would probably mean the ousting of Communists from leadership. I felt quite strongly that this was not the important thing. What was important was that the workers in Oshawa should win the strike and, in the winning of it, become an integral part of the automobile workers' organization in the whole of North America. So we decided to offer leadership and direction of the strike, which meant the leadership going to the UAW.[23]

Buck notes that winning the strike and establishing industrial unionism were long-term advances that outweighed the short-term setbacks for Communist organizers:

> The men who had worked for years underground building up that small, but vital union ... were all eliminated, and new people were brought forward; first by appointment, later, by elections ... This created some hard feelings among our own Party members in the automobile industry, and it required a lot of work to convince them that this was still better, that now they must start fighting all over again to win the confidence of the workers. They did and after awhile our people came back into the leadership.[24]

Who Called the UAW?

There have been competing accounts about who made the critical call to Detroit that led to Hugh Thompson being sent to Oshawa, but it is most likely that the call was made by Bill Gelech, a Communist who was a member of the Unity Group. Ethel Thompson is very clear that "Bill Gelech, well that's the guy that was the instigator of bringing Hugh Thompson over here and he was part of the Unity Group."[25] J. B. Salsberg describes early organizing meetings taking place in the unfinished cellar of Bill Gelech's house.[26] By Art Shultz's account, "There was two groups. Thompson came here on the invitation of the left group."[27] The "two groups" referred to by Shultz were the "left group" that included U.K. immigrants who identified with the Independent Labour Party and Communists. The other group was centred around supporters of the CCF, many of whom were not workers organizing for the union. The CCF prior to the Oshawa strike had focussed on electoral politics, not union organizing. Shultz's account is reinforced by this detail— Shultz says that later Thompson showed him a piece of paper "that the group that had invited him a list of people that they wanted, a list of officers of the local union. They didn't quite get there and when the charter was set up, it was divided between the two caucuses."[28] This seems to verify that it was the Unity Group that sent the invitation that resulted in Thompson arriving in Oshawa, and that it included the list of names that the Unity Group had drawn up to be charter members of the local union. George Burt also confirmed in an interview in 1963 that, "Several days before the meeting [that took place on February 19, when the body shop walked out] a committee who had been meeting in secret sent a request to the UAW in Detroit for help. While we were meeting the company about our strike, Mr. Hugh Thompson arrived on the scene."[29]

Abella's account is that Allen Griffiths "an active member of the CCF and opponent of the Unity Group, took it upon himself to phone the UAW office in Detroit for help." Abella describes Griffiths as a worker in the GM body shop, which seems unlikely since Pendergest noted that Griffiths in 1937 was a retired life insurance agent[30]. Abella also says that "at the same time a call went out from Communist party headquarters to the UAW pleading for an organizer to be sent to Oshawa."[31] Abella is the only researcher of the Oshawa strike to claim

937 *The Indianapolis Times*
Jan 7, 1937

Directs Anderson Strikers

Hugh Thompson (above), is the Anderson leader of the United Automobile Workers of America strikers, and from an office over a clothing store in Main St. directs activities of union men amounting to 12,000 idle from two General Motors Corp. plants there.

In January 1937, Hugh Thompson was leading 12,000 workers on strike at two GM parts plants in Anderson, Ohio, one of them a sit-down strike. (*Indianapolis Times*, January 7, 1937) it was Griffiths who called the UAW. It makes no sense that Griffiths would contact the UAW if he was an opponent of the Unity Group, which had been working since at least the previous November with the objective of joining the UAW. In a letter to Local 222 in 1951, Thompson mentions getting a call from Griffiths at the Genosha hotel after he arrived in Oshawa, but does not mention anything about Griffiths calling Detroit. Pendergest notes that Millard told him in an interview that Griffiths had arranged for the body shop workers to hold their meetings in the CCF hall, and Millard also claimed that it was Griffiths who contacted the UAW. However, Pendergest also points out that "Allen Griffiths was a neighbour of Millard and a very active CCFer," which could be a reason that Millard, speaking many years later, might want to promote Griffith's role. It is Pendergest's conclusion that it was a member of the Unity group "who was the instigator of the move to get Thompson. He was Bill Gelech, a known communist."[32]

Hugh Thompson, Seasoned and Courageous Organizer

In the wake of the Flint Sit Down Strike UAW organizer Hugh Thompson had been assigned to Grand Rapids, Michigan, to assist with the organizing of a General Motors parts plant. He had only been there three days when he was contacted by UAW Secretary-Treasurer George Addes and told to go to Oshawa. Thompson said, "I drove all night with my wife and child and arrived there the next morning and started organizing the huge General Motors plant in that town."[33]

Who was this organizer who played a key role in the whirlwind of organizing and strikes over the next two months?

Before arriving in Oshawa, Hugh Thompson had a very long history of political and union activism. Thompson was born in Ireland in 1902, where "working on a farm and as a weaver he was exposed to unionism at an early age."[34] When he was just ten, he took part in a major weavers' strike in 1912, and while doing picket duty he confronted a strikebreaker who hit him over the head with a rock. Thompson later was a member of the Irish Republican Army (IRA) before immigrating to Canada in 1922, and then later to the U.S. He wasn't the only IRA veteran who went on to play a role in organizing the UAW.[35]

Thompson worked at, and was fired from, Michigan Stamping and several other auto parts companies for talking union in the late 1920s.

Anderson Armory Too Small for Rally of Army of Strikers in General Motors Plants

"When union and non-union automobile workers on strike and idle because of closed Anderson plants yesterday tried to get into the National Guard armory to hear Hugh Thompson, strike leader, explain objectives, they found the hall too small to accommodate all of them. At the left, a crowded side entrance. Police Chief Joseph Carney is shown next stopping a worker who wanted to get in ... After the meeting strikers visited the Guide Lamp Co. where a sit-down strike is in progress and were entertained (third from left) by the strikers' band ... The photo at the right shows Mr. and Mrs. Harold Holloway, separated by the strike since last Thursday, embracing through the iron fence." (*Indianapolis Times*, January 5, 1937.) January 5, 1937.

He eventually was hired at Murray Body in Detroit as a trimmer. Thompson said, "During that time I recall a strike called by the Auto Workers Union, which was a communist-dominated union headed by a man named Raymond."[36] Thompson had been made a supervisor, and told this story to Jack Skeels, as part of the Oral History Project on the development of unionism in the auto industry:

> All of the boys walked off in the trim shop, and I remember during the strike going to the hole. This was the end of the line where the skilled men were to repair any failures on the part of the assemblers on the line. I found everyone of these men there and I ordered them out of the plant, calling them some names for scabbing on their own brothers. They told the superintendent and the superintendent fired me instead of the scabs.[37]

Thompson was later rehired at Murray Body, and in 1933 he signed up 230 workers to the union, believing that union organizing would be protected under the terms of the proposed NRA bill. Of course he was fired again, but over the next few months he succeeded in signing up enough workers to get AFL charters for federal unions at Murray, Dodge, Briggs, and Studebaker in South Bend, Indiana. "These were the four original locals of what is now known as the UAW-AFL-CIO."[38]

Following this, Thompson became one of the first paid organizers in the auto industry, first for the AFL and then for the UAW.[39]

At the time of the Flint sit-down strike, Thompson's assignment in the UAW battle with GM was organizing at two GM parts plants in Anderson, Ohio—Guide Lamp with 3,000 workers and Delco-Remy with 8,000. The union commenced a sit-down strike at Guide Lamp on December 31, 1936, but was soon faced with organized threats and violence. Anderson was basically a company town, and GM officials and local politicians organized a Citizen's League as an anti-union force. Thompson received a letter warning him and his organization "to get out of Anderson, and do it now, while getting is safe. We don't need your trash in Anderson." The letter was signed, "Yours the Gang Who Mean Business."[40] The Citizen's League organized a mob of thousands armed with clubs and iron bars that destroyed the union offices, beat up some union supporters and laid siege to a hall where a meeting had been planned. "I was informed at my home by the chief of police ... that I had better leave town before I got hurt since there was a mob of 3,000 people preparing to lynch me. Rather than leave town, I walked across the square to our office ... The mob gathered around the office and the police would not break them up. I saw the rope by which I was to be hung—and that is not a good feeling."[41] Thompson was able to get out of Anderson in one piece, and not long after, those plants were successfully organized.

Thus, when Hugh Thompson came to Oshawa with his wife and young daughter, they had already been through years of difficult battles, and Thompson was experienced and cool under pressure. Mrs. Thompson played a significant role in the organizing of Local 222, helping to run the Local 222 office, and signing up members. It was definitely a family affair—their 2 ½ year old daughter, Sheilah Ann, featured in a *Toronto Daily Star* front page photo with her father part way through the strike.

Thompson addressed criticisms that the CIO was not wanted or needed in Oshawa to the *Financial Post*, explaining that he was responding to a desire for union organization by GM workers who had appealed for aid to UAW headquarters in Detroit. "We weren't quite ready to branch into Canada because we were still involved in the battle in the United States. But we would have come eventually, and when we got the hurry-up call for help, I went to work."[42]

"Whatever Is Best for Charlie Millard"

The newly elected President of Local 222, Charlie Millard, was a very different person from Hugh Thompson. Millard had no union organizing background at all, not even in the Oshawa GM plant. As a former failed small businessman, he also did not have a working-class outlook. Thompson's only goal in Oshawa was the success of the union organizing effort. In contrast, there is evidence that self-advancement was a prime motivating factor for Millard.

Just prior to Hugh Thompson's arrival, some indications arose of disagreement about the political strategy of the union organizing between supporters of the CCF and the left (Unity Group and Communist Party). J. B. Salsberg, the leading Communist Party union organizer at the time, described the sequence of events in his interview with Carole Condé and Karl Beveridge. "I was at home and 2 or 3 cars filled with auto workers from Oshawa came to my house ... they said, Joe, she's breaking out tomorrow—there'll be a strike tomorrow."[43] Salsberg says that there was concern about Charlie Millard at this time— "they suspected him of wanting a Canadian union." Salsberg's opinion was "that the issue wasn't now a Canadian union, with labour rising the way it does in America in auto to now talk of anything else but a link with Detroit is senseless, it would be most divisive and destructive."[44]

Salsberg noted that Millard was not known to the activists who were leading the organizing effort. "Millard was an autoworker but wasn't involved in the organization, I was told. When he first appeared on the scene, I said, who the hell is this guy? He was teaching a bible class in a church, and he's quite intelligent but he hadn't been around."[45] Although not involved in the effort to establish a union at GM, Millard had been active in the Oshawa CCF, and, as mentioned, he had failed as a businessman. Starting as a carpenter, he had established a company manufacturing door frames and had several employees.[46] The C. H. Millard Company went out of business early in the Depression, and Millard ended up working at General Motors. Millard was active in the early years of the Oshawa CCF and was an unsuccessful CCF candidate for municipal office in 1935 and 1936. Within the CCF, Millard was part of the dominant executive group that opposed efforts by the Communists to establish a united front.[47] Pendergest judged that at the time, "the control of the party lay with the middle class club section and the intellectuals and pseudo-intellectuals at Toronto."[48]

A good indication that Millard did not have a working-class outlook is given by Daniel Benedict in his article, "Goodbye to Homer Martin." Benedict states that "Millard was a Mason" and "thought that he was able to get concessions from employers who were also members of that order." Benedict also points out that although Millard "spoke strongly against employers and governments, some of them thought him an 'easy mark.'"[49]

Millard also developed a reputation for self-promotion—William Noble, a prominent CCF member at the time, told James Pendergest that Millard had no fixed political principles, but would move left or right according to "whatever is best for Charlie Millard."[50] Nevertheless, he always seemed to "compete and conflict" with Communists,[51] and in his later union career as CIO Ontario director, he successfully worked to ensure "that the Communists were removed from SWOC [the Steel Workers Organizing Committee]."[52]

In the year before the Oshawa strike, Millard was also President of the Oshawa Ratepayers' Association,[53] and prominent in the United Church, including being superintendent of the Church's Oshawa area Sunday schools.[54] Thus, he was quite well known, even though he had not been involved in the early efforts to organize a union at GM. With the likelihood of major walkouts at GM about to break out, the organizers were concerned about Millard's potential influence, particularly if he opposed affiliation with the UAW and CIO. Salsberg says that he was able to bring a CIO organizer for the Rubber Workers' union with him to Oshawa to respond to the potential challenge. The CIO rep was able to speak "for the CIO and we saved the day." Then Salsberg says, "I was in touch with Detroit and said, you've got to send somebody right away and they sent Thompson."[55] Nevertheless, the Communists felt a broader united front was necessary to the successful establishment of a UAW local in Oshawa, and not only were willing to work with the CCF, but also to deliberately play a low-profile role in the organizational work. Salsberg stated that the Communists were willing to do a lot of the organizational work, and that "while of course they wanted to influence the workers ... there was no objection to working with the CCF."[56] Salsberg noted that "Millard became President because he was a good speaker," and his only concern with Millard and the CCF was "that they don't try to lead or direct this lava that came from this eruption in the direction of a narrow channel of so called Canadian unionism."[57]

In other words, Millard was acceptable as a leader if he supported organizing under the UAW banner. The decision for the Communists to step back, and allow Millard and others connected to the CCF to play a leadership role, along with officials of the UAW, was a strategic decision in the greater interest that the Oshawa workers, in the previously quoted words of Tim Buck, "win the strike, and in the winning of it, become an integral part of the automobile workers' organization in the whole of North America."[58]

February 19, 1937 – Body Shop Walkout

Although there are differing accounts of how Thompson was invited to Oshawa, there is little dispute about what happened next. On February 19, 1937, the body shop workers carried out their threat to strike, and about 250 of them walked out. Union organization in the GM plant was strong enough at this point that management took no action against the workers who walked out. Instead, four delegated workers, including George Burt, met with Harry Carmichael (GM VP and General Manager), Louis Fine and O. E. Jeanette of the provincial Department of Labour, and the Mayor of Oshawa, Alex Hall. The delegates reported back to the rest of the workers at the CCF Hall, where they agreed to return to work and try out the new production rate for two weeks.[59] That was the same day that Hugh Thompson had arrived in Oshawa, and when he heard about the meeting, he headed over and was able to address the workers present.

The Organizing Campaign – February 19 to April 7

Despite opposition from Louis Fine, Hugh Thompson was able to speak to the sixty or so GM workers meeting at the CCF hall. It was just a week after the momentous victory at Flint, and Thompson was able to convey the goals and accomplishments being achieved under the leadership of the CIO and UAW. A most remarkable union organizing steamroller began that day when all the workers present signed UAW membership cards within fifteen minutes.[60] The union effort was extremely well organized under Thompson's leadership.

Picket line at the Coulter Mfg. Co., Oshawa. After a short strike,
the workers won wage increases, seniority, recognition of an "Employees'
Committee," a steward system, and re-employment of all employees
both day and night shifts. (Walter P. Reuther Library)

We held meetings by departments every night, allowing one hour for each
department, starting at 6:00 o'clock through 10:00 o'clock at night and
sometimes we held departmental meetings for organizational purposes
after 4:00 p.m. I explained what the UAW-CIO stood for and answered the
questions and Mrs. Thompson signed the members.[61]

In less than a week, over 1,000 workers had joined and others were
signing at the rate of 200 a day. Thompson twice ran out of application
forms.[62] By Thursday, February 25, an overflow crowd at the Legion Hall
listened to speeches by Thompson and Sam Kraisman of the
International Garment Workers expounding the goals of the new union
movement. Kraisman notably called for unions to increase wages and
decrease hours and to divide hours so that there was not a single
unemployed auto worker. He declared that governments and employers
wanted a surplus of labour as a threat to keep down wage levels and
weaken unions, and that unions had a duty to the unemployed to
eliminate unemployment.[63]

The enthusiasm for industrial unionism quickly spread beyond
workers at General Motors. The UAW secured their first contract at
Ontario Steel Products, a manufacturer of auto springs, on March 15.

KEEP IRONS RED HOT FILL HOSE WITH LEAD IN PLANT AT SARNIA

Workers Ready to Stave Off
Rumored Attack in
Night

ARREST ORGANIZER

Thirty Vigilantes on Guard
Outside—Extra Provin-
cial Police Arrive

Special to The Star
Sarnia, March 5.—Thirty youthful vigilantes recruited from nearby
farms, who stood guard most of the
night over the scene of the battle
between strikers and faithful employees on Wednesday at the
Holmes' Foundry, were gon to-day
and the plant was defended by 27
provincial policemen, rushed here
since yesterday after a rumor that
strikers were gathering for a coun-
ter-attack.

The front page of the *Toronto Daily Star*, March 5, 1937, describes vigilante violence used against sit-down strikers at the Holmes Foundry in Sarnia.

The agreement raised wages by about $1 a day (to a minimum of 45 cents per hour), recognized seniority, and provided that "no employee shall be discharged without his case being first taken into consideration between the management and committees of the union."[64] This demonstration of quick material benefits spurred the organizing efforts, and unionization next was achieved at Coulter Manufacturing after a short strike. The Coulter contract featured wage increases, seniority, recognition of an "Employees' Committee," a steward system, and re-employment of all employees, both day and night shifts.[65] The impetus for the strike had been the announced layoff of the night shift. Meanwhile, the Steel Workers Organizing Committee, led by Dick Steele and other communists, was organizing city steel plants, and "even the baker and dairymen drivers, garage and service station employees, store workers and barbers were organizing."[66]

Vigilante Violence at the Holmes Foundry
Sit-Down Strike – Sarnia

While union organizing was ramping up in Oshawa, a shocking event in the Western Ontario border town of Sarnia revealed the violent actions that anti-union forces were prepared to use to prevent workers establishing an industrial union. It also demonstrated clearly that the Ontario government, headed by Liberal Mitch Hepburn, would back the anti-union forces to the hilt. Newspaper headlines warning that strikebreakers "keep irons red hot, fill hose with lead" and "Hepburn will permit no 'sit-down' strike" clearly revealed the nature of the class forces that the Oshawa workers were about to challenge.

The Holmes Foundry was a subsidiary of an American company established in 1918 that manufactured engine blocks. "Job conditions were harsh. With little ventilation, the men finished shifts covered in dust, but weren't provided with showers. And with no lunch area, they ate meals in the same room as makeshift and unsanitary toilet facilities."[67] Many of the workers were Italian, Polish, and Slovak immigrants. Several of them lived in company-provided shacks on Berkley Row, a short street that ran alongside the factory. A group of the immigrant workers were members of the Amalgamated Iron, Steel and Tin Workers union, and were being assisted in a unionization drive by Milton Montgomery, an Ontario representative of the Steel Workers Organizing Committee. The workers presented management with demands for an eight-hour day, showers, toilets and a lunchroom, a daily wage of $5, and recognition of the union. Management refused to negotiate.

Sarnia is barely 100 kilometres due east of Flint, Michigan. Clearly inspired by the victorious conclusion to the historic sit-down strike in Flint just twenty days earlier, a group of seventy workers at the Holmes foundry began a sit-down strike on March 1, 1937, although this was not authorized by the union leadership. The sit-downers were all immigrant workers, and there had been tension in the plant between them and the Canadian-born workers. The management and others were able to organize a mob of 300, mostly composed of people who did not work in the plant, to attack the strikers armed with clubs and bullwhips. Anti-immigrant racism was used to incite the mob. After a pitched battle inside and on the plant's roof, the strikebreakers prevailed, leaving more than fifty workers injured, some of them fighting for their lives. Some of the strikers fled to the homes on Berkley Row, but they were followed, dragged into the street, and beaten. Many of the homes were looted and trashed. While all this was happening, the Sarnia police stood by and did nothing. Their excuse was that the plant was in Point Edward, which was outside their jurisdiction. However, once the battle was over, the police stepped in and arrested sixty-six of the strikers and charged them with trespassing. They were jailed and denied bail. Later, Montgomery was arrested and charged with assault, although he had not been part of the battle.[68] Appearing in Sarnia court to represent the strikers and their supporters was J. L. Cohen, counsel for the Canadian Labour Defence League, who we will meet again in Oshawa.[69]

Once the strikers had been removed from the plant, management set the "loyal" workers to work producing weapons, including cutting a 1,000-foot length of hose into 15-inch lengths that were filled with molten lead to produce blackjacks. "In addition, iron missiles were distributed at strategical points throughout the foundry and yard-length iron rods were placed in salamanders of burning coke with one end always red hot for action."[70] These brutal weapons were prepared to be used if strikers returned to the plant. In addition, "thirty youthful vigilantes recruited from nearby farms" stood guard in front of the plant overnight. They were under the leadership of the brother of William Guthrie, a Liberal member of the provincial parliament.[71]

Sam Lawrence, the lone CCF member in the Ontario Legislature at the time, demanded the Attorney General investigate the failure of the Sarnia police to intervene in the riot. Premier Mitch Hepburn immediately jumped to his feet and proclaimed:

> Those who participate in 'sit-down' strikes are trespassers, and trespassing is illegal in this province. There will be no 'sit-down' strikes in Ontario. This government is going to maintain law and order at all costs, and I have no sympathy for 'sit-down strikers.' I have more or less sympathy with those who attempted to eject the sit-down strikers.[72]

Hepburn's words signalled approval of the vigilante violence inflicted on the striking workers, that cast a shadow over the coming battle between General Motors and its workers in Oshawa.

March· 25ᵗʰ 1937

The meeting opened at 8:29 in the Collegiate auditorium with Mr. C. H. Millard in the chair. about 2000 being present.

The honour guests of the evening were Mayor Alex. Hall and Alderman Alex. M°Leese. + Ed Hall 2nd Vice Pres. of the U. A. W. A.

Mr. Millard addressed the audience until Mr. Hugh Thompson and Mr Ed. Hall 2nd. Vice. Pres. of the U. A. W. A. arrived. (who were welcomed by an overwhelming ovation.) Both the mayor and Mr. Ed. Hall gave fine addresses.

Mr. Thompson then read out the results of the election of Officers.

		VOTE.
Pres.	C. H. Millard	718
Vice. "	E. E. Bathe	300
Treasurer	G. Burt	631
Rec. Secty.	W. Harmer	761
Trustees	G. Day	977
	G. Frise	557
	J. King	380
Searg. At Arms	H. Farrow	accl.

For Financial Secty. it was necessary to have another vote between A. Shultz and J. Owens it was agreed to vote by the Show of hands. – Mr. Shultz won by a large majority.

The Local 222 minute book entry for March 25, 1937, describes a membership meeting of 2,000. UAW VP Ed Hall and Hugh Thompson spoke, and the results of the election for Local 222 executive offices were announced. (Local 222)

The *Evening Telegram* reported that the GM Oshawa workers had elected 300 stewards who held a banquet at the Genosha Hotel on March 25, 1937, prior to the mass membership meeting. Pictures included three women stewards (top centre): Nora Adams, Mabel Davidson, and Alice Sugden. Gertrude Gillard, sole woman member of the bargaining committee is lower left.

Rank and File Strategy in Oshawa

The union strategy in Oshawa was built around the active involvement of the workers themselves. The newly chartered Local 222 held a meeting on Sunday, March 14, 1937, with an attendance of 900 members. Nominations were taken for eight executive positions of the Local Union, and 175 members were nominated.[73] After a week of voting, the winning candidates were announced at a meeting on March 25 in the auditorium of the local high school, Oshawa Collegiate and Vocational Institute (OCVI). About 2,000 members were present and heard guest

Members of the bargaining committee leaving after GM management failed to
show for a scheduled meeting on April 8, 1937, the first day of the strike. Front:
F. P. Palmer, Pat Murphy, C. H. Millard, Gertrude Gillard. Back: Geo. Frise,
William Walker, George Day, E.E. Bathe. (*Toronto Daily Star,* April 9, 1937, p3.)

speakers that included Oshawa Mayor Alex Hall, and UAW International Second VP Ed Hall.[74] This is a remarkable level of participation considering that there was not even a contract with GM in place
at that time.

Organizing was taking place at the Windsor and St. Catharines GM
locations at the same time. Bill Gelech was fired by GM in March for
assisting in St. Kitts. According to Heather Robertson, "Gelech had
asked for a half-day off, saying that he didn't feel well, but then he had
driven to St. Catharines and delivered a rousing union speech to
Ukrainian workers at the GM engine plant. Speaking in Ukrainian was
enough to get anyone fired, and General Motors had acquired a thick
file of RCMP surveillance reports on Gelech."[75] Despite later efforts by
the union and their counsel J. L. Cohen, Gelech was never rehired.

Even more important than the systematic campaign to sign up members was the organization of the union on the shop floor. A chief steward was chosen for each department in GM, and each chief steward had a number of stewards under their leadership. Several newspaper accounts during the strike document meetings of up to 300 stewards or more. Stewards were maintained as a vitally important part of the union's structure in the following years, and Shultz highlights the role they played in collecting dues (when there was no dues check-off) and education, with the goal of having one steward for each group leader and supervisor—or about one steward for every fifteen to twenty-five workers.[76] If there were in fact close to 300 stewards out of the GM workforce of 3700, that would be about a ratio of 1 to 15 or better.[77]

On March 25, the day of the mass membership meeting, the newly established stewards' body was already organized enough to hold a celebratory banquet in the Genosha Hotel, where "over three hundred stewards dined to hear from members of the bargaining committee, including Gertrude Gillard."[78]

Irving Abella did not understand the role and importance of the stewards. Abella incorrectly stated, "Stewards were nominated from each department to represent the men on the union bargaining committee."[79] In fact, the bargaining committee was a completely different structure, initially including only seven members. Charlie Millard sent a letter to GM Canada executives Carmichael and Highfield on March 31, 1937, noting, "By direction of the chief of stewards, Local Union No. 222, I am presenting to you this request. That you meet with this committee, namely C. H. Millard, Miss Gertrude Gillard, E. E. Bathe, Geo. Day, Wm Walker, Patrick Murphy, Frank Palmer and Hugh Thompson."[80] The role of the stewards is noteworthy—it is the chief of stewards who directed who the members of the bargaining committee were. Highfield's reply was that he would meet with the first seven, "at any time you suggest but positively will not meet any person not an employee of General Motors." Nowhere in Abella's writing is there any indication that he understood that there were 300 stewards, or what the implication of that fact was for the strength of the union at the point of production.

While Gertrude Gillard was the sole woman on the bargaining committee, there were also a significant number of women stewards. The representation of women workers in the Local Union and in the workplace is noteworthy and is likely an indication of left-wing influence. Communists in particular were diligent about advocating for equal rights for women workers. Irving Abella, however, completely omitted any mention of Gertrude Gillard, women stewards, or even any mention of women workers.

Within a month, virtually the entire GM workforce was signed up as UAW members, and preparations were made to bargain with GM management. The Flint sit-down strike had ended on February 11, but it was not until March 12 that a collective agreement was signed between GM and the UAW that settled the basic issues of seniority, a grievance system, and union representation. On February 11, GM had agreed to recognize the UAW as the representative for all UAW members, and as the sole bargaining agent in seventeen GM plants in the U.S.

Bargaining with GM Oshawa

The first negotiation sessions took place from March 18 to 23 between GM officials and the bargaining committee members led by Millard, but without the participation of Thompson. The demands presented by the union closely tracked the agreement signed in the U.S. on March 12, 1937—a grievance procedure, an eight-hour day/forty-hour week with time and a half for overtime, seniority, and minimum wages. In addition, the union asked for abolition of the efficiency system, five-minute breaks each morning and afternoon, a union notice bulletin board, vending machines, payday every other Friday (instead of twice a month at the company's discretion), and a contract that expired September 1, 1937—the same date as the U.S. contract.[81] Nothing was resolved, and management was resistant to having Thompson included. Ed Hall, UAW 2nd VP, announced at the Local 222 membership meeting on March 25 that Millard had been appointed as a UAW representative to assist Thompson. Hall also said that he had met with C. E. Wilson, an executive VP of GM, and that Wilson had called the Oshawa plant manager to urge a more cooperative approach.[82]

The stewards' body played a leading role in the battle with GM. On Tuesday, March 30, a mass meeting of stewards decided they would call for a walk-out on Thursday unless Thompson was included in the bargaining committee. The threatened strike was postponed when Thompson agreed that Millard would represent the union in the negotiations, with Thompson available for consultation.[83] Then, on Thursday evening, the shop stewards voted to give Thompson authority to call a strike. He received the same authority from the UAW locals representing GM workers in Windsor (Local 195) and St. Catharines (Local 199), which showed that the battle was more than a local Oshawa issue.[84] There were common threads between the union organizing in all three locations. One thread was historical—in all three locations Communists had played a prominent role in the organizing efforts in the preceding decade. Another thread was organizational—workers had chosen to join their efforts through affiliation with the UAW, and organized UAW local unions.

At the next bargaining session on Friday, April 2, GM management objected to meeting with Millard now that he was a representative of the CIO and said he was no longer an employee on leave of absence. Labour Minister David Croll held a sidebar discussion with the two GM officials and mediator Louis Fine, in which he made the following revealing statement:

> I can read men and as I look at that bunch in the next room, I can tell by the eyes of most of them that they are a bunch of fanatics. As for Millard, I think he is a weakling who can't do anyone much harm.[85]

This judgement that Millard was weak, and thus better for GM and the Ontario government to deal with, may have been a factor in the efforts to prevent Thompson from playing a more direct role in the negotiations. Of course, the influence of the Ontario Premier, Mitch Hepburn, was also a major factor. Hepburn had expended tremendous effort to prevent GM from recognizing the CIO in any way, portraying it as a threat to Ontario's economy—particularly the northern mines run by Hepburn's friends and in which he had investments.

Negotiations continued over the next several days, with Millard representing the union, but no real progress was being made. Millard was in regular contact by phone with Thompson, who had returned Monday from a conference with Homer Martin in Detroit. Premier Hepburn was being kept fully informed of the state of negotiations in Oshawa, and when he learned that a settlement favourable to the union was imminent, he cut short his vacation in Florida and hurried home. Hepburn contacted both the mediator and GM management to urge them to resist the union's demands. When GM management then reverted to a harder stance and refused to negotiate with Millard as long as he was "a representative of the CIO," it brought negotiations to an end.[86]

On Wednesday evening, April 7, "almost three hundred plant stewards met" for five hours. They were fed up with the delays and had received strike approval from UAW headquarters. Plans were made for a strike, set to commence at 7:05 a.m. Thursday morning, five minutes after the start of day shift.

Chapter 5

The Strike

In little more than one month, from February 15, the date of the first walk-out, until March 18, the beginning of negotiations with General Motors, incredible work had been done in union organization in Oshawa. Not only had almost all GM workers signed up as members of UAW Local 222, but they had also established the functioning framework of a democratic organization, based on regular well-attended meetings of stewards and the membership, as well as shop-floor representation by stewards in every area of the GM plant. GM had even been forced to accept a role for stewards in the handling of grievances on a trial basis from mid-March.[1] There was an upsurge in union organizing in Oshawa in many industries, and Local 222 signed contracts with two supplier companies—Coulter Manufacturing and Ontario Steel Products.

Once the strike began on April 8, the union leadership built on this framework. The engagement of union members was a priority, and all major decisions were made by mass meetings of either the stewards or the full membership. Community support was expanded and strike supporters arrived in Oshawa from across Ontario. The strikers found ways to counter hostility from much of the media and ferocious attacks from the provincial government of Mitch Hepburn. Solidarity was enhanced by ensuring that women workers were represented on the GM bargaining committee and that women, whether workers or relatives of workers, were engaged in providing support for the strike through the establishment of a Ladies' Auxiliary (an organization of women partners or relatives of workers that engaged in strike support activities).

It was critical to the success of the strike that the GM workers were members of the UAW—not just because of the inspiration of the victory of the Flint sit-down, but because of the principles expounded by the UAW/CIO, because of the attention and solidarity shown by the UAW leadership; and because of the ability of the UAW leaders to intervene with the Detroit executives of General Motors U.S.—the parent company of the wholly owned subsidiary, GM of Canada.

Stewards Were Key

A special point should be made about the role of the stewards' body leading up to the strike, and especially during the strike. The union had built an unprecedented network of union representatives throughout the workplace. Charles Millard told the *Toronto Daily Star* on the day of the walkout that "all arrangements for picketing were in the hands of the 300 stewards and 52 chief stewards of the workers."[2] Three hundred stewards in a workforce of 3,700 means one steward for each twelve to fifteen workers, an extraordinary number. The goal was to have one steward for each supervisor's group. Stewards were not full-time union officials but worked along with everyone in their group. By the time the strike began, the stewards in Oshawa were already establishing themselves as a mechanism for workers to challenge management decisions in the workplace, and as an effective channel of communication between rank-and-file workers and union leadership. The organization of a system of stewards as an effective shop floor presence for the union was key to UAW organization. H. A. Logan noted that stewards were an important feature of the UAW promotion of "rank-and-file democracy." "In the administration of agreements attention has already been called to the prominence of the shop stewards, workers among other workers and hence in closest contact with attitudes and interests and opinions in the shop." William Weinstone listed as a factor in the success at Flint was that the "leaders ably prepared for the strike by the development of a shop steward system."[3]

Pendergest notes that workers "were recognizing that the company started to treat them better once they had an organization and thus, they were more willing to support the union's demands."[4] The stewards would provide the backbone of the strike efforts. Abella's lack of understanding of the stewards is puzzling but telling. Referring to the first

Three of the newly elected stewards at the March 25, 1937, banquet: Isobel Baird,
Barbara McGregor, Margaret O'Donnell. (*Toronto Daily Star*, March 26, 1937)

bargaining session with GM on March 18, 1937, he states "The union
was represented by Charles Millard and stewards elected from each
department in the plant."[5] The bargaining committee of seven (at this
meeting) was clearly very different from the mass stewards' body that
was already in existence and functioning. Many contemporary news
articles referred to regular stewards' meetings of 200 to 300 taking
place, so Abella's neglect of this vital organization of workers in the
workplace must be symptomatic of his perspective that only the leaders
are significant, and that "the average union member ... plays an
unimportant role in the affairs of his union."[6]

Stewards worked alongside everyone else. They only had time away
from their job when they were actively representing somebody and
dealing with management. The stewards' system at GM Oshawa was
not unique to that plant, or to the city of Oshawa; it was a fundamental
objective of the early UAW in their organizing efforts everywhere. One
example is the Houdaille unit of Local 222. Bill Rutherford, the long-
time chairperson of that unit and a left winger, in speaking about a
contract negotiated in the early 1940s, stated:

> It was a good contract. We recognized the stewards right off the bat.
> Stewards got time off. Not like GM ... every time the company made a
> new foreman down in our plant I made a new steward, you know, and he
> had time off the job.[7]

Unlike the first GM contract, which did not include explicit mention of stewards, the first Canadian UAW contracts with Ford and Chrysler did. The 1942 contract between UAW Local 200 and Ford of Canada provided for a plant committee of thirteen committee members and 50 stewards for a workplace of about 7,000. Don Wells stated in his study of Local 200 that there were also sub-stewards for every fifty or so workers. "These latter played a critical role. While they collected dues and signed up new members, they communicated union policy to the members (and the members' concerns to the leaders) on a daily basis."[8] Wells also pointed out the prevalence of direct shop-floor action in many UAW plants in the U.S. at that time "and shop stewards often played a central role in it."[9] The first contract with Chrysler in Canada specified recognition of twenty-three stewards and ten members of the plant committee.[10] Nelson Lichtenstein noted that workplace disputes over speedup, favouritism, and discipline at GM U.S. plants had increased by 1940. The fundamental commitment to a philosophy of rank-and-file unionism provided a basis for an effective response:

> To resolve such workplace conflicts, the industrial union movement had a clear and unambiguous solution: scores, even hundreds, of wide-awake shop stewards in each factory, mill, and office. The UAW called these worker-spokesman-organizers "a weapon of democracy" powerful and numerous enough to overthrow the foreman's "small-time dictatorship" and establish a "democratic system of shop government." In a brilliantly educative 1940 pamphlet, "How to Win for the Union," the new UAW Education Department defined the shop steward as "at once a diplomat negotiating with a foreign power and a general preparing his troops for possible conflict."[11]

Having the most extensive possible steward system was a **principle** that derived from a left-wing class analysis. It aimed at creating the widest and deepest engagement of workers in the struggle with corporate owners, and centring that struggle in the workplace, at the point of production. The Communist position was clearly laid out in William Weinstone's pamphlet about the Flint sit-down strike, where he argued that consolidating the gains of the strike would require "above all the establishment of an efficient shop steward system."[12] Thus, it is not surprising that unions with the most left-wing, or Communist, leadership put a high value on establishing a large and militant body of stewards and consistently achieved higher levels of shop floor representation. This included the United Electrical Workers (UE), the Farm Equipment Workers Union (FE), the United Packinghouse Workers of America (UPWA) and many Locals of the UAW, although leadership in the UAW was divided and featured contests between left and right for leadership at both the national and local level. UE leader James Matles stated, "the ideology of rank-and-file unionism is spelled out in the UE constitution."[13] Matles noted the first national UE contract with GE:

> Laid down the blueprint of the UE grievance machinery and shop steward system, ingredients of rank-and-file industrial unionism which were to remain characteristic of the union's functioning over the years. Both parties agreed on an arrangement of one steward to one foreman; on the desirability of bringing up and settling grievances at that level, on the shop floor; on processing unresolved grievances to the next level of local union leadership and plant management and, if still unsettled there, to top UE and GE officers; on a pledge of no strikes or stoppages while a grievance was in the works, nevertheless reserving the right of the workers to take strike action if the grievance procedure had been exhausted and a grievance had failed to be settled to their satisfaction at the highest level.[14]

According to labour historian Toni Gilpin, the Farm Equipment Workers Union was another union whose key leaders "were members of, or sympathetic to, the [Communist] Party when the union was founded, and that remained the case for years afterwards. Their Communist Party involvement provided them with a grounding in Marxist analysis, a dedication to racial solidarity, and a belief in perpetual class conflict that would shape their worldview and define all aspects of their engagement with International Harvester."[15] In that ongoing class struggle, notes Gilpin:

> Frontline leadership makes all the difference, and thus the FE fought to maintain a large and unfettered steward body. Stewards serve as first responders for aggrieved workers in disputes with management, and within the FE, they were regarded as "rank and file generals" on perpetual duty to keep the membership organized and battle-ready. "Shop stewards are the key to a union's success or failure," the FE had declared back in 1940 … FE contracts, therefore, established a sizable steward presence—on average, the union claimed, one for every thirty-five to forty workers—vested with unusual freedom.[16]

The contract language that FE negotiated was strong enough that an arbitrator in 1948 ruled that there was a "clear contractual commitment" to paid time off for FE stewards, and further, there was "no limit to the amount of allowable time" they were entitled to."[17] Gilpin contrasts the FE commitment to "a large, mobile and autonomous steward body" regarded as "the backbone of the union", to the changing practices in the UAW under Walter Reuther's presidency and the "Treaty of Detroit" contract with GM in 1950, which "sharply limited where UAW officials could go within GM plants and how much time they could spend handling workers' complaints, and allowed for only one union representative on the shop floor for every 250 General Motors workers."[18]

According to the pamphlet "The Bosses' Boy: A Documentary Record of Walter P. Reuther" issued by opponents of Reuther ahead of the 1947 UAW convention and election, some of the move towards cooperation with management and limitation of shop floor representation and militancy began in the GM plants when Reuther was head of the UAW's GM department even before he became president.[19]

Another great example comes from the period when the massive Armour meatpacking plant in Chicago was being organized by the Packinghouse Workers Organizing Committee (PWOC) Local 347. The PWOC was the precursor of the UPWA. Historian Rick Halpern reported that, "By mid-1938, almost every one of the plant's one hundred departments contained a head steward with seven to twenty assistants, depending on the size of the department." These stewards extended the presence of the union throughout the plant. The Local 347 activists also believed that the extensive shop floor organization was a guard against corruption. Halpern quotes a PWOC activist, Jesse Prosten, who explained, "We felt that the employers always bought us out ... They bought the officers of the union in the old AFL style. So we had one steward for every ten people. We figured, well, if you're going to buy some you can't buy them all." The shop floor power of these stewards was remarkable. "Local 347 developed a tactic, referred to as 'whistle bargaining,'" noted Halpern. "Each steward wore a whistle around his or her neck. Whenever a supervisor declined to discuss a grievance, the steward gave a blast on the whistle and the department halted work. When the issue was resolved, the steward whistled twice and production started up again."[20]

UAW Local 248, which represented workers at Wisconsin's largest industrial plant located in the Milwaukee suburb of West Allis provides another example. The historian of Local 248, Stephen Meyer, notes that "Within the UAW, the Allis-Chalmers local had the solid reputation of a Red local in the late 1930s and early 1940s."[21] The resulting steward system that was created in Local 248 had the same militancy and dense network of stewards that was seen in UE and FE. In 1937, the Local recording secretary, Julius Blunk, described the setup to a National Labor Relations Board panel. Meyer notes there was a large number of union representatives, as was typical in many smaller UAW shops "such as Chrysler, Nash, and Packard." The Allis-Chalmers local had existed before affiliation with the UAW, and used different terminology than other places—the lowest level of representative was called the "committeeman," and represented twenty-five to fifty workers. Above the committeemen were "stewards" who represented plant divisions. (This is the opposite of how the terms "steward" and "committeeman" were more commonly used.) Blunk testified that "the stewards structure parallels the setup of management. The committeeman equals the foreman; the steward of the division equals the superintendent, or rather parallels the superintendent." In total there were about 225 committeemen for the plant and 265 union representatives in total.[22]

These examples show there was a widespread commitment within the UAW and other industrial unions with left-wing leadership to a large, militant, active representation structure that aimed at having one union rep for each supervisor. Hugh Thompson brought this philosophy of rank-and-file unionism with him when he arrived in Oshawa, and the existing network of experienced, left-wing union organizers in Oshawa were well placed to adapt it to the Oshawa GM plant in short order. As negotiations were taking place with the Oshawa GM management, the stewards were ready. When the negotiations broke down, the stewards acted.

Hugh Thompson expressed the feeling of the GM workers clearly when talks broke off on the evening of April 7—"We are through fooling around." The actively functioning stewards' body gave the local union the strength to respond to GM's delaying tactics. The decision to strike was arrived at "following a five-hour conference of union stewards"

Hepburn's vain attempt to hold back the CIO tide—
Toronto Daily Star editorial cartoon, April 12, 1937.

that went until 1:05 a.m. on April 8, 1937. Approval to strike had been granted from UAW headquarters in Detroit. Exactly six hours later, the workers conducted a coordinated walkout, five minutes after clocking in to work.[23] Picketing was well organized, "Picket lines are 40 at a time in front of every gate. Every six hours 40 others take their places." Even though the decision to strike had been made only hours before, "At noon the picket lines were fed as they walked. Sandwiches were brought in crates by union workers, and the men drank coffee from white mugs as they walked in their oval chain."[24]

Hepburn's Goal – Stop the CIO

Even before the strike began it was clear that Mitch Hepburn was personally committed to thwarting the union to a degree that was unusual for a premier of Ontario. Although it was not public knowledge at the time, Hepburn made several unsuccessful efforts to have Hugh Thompson arrested or deported starting soon after Thompson arrived in Oshawa.[25] Hepburn had been publicly vowing to stop the CIO from gaining a foothold in Ontario for some time, including in his inflammatory remarks in the legislature supporting the anti-immigrant vigilantes who had violently attacked sit-down strikers at the Homes Foundry in Sarnia on March 3, 1937.

Hepburn's extraordinary hatred of the CIO and its organizing efforts in Ontario was both ideological and personal. Hepburn's background was as proprietor of his family's onion farm in St. Thomas, "where a feudalistic client-patron relationship with workers provided him with no understanding of industrial disputes and the aims of organized labour."[26] Hepburn had employed pro-labour rhetoric when he ran for premier in 1934, but in reality, his victory was cemented through friendship with political and corporate leaders such as George McCullagh, publisher of *The Globe and Mail*. Pendergest revealed that McCullagh

> [H]ad purchased a block of shares in Hyslop Gold Mines for himself and for Hepburn. (Of course, the latter's name did not appear anywhere in the transaction.) The stocks had done well and a good deal of money stood to be made. Hepburn was listening very closely to McCullagh's advice on both economic and political matters. This relationship partly explains the Premier's concern over the C. I. O. moving into the mining areas of Northern Ontario.[27]

It is likely that it was Hepburn's intervention that ensured that the initial negotiations between the union and GM failed. GM of Canada had no compelling reason to resist reaching an agreement with the union after the parent company had settled with the UAW in the U.S. on February 11. In fact, the Oshawa plant was already recognizing the role of union stewards in taking up grievances from about mid-March.[28] Hepburn played a personal role in urging GM not to recognize the CIO in any form or deal with Thompson, which seriously obstructed the negotiations.

When Hepburn learned that an agreement between Local 222 and GM of Canada was imminent, he rushed back early from vacation in Florida, on April 7, and phoned GM Vice-President George Chappell. GM then announced they would no longer negotiate with Millard as long as he represented the CIO, nor would it sign a written contract with the new union.[29] This precipitated the strike.

Thursday, April 8 – Day 1 – The Stewards Call a Strike

As soon as the strike began, Hepburn went on the attack against the union. At a press conference, he deplored "that the employees of General Motors have seen fit to follow the suggestion of the CIO-paid propagandists from the USA to desert their posts," and claimed the strike was, "the first open attempt on the part of Lewis and his CIO henchmen to assume the position of dominating and dictating to Canadian industry." Most of the Ontario media supported Hepburn, praising him for opposing the CIO before "it can extend into all the major industries of Ontario and wreak havoc in its wake."[30] One *Toronto Daily Star* front page headline stated, "Province to Back G.M. in C.I.O. Fight," noting "All the resources of the province will be thrown behind General Motors Corporation in its fight against the dominating influence of John L. Lewis and his Committee for Industrial Organization, the *Star* learned today at Queen's Park."[31]

Hepburn's declaration of war against the Oshawa strikers included overruling an earlier promise of relief from Labour Minister David Croll. Hepburn told the press, "Should this strike continue for an indefinite period the cabinet at a special meeting today decided that no relief will be granted in any form whatever."[32] It was time for a showdown, Hepburn said, "We were advised only a few hours ago that they are working their way into the lumber camps, the pulp mills and our mines. Well, that has got to stop —and we are going to stop it. If necessary, we'll raise an army to do so."[33]

Once the strike started, Hepburn telegraphed federal Justice Minister Ernest Lapointe with a request for the deployment of RCMP officers because the situation in Oshawa was, "becoming very acute and violence anticipated any minute." Lapointe dispatched one hundred men, but they were to be stationed in Toronto, not Oshawa, to be used only if necessary.[34] Hepburn also ordered the mobilization of Ontario Provincial Police officers.

Media coverage of the strike was extensive. The *Star* had a banner headline about the Oshawa strike every day until the strike was settled. The April 8 issue of the *Toronto Daily Star* headline declared "3,700 Motor Workers Strike at Oshawa." There were seven separate articles about the strike that started on page 1 and another article and five photos on pages 2 and 3. Women strikers were featured in several articles and some of the photographs. According to the *Star*, union officials said that 260 women workers were on strike (an article a few days later claimed there were 500). One story reported that one hundred RCMP officers were on their way, as well as sixty provincial police.[35] Meanwhile, General Motors sent workers home from the Windsor plant about 9 a.m. The Windsor plant assembled engines for Oshawa. The GM subsidiary in St. Catharines, McKinnon's, continued in operation.

Frederick Griffin – Insightful Reporter

The lead *Toronto Daily Star* article on April 9, 1937, was bylined by Frederick Griffin, who was the *Star*'s key correspondent from Oshawa all through the strike. Griffin's articles were detailed and insightful, and provide a good window into events as they happened. Griffin's 1946 obituary in the *Star* noted that, "in his insatiable passion for truth he spent hours digging into backgrounds and motives ... He would not rest with a surface skimming. He had to know what went on beneath." Griffin's reporting was also informed by a belief that "society was being remade and his heart burned to play some part in the remaking, if only as a humble historian." Five years before the Oshawa strike, in 1932, Griffin had spent several weeks in the Soviet Union writing feature stories for the *Star* that "were hailed as among the first honest and factual reporting of that great Communistic experiment," in the same obituary.[36] When his features were published in book form, one of the chapters was titled "When Worker is Boss," perhaps foreshadowing a bit the power that would be exercised by Oshawa autoworkers and chronicled by Griffin in 1937.

Frederick Griffin may well have felt an affinity with Hugh Thompson —both had immigrated from Ireland as young adults.

"GM workers picketing after walking out five minutes after the start of shift,"
April 8, 1937. (Toronto Archives Fonds 1266, item 44073)

"Local 222 membership meeting at the Oshawa Collegiate on the first day
of the strike." (Toronto Archives Fonds 1266, item 44082)

When the union bargaining committee arrived at the GM offices on the afternoon of April 8 for scheduled talks, no one was there, so no negotiations took place that day. In the evening, the union called a membership meeting at Oshawa Collegiate. Three thousand people attended and were addressed by Hugh Thompson and Mayor Hall—who rejected the need for outside police. The union offered to provide Union Police to help keep order. Liquor stores were closed for the duration of the strike at the request of the union.[37]

An indication of the preparation of the Local membership to carry out a potentially long strike was the evidence of workers cutting back their spending and putting so much of their April 7 pay cheques into savings that it was referred to as a run on the bank—in reverse. The *Toronto Daily Star* described it this way:

> It was noted yesterday and to-day that there is unusually little buying as if the strikers and their families were conserving their funds. They have begun the strike with considerable money available, following the biggest pay-day in General Motors' history. March was also a big pay month.
>
> Yesterday morning, following the commencement of the strike, it is reported that there was a considerable run on the bank for the first hour and a half. But it was to put money in, not to take it out. Heavy depositing was done by the striking workers, who evidently intend to eke out their last earnings.[38]

Friday, April 9 – Day 2 – Millard Steps Offside

On Friday afternoon, Millard contacted Hepburn and asked to meet him with a group of workers. Hepburn agreed and held a meeting in his office with Millard and four others. While one of them was a member of the union bargaining committee, three of them were not.[39] This step by Millard was offside—he was acting without authorization from the rest of the union leadership or the stewards. Millard certainly received a friendly reception from Hepburn, who invited the media into his office after the discussion and praised Millard's group. According to the *Toronto Daily Star* reporter, the five strikers sat close to Hepburn's desk, "and they, the premier, and Louis Fine from the department of labour, were wreathed in smiles. There was distinctly an air of relief in all faces in contrast to the tension of the night before, when the premier issued a statement condemning the C.I.O. for destroying Canadian industry."[40] Hepburn implied a deal was close:

> "I think we have good news for you," he said smilingly to the reporters, and several of the workers nodded in agreement. "These gentlemen, along with Mr. Millard, resumed negotiations with the government this afternoon, and we believe we've made progress."[41]

Hepburn announced he would meet GM executives in the morning, and Millard would bring back his group later in the day "with any additions he may care to make to it." He expressed hope that they could reach an agreement then, and noted, "These men have been quite reasonable in their demands, very reasonable in fact. I don't think we are very far apart now. Hepburn also announced that Millard had agreed GM could send trucks across the picket line to pick up replacement parts to service vehicles."[42]

On the face of it, this seems like an effort by Millard to take control and compromise the demands of the strike. It was a shocking affront to the unity of the strike for anyone, especially the Local Union President, to negotiate with a small, hand-picked group rather than the elected negotiating committee. It is even more problematic considering that Millard was never trusted by the left because of his political outlook and lack of involvement in the union before February 1937. It is also odd that Hepburn, in front of the press, asked Millard if he wanted to add anything, and Millard stated, "I don't wish to say anything but that we expect recognition of our status in the international union."[43] Hepburn did not react, despite his virulent opposition to any recognition of the international union up to this point. There were reports that Hepburn was going to urge GM to sign an agreement as long as Millard signed for the union rather than Thompson. Likely, Hepburn believed that he could get Millard to agree to a deal that did not recognize the

GM strikers in front of the plant, April 9, 1937. (Oshawa Museum A016.12.7)

international UAW. It certainly seems at this point that Millard had justified the earlier assessment by Hepburn's Labour Minister: "As for Millard, I think he is a weakling who can't do anyone much harm." Some reports indicated that Hepburn's goal might be to promise workers improved wages and working conditions and get them to return to work individually on those terms.[44] The next day, Hepburn told the press, "I have considerable admiration for the employees' committee who sat in yesterday with me." He said that he believed if the same committee had carried on, they could have reached a satisfactory arrangement, but that "General Motors have gone as far as anyone could reasonably expect them to go."[45] However, things did not "carry on" with the unrepresentative "employees' committee" thanks to the swift response of Hugh Thompson and the stewards.

Millard's individualistic action in breaking ranks with the elected leadership could have been a serious setback for the union. It could have led to conflict and disunity in the union leadership or undermined the goals of the strike. However, the potential crisis was handled in the best way possible—by taking the issue to the rank and file—in this case to the stewards. Friday evening Hugh Thompson met "two or three hundred Oshawa union stewards behind locked doors and after two hours of conference, from which came frequent applause, he came out" and made some significant announcements. The *Star* reported that Thompson declared heatedly that, "The committee which visited Toronto had no power to discuss terms or reach an agreement. He [Millard] and that committee which went with him had no power in the world, no right, to make a decision." In particular, Thompson announced that the stewards had made these significant decisions— that "anyone going to work at the request of General Motors are strike breakers, regardless of what they may think." Further, "the stewards, at their meeting, decided that at the conference to be held with Premier Hepburn at the parliament building [April 10] with a workers' committee, he [Thompson] was to attend as a member." "I am also," he added, "to attend on any future conference with General Motors and be a member of the committee."[46] The collective body of the union stewards had repudiated Millard's attempt to operate without authorization and issued a remarkable public dressing down to their Local President. Millard didn't publicly step out of line again for the rest of the strike.

Saturday, April 10 – Day 3 – Rally of 3,000 Greets Homer Martin

On Saturday morning, a confrontation on the picket line was defused when Hugh Thompson convinced picketers to maintain discipline and allow GM to pick up a few truckloads of parts. Then the bargaining committee headed to Hepburn's office with Hugh Thompson. Significantly, this was now the full bargaining committee, not the rump group Millard had taken on Friday. Thompson waited in the corridor while Millard asked for him to be accepted as a member of the committee. Hepburn declared he would not meet Thompson under any circumstances. At that, Millard said there was nothing left to discuss and the meeting was over.[47]

After the meeting broke down, the committee went to the Toronto airport to meet UAW President Homer Martin who was flying in from Detroit. Some carloads of strikers from Oshawa also arrived, and a cavalcade of more than a dozen cars headed for the strike battleground. By the time they reached Oshawa, the procession included some fifty vehicles following the flag-draped convertible carrying Martin. Three thousand people met the cavalcade and, led by a band, the crowd circled the GM plants and stopped in front of the Genosha Hotel, where Martin gave an impassioned speech standing on the hood of his car. Police Chief Friend judged it the largest demonstration in Oshawa's history.[48] Felix Lazarus, writing for the *New Commonwealth*, described the changed atmosphere in Oshawa:

> Oshawa has fallen! One week ago it was known as "The Home of General Motors." Today it belongs to the United Automobile Workers, International Union ... Never in the history of the Canadian Labour movement has a town so completely been captured by the sentiment of trade unionism ... the workers in their Sunday best flaunt their union-buttons to the public eye and every second person one meets wears a button. This town has certainly gone union, and with a vengeance.[49]

Three thousand strikers at a mass union meeting that night at OCVI gave a vote of confidence to Hugh Thompson as a bargaining representative for the union.[50] The meeting was addressed by Homer Martin, who stated that he was going to arrange for the International union reps in Oshawa to meet GM Oshawa plant managers, to establish that "the agreement reached in the United States shall apply to the plants in Canada, as was agreed to by Mr. Knudsen."[51] Martin argued that the February 11, 1937, agreement between GM and the UAW applied to union members in Canada also, because it included the clause, "The Corporation hereby recognizes the Union as the collective bargaining agency for those employees of the Corporation who are members of the Union."[52] Martin promised the Oshawa workers:

> The International is squarely behind you with every bit of resource and strength we have, and if they don't make cars in Canada under union conditions, they won't make them at all in the United States![53]

On April 10, 1937, a cavalcade accompanied Homer Martin from the Toronto airport to Oshawa. Here the crowd is addressed by Mayor Hall and Hugh Thompson in front of the GM plant. (Toronto Archives Fonds 1266, item 44094)

Women strikers picketing on April 10, 1937.
(Toronto Archives Fonds 1266, item 44097)

GM strikers show their defiance, April 10, 1937. (Oshawa Museum A016.12.8)

The *Toronto Daily Star* reported "It was understood that Martin had discussed the Canadian situation yesterday [April 9] with William S. Knudsen, Executive Vice-President of General Motors."[54] Knudsen was the key negotiator for GM with the UAW, and the one who had signed the historic February 11, 1937, agreement that ended the Flint sit-down strike. Ed Hall, UAW Vice-President, responded forcefully the same day to Hepburn's attacks on the CIO as "foreign agitators," by stating that if Hepburn "were as interested in protecting citizens of his country from exploitation by foreign interests as he is in protecting the exploiters, this strike would not be necessary."[55]

The Saturday meeting was also an opportunity to demonstrate growing support for the strike from the labour movement and public. The Toronto District Trades and Labour Council (TTLC), the largest AFL labour council in Canada, invited Local 222 to affiliate, despite the friction at the time between the AFL and the CIO (The CIO-affiliated unions had been suspended by the AFL in the fall of 1936). The invitation was accepted on the spot. TTLC Secretary John Buckley announced that "not only has the Toronto Trades Council formed a strike committee to throw all its resources into the fight on behalf of the automobile workers, but immediately strike committees will be formed in every town and hamlet of Canada." Buckley added, "If the premier has thrown the weight of the government behind the vested capitalist interests, then I say to the government we will be compelled, as trade unionists were in Great Britain in 1905, to participate in politics and take over the government of this province."[56] George Watson, Vice-President of the TTLC spoke to the need for unity. "This is not a question of C.I.O. or American Federation of Labor. It involves the entire working class of this Dominion, as to whether they can organize into any organization they see fit. Organized labor must throw all its differences into a hat and fight as a solid body for labor and labor alone."[57]

Leading up to the strike, and in its first few days, the International UAW had shown great attention to the battle, and provided significant support to the GM workers in Oshawa, especially when consideration is given to all of the other ongoing battles they were involved in. The 3,700 workers at GM Oshawa were a small fraction of the more than 100,000 GM workers in the U.S. and Canada at that date.

UAW support began with the dispatch of UAW organizer Hugh Thompson on February 19. While Thompson led the organizing efforts, assisted by his wife, there were other UAW and CIO representatives who also provided assistance over the next two months. Charles Millard was appointed as a UAW rep. The UAW Executive Board granted a charter to Local 222 on March 2, 1937. UAW VP Ed Hall spoke to a meeting of 2,000 Local 222 members on February 25 and noted that he had met with C. E. Wilson, an executive VP of GM, and arranged for Wilson to call the Oshawa plant. On April 4, Thompson conferred with UAW President Martin about the Oshawa organizing. Martin made a major appearance in Oshawa on the third day of the strike, April 10. Martin had also spoken to a senior GM executive, Knudsen, on April 9, and Ed Hall made a public statement countering Hepburn that day.

At the same time that the organizing battle was happening in Oshawa, in the United States the UAW leadership was trying to cope with an unprecedented wave of sit-down strikes, police and court actions, and organizing. The forty-four-day Flint sit-down strike ended on February 11, and the UAW leaders immediately sat down to negotiate a contract. It took tremendous effort to win recognition of seniority and a grievance procedure which were viewed as fundamental challenges to management's rights, but these key building blocks of workers' rights were achieved, and an agreement was ratified on March 12, 1937.[58] Significantly, the eventual agreement in Oshawa largely mirrored the U.S. one. Even before the GM deal was concluded, massive sit-down strikes hit the Chrysler plants in Detroit, as well as dozens of others. It wasn't until April 11 that *The New York Times* announced that sit-down strikers had left the Hudson motors plant after thirty-three days, and that 90,000 workers would be returning to their jobs from Hudson, Chrysler, Briggs, and Reo. An injunction application to evict and arrest 6,000 Chrysler workers from eight plants, and which would also make possible the arrests of Homer Martin and John L. Lewis, was dismissed.[59] Mortimer reports that "The storming of the GM citadel had set in motion a wave of revolt against the open-shop employers that could not be contained .... At one point, eighteen sit-down strikes were going on simultaneously ... I was kept busy going from one sit-down strike to another, and seemed to spend all day every day trying to keep up with the unbelievable upsurge of sentiment for the CIO."[60] Despite this explosion of strikes and organizing, threats of injunctions and arrests, and other pressures on the UAW leadership in Detroit, they did not neglect the strikers in Oshawa.

Sunday, April 11, 1937 – Day 4 – Support Rally of 7,000

On Sunday afternoon, after Homer Martin had departed, a mass rally of 7,000 people was held in Oshawa's downtown Memorial Park. In addition to Hugh Thompson, speakers included two representatives of the Toronto District Trades and Labour Council. TTLC President John Noble spoke about the importance of resisting Hepburn's attack on the right of workers in Oshawa to belong to the union of their choosing. He said, "If we allow this act of Hepburn's to go unchallenged, it will spread. It is only an echo of what has been going on in the province of Quebec."[61]

Monday, April 12, 1937 – Day 5 – Women Strikers in the Forefront

On Monday evening, two meetings were held. At an organizing meeting, workers from the parts and service department agreed to join the union and the strike, as did the remaining non-union members of the maintenance department. At least 156 workers signed union cards. As a result, on Tuesday morning no hourly workers crossed the picket line to enter the parts and service building, only fifty-eight supervisors dressed in business suits who began loading a truck while being jeered.[62]

The other Monday evening meeting was of the 300 stewards. Millard announced after the meeting that the stewards had decided to organize the 300 office workers in GM's main office, in response to numerous requests.[63] The key story from this stewards' meeting was the response to news reports that Hepburn was demanding loyalty from his cabinet ministers and threatening to dismiss Labour Minister David Croll and Attorney General Arthur Roebuck, and that Federal Labour Minister Norman Rogers had offered his offices to help mediate the dispute, if requested by both GM and the union. In response the stewards adopted a resolution, which they released to the media. The *Toronto Daily Star* reported the resolution this way:

> Since Premier Hepburn refused to recognize a committee of employees, and whereas the federal department of labor has expressed willingness to act as conciliator in this dispute, be it resolved that the steward body go on record as accepting the offer of the Dominion government's department of labor as expressed by the Mayor of Oshawa (since the move was through the medium of Mayor Alex Hall) and that a vote of confidence be given the Ontario minister of labor, Hon. David Croll, for his good work in the

Rally of 7,000 supporters of the GM strike in Memorial Park, Oshawa.
(Oshawa Museum A016.12.1)

Hugh Thompson speaks to the rally of 7,000 at Memorial Park, April 11,
1937. (Toronto Archives Fonds 1266, item 44117)

Women strikers marching on April 15, 1937. (Oshawa Museum A016.12.5)

beginning of negotiations with General Motors Corporation, expressing regret that he was not given a free hand to continue along the lines on which he so well began.[64]

This action effectively countered Hepburn's attempt to bypass the union leadership and mediate an agreement between GM and workers. It also infuriated Hepburn, who protested the "unwarranted interference" on the part of Rogers and stated that he was confident GM "will not be party to such a treachery."[65]

Recognition of the important role of women in the strike was evident in stories and photos in the *Toronto Daily Star*. One article featured an interview with Gertrude Gillard, who "represents women on Oshawa Strike Committee." The *Star* noted that the 500 "average young women working for a living" a month ago, were now "a militant group fighting for a principle." Gillard represented the women on the union bargaining committee, and told the *Star*, "Of course the girls will stick. They know what they're striking for and they'll see it through. None of

THE TORONTO DAILY STAR, TUESDAY, APRIL 13, 1937

The *Toronto Daily Star* featured the women strike supporters making sandwiches and delivering coffee and food to the picket lines. This was the beginning of the Ladies' Auxiliary. (*Toronto Daily Star*, April 13, 1937, p3.)

them that I have talked to has ever suggested we go back to work or has ever expressed any doubt in the cause." Gillard added, "And any of the wives of strikers I've talked to seem anxious that their husbands stick the strike out to the finish. They seem to realize it will be the best thing in the long run."[66] Given the attacks on the CIO and Hugh Thompson by Hepburn and the media, it is noteworthy that Gillard affirmed, "We think Hugh Thompson is an A1 man. We believe he has wonderful control. I don't see how there can be any doubt as to the outcome of this strike. We've affiliated with the right organization and we seem to have the right backing."[67] Beside the interview with Gillard, the *Star* featured photos of women preparing large stacks of sandwiches and distributing coffee and sandwiches to the picket lines.

April 12 was also the day that the Supreme Court of the United States upheld the constitutionality of the Wagner Act (National Labor Relations Act, (NLRA)). There had been expectations in some quarters that the NLRA would be struck down, similarly to the Supreme Court's decision to nullify the National Industrial Recovery Act in 1935. This Supreme Court decision was a boost for the labour movement in the U.S., and particularly for the CIO, since the NLRA enshrined collective bargaining and union representation rights in law. The decision was news in Canada as well, and the front-page story in the *Toronto Daily Star* was headlined "National Labor Relations Act Upheld By U.S. Court" with a subhead that was very relevant to the ongoing battle in Oshawa, "Right of Workers to Choose Own Unions Is Recognized."[68]

Tuesday, April 13 – Day 6 – Hepburn Asks for More Mounties

On April 13, Homer Martin was again putting pressure on GM U.S. executives. According to the *Toronto Daily Star*, "at this hour [a] conference was actually going on in Detroit between Homer Martin ... and William S. Knudsen ... the subject is the strike here and the possibility of ending it." However, the *Star* also reported that while admitting Homer Martin "has endeavored to use the agreement with the General Motors Corporation of the United States as a lever to have pressure brought by that organization on the General Motors of Canada to settle the Oshawa strike, a spokesman for the U.S. company definitely denied that any influence is being exercised in respect to the Canadian situation."[69]

At the same time, Hepburn told the press that he was demanding cabinet support for his stance on the Oshawa strike, and any cabinet member who disagreed would be asked to resign.[70] On the morning of

April 13, Hepburn had wired federal minister Ernest Lapointe claiming that the situation in Oshawa was becoming more tense and requesting that at least an additional one hundred RCMP officers be dispatched to Toronto to be available. Hepburn was not satisfied with Lapointe's reply that he would discuss the request with his colleagues the next day before deciding. Hepburn then sent a note to the Lieutenant Governor requesting an amendment to the regulations governing the Ontario Provincial Police to permit the appointment of "Special Constables" with jurisdiction in any part of Ontario.[71]

Wednesday, April 14 – Day 7 – Hepburn Demands Resignations, Hepburn's Hussars, Local 222 Veterans March, Mayor Hall Issues an Ultimatum

On the seventh day of the strike, Hepburn ramped up his campaign to defeat the CIO in Oshawa. This involved whipping up anti-Communism, trying to create a fear of impending violence, clamping down on any dissent, and announcing the recruitment of 200 special "law-and-order" provincial police that he could use to intervene in the strike.

The headline news was Hepburn's demand that Cabinet Ministers Croll and Roebuck resign, which they did later that day. In a letter dictated in the presence of the *Toronto Daily Star* reporter, Hepburn told the two ministers, "you are not in accord with the policy of the government in fighting against the inroads of the Lewis organization and communism in general."[72] Hepburn told the *Star* that it was "a fight to the finish" and that "we know that the Communists are standing by, by the thousands, ready to jump in at the first sign of disorder. If the C.I.O. wins in Oshawa, it has other plants it will step into. It will be in the mines, demoralize that industry and send stocks tumbling."[73]

The Premier further announced that because of the Communist threat he had given orders for 200 extra men to be recruited to the provincial police force, "and we may call for more, too." The new recruits would not be equipped with revolvers "unless the situation warrants it," said Hepburn.[74] While the force was never deployed, it was a useful gambit to grab headlines and create the belief that Communists were a serious threat and there was imminent danger of violence. The special force was quickly dubbed "Hepburn's Hussars," and sometimes the "Sons of Mitch's."[75]

The union was responding on a number of fronts. GM Canada had expressed concern about losing export sales. Because of high domestic tariffs and favourable Commonwealth trade rules, GM shipped vehicles assembled in Canada to the U.K. and some other Commonwealth countries. Sales to the U.K. were estimated to be 50% of Canadian sales. When GM of Canada vice-president Harry Carmichael floated the idea of replacing export sales of Oshawa-built vehicles with vehicles assembled in the U.S., the response was forceful. UAW vice-president Ed Hall was quoted in the *Star*:

> If that is done, it would place the union workers in the United States plants in the role of strike-breakers. If that happens, we will spread the strike to the United States plants. It will be a strike of principles. It is up to General Motors."[76]

Hall added a comment that "Premier Hepburn's action in demanding the resignations of two members of his cabinet because they did not agree with him can be construed as nothing but dictatorship ... Premier Hepburn wants to be another Hitler." UAW officials were still putting pressure on the Detroit executives of GM, and Ed Hall stated that "General Motors has agreed to deal with the union, with Hon. Mr. Rogers as mediator, if Mr. Rogers will agree." Hall attributed this statement of agreement to C. E. Wilson, Vice-President of GM in Detroit.[77]

Hepburn's threatening action of enlisting veterans, among others, in his new special police led to a demonstration of war veteran members of Local 222, many wearing berets and sporting medals, who marched to the cenotaph in Memorial Park, laid a wreath, and with a roar passed this resolution addressed to Premier Hepburn:

Five hundred ex-service men, veterans of the great war, who are members
of the Oshawa local 222 of the International union, United Automobile
Workers of America, affiliated with the C.I.O. under the leadership of John
L. Lewis, hereby vigorously protest against your enlistment of veterans of
the great war for possible use against old comrades who are now peacefully
fighting for their rights as labor men and free citizens of Canada in the
strike at the Oshawa plant of General Motors.[78]

Additional criticism of Hepburn and support for the strikers came
in statements from Ernest Woollon, past president of the Toronto
Trades and Labour Council, and from UAW Local 195 in Windsor
whose statement asserted that "the General Motors strike would have
already been settled in Oshawa and local General Motors workers
would have been back at work, also, if Premier Hepburn had not inter-
fered in the negotiations."[79]

At some point during the day the stewards met and voted that they
did not want Hepburn to play a role in mediating the strike issues.
Reportedly the stewards had heard from UAW vice-president Ed Hall
that Canadian officials of GM could "settle the strike in five minutes
as far as they were concerned if Premier Hepburn could be eliminated
from the picture."[80]

The final decisive action of the strikers in reaction to the events of
the day came at a mass meeting held that evening with an attendance
of 3,000 members of Local 222. The meeting passed resolutions deplor-
ing the sacking of Croll and Roebuck. The main resolution passed at
the meeting denounced Hepburn's actions and statements that "threatened to destroy trade unionism and to raise an army to suppress the
growth and spread of legal trade unionism in Ontario;" and that
opposed "the legal right of labor to choose its own organization and
elect its own representatives to negotiate for it." The resolution noted
that Hepburn's "massing of police forces is entirely unnecessary, in view
of the discipline and peace which have marked this strike since its
inception, and can only be construed as a provocative measure." The
resolution concluded with this statement:

Therefore, be it resolved that members of local 222, United Automobile
Workers of America, Oshawa, go on record as condemning these policies
and as refusing to conduct any negotiations as long as Premier Hepburn is
a party to them, and we further respectfully request that he withdraw from

To protest Premier Hepburn's private militia, 500 members of Local 222 who were veterans marched to the cenotaph in Memorial Park. April 15, 1937. (Toronto Archives Fonds 1266, item 44159)

The veterans passed a resolution to Premier Hepburn that they "hereby vigorously protest against your enlistment of veterans of the great war for possible use against old comrades who are now peacefully fighting for their rights as labor men and free citizens of Canada in the strike at the Oshawa plant of General Motors." (Toronto Archives Fonds 1266, item 44160)

any participation in this dispute, because of his avowed bias, and allow the Dominion department of labor to act as mediator."[81]

Mayor Hall's "Ultimatum"

Despite the strong demonstration of unity and resolve from the ranks of the strikers, there was another attempt to undermine and weaken the strike that day—it came from Oshawa Mayor Alex Hall. A *Toronto Daily Star* front page headline read "Ultimatum to U.A.W. from Oshawa Mayor Demands U.S. Strike." Hall's message was provocative in the extreme, and clearly designed to grab headlines. It also posed a potentially serious problem for the success of the strike. Hall sent first a telegram, and then a letter to UAW President Homer Martin, and released both to the media. Hall's letter claimed that the strike "could be settled within half an hour's time except for the point that the General Motors will not recognize the International union." Hall blamed the International UAW for the impasse, claiming that international united action was required and "to date such has not been forthcoming." Hall deliberately set out to create splits in the union by claiming that "Canadian workmen [are] losing, while American workmen are gaining." Then came this inflammatory threat:

> Unless an agreement is negotiated between the General Motors and the union in Oshawa before the end of this week I am demanding that the members of your union in the United States go out on strike ... Unless the agreement is signed so that these men can start to work Monday morning, I expect the General Motors plants in the United States to close Monday. Failing this I am calling a mass meeting of all citizens of Oshawa, and laying all the cards on the table. I shall tell them that they are being fooled and hoodwinked, and that the international union is not playing the game with them.

Hall's goal, stated in his telegram, was to get Canadian workers "to abandon recognition of the international union idea." The telegram concluded, "Consider this as an ultimatum."[82]

Since the key issue at this point of the strike was getting GM to recognize the union, Hall's attempt to get workers to give up on the international union because they were being "fooled and hoodwinked" was potentially hugely damaging. It is telling that he had not a word of criticism of Hepburn in his letter, despite everyone recognizing that the attempt to prevent an agreement was being driven by the Premier. Hall's grandstanding in effect supported Hepburn by portraying the international as unwilling to help the Oshawa strikers. Hall's threat to call a mass meeting of "all citizens of Oshawa" could be read as a call to anti-union forces to show up and try to destroy the strike.

Thursday, April 15 – Day 8 – UAW and GM Meet in Detroit, Hepburn Meets the Communist Party in Toronto

Mayor Hall's ultimatum demanding that the UAW call a strike against GM in the United States had no credibility, since it was not supported by either strike leaders or strikers. The *Toronto Daily Star* interviewed five strike leaders who unanimously rejected Hall's remarks and, in the words of chief of the stewards and bargaining committee member George Day, expressed confidence in Homer Martin "as a leader and feel that he knows whether or not to call a strike in the United States at present. The union here is 100 per cent behind him in whatever he does." Hans McIntyre, secretary of the stewards, pointedly asked, "Since the Ontario government has stepped in and taken the negotiations out of the hands of General Motors, why should Mayor Hall have stepped in with such an ultimatum anyway?" Charles Millard told the *Star*, "We are satisfied that a strike will be called over there if it becomes necessary." Millard was asked by reporter Frederick Griffith, "If the strike is not called, will the strikers here accept his [Hall's] demand that they forget the international union and settle the affair themselves as a local group?" Millard replied, "Not a chance in the world ... We have in Oshawa a great respect for and confidence in our general president Homer Martin. I believe it would take more than the mayor's letter to weaken our allegiance." As McIntyre phrased it, "If Mr. Martin does not call a strike, I am confident that he will give us a very definite reason that will satisfy us of his sincerity." The *Star* found nobody with a dissenting view, and all the remarks expressed provided evidence of a mature thoughtfulness and understanding of the situation that must have come from broad democratic discussions.[83]

The UAW International officers also responded to Hall's ultimatum. Homer Martin affirmed his position that the agreement signed by GM in the U.S. applied to Canadian plants but did not commit to calling U.S. workers out on strike. A meeting took place in Detroit between top U.S. officials of GM and top leaders of the UAW, and a joint statement was released:

> In a meeting held at the General Motors Building here at Detroit the situation in Canada was discussed. After due consideration it was agreed the problem should be settled between General Motors of Canada officials and the committees representing the various local unions involved.
>
> Those at the conference were C. E. Wilson, vice president; H. W. Anderson, director of industrial relations, and Floyd Tanner, director of manufacturing, for the corporation.
>
> Homer Martin, president; Ed Hall and Wyndham Mortimer, vice presidents, for the U. A. W. A.[84]

Despite the sparseness of details in the statement, Hepburn immediately claimed the arrangement was a "surrender" by the CIO of its attempt to enter Canada and a success for his own campaign to stop the CIO and communism. Hepburn invited GM of Canada officials and strike leaders, including Millard, to his office for 11 a.m. the next day (Friday, April 16) for talks. Mayor Hall was also quick to read into the announcement vindication for his effort to undermine Oshawa workers' affiliation to the international union. Hall stated, "The invasion of foreign intervention for international advantage need not now be considered ... the Oshawa men must make their own agreement without consideration for Mr. Martin ... I am hoping that from this situation will be born a great Canadian union."[85]

Millard responded to the invitation from Hepburn by noting that it would be voted on by the stewards before it was accepted. He rejected Hepburn's interpretation of the Detroit statement by adding "if Premier Hepburn negotiates with us he will really be recognizing the C. I. O., because we are affiliated with it."[86] Abella stated that Millard, in response to Hepburn's invitation, "demurred until Martin, who was due in Oshawa that same day, could explain to the angry members of his union why he had reneged on his promises."[87] Abella's reference to "angry members" is not supported by a single source. Abella also completely omitted Martin's publicly stated reason for waiting to respond to Hepburn: "I can't confer with the Premier unless the stewards instruct me, in view of the resolution passed by the strikers on Wednesday night asking the Premier to step out of the picture as negotiator."[88] Even more concerning is Abella's description of the Detroit agreement. Abella stated that Hepburn had been informed that at a meeting with GM executives in Detroit, "Homer Martin had agreed that the Oshawa strike 'should be settled on a Canadian basis without recognition of the CIO … and that it should be settled between company officials and the various representatives of the local unions involved.'"

First, "without recognition of the CIO" is not wording that is included in the official joint statement released after the Detroit UAW-GM meeting. Yet, Abella included it in quotation marks. The footnoted source for this paragraph in Abella's article is *The Globe and Mail*, April 16, 1973. However, the words "without recognition of the CIO" did not appear anywhere in *The Globe and Mail* either. *The Globe and Mail* article stated that agreement had been reached "that the critical strike at Oshawa should be settled between the Canadian motor company's officials and the local Oshawa union." *The Globe and Mail* also quoted directly from the joint announcement that the issues "should be settled between the General Motors of Canada officials and the committee representing the various local unions involved."[89] There is an important distinction between saying the strike will be settled by the local union(s), and saying the strike will be settled "without recognition of the CIO." Even *The New York Times* acknowledged that "This seemed to be one of those "face-saving" devices which would enable both sides to claim victory. Premier Hepburn and the company would thus be able to say that they had stopped the C. I. O. drive in Canada, while the union could assert that it did not make any difference whose signature was on the contract, if the company signed it would recognize a local of the U. A. W. A. and through it the international union and the C. I. O."[90]

The *Toronto Daily Star* had reported earlier in the day in a story bylined from Detroit that, "Officers of the U.A.W. union and General

Motors officials conferred here to-day in an attempt to settle the Oshawa strike." The story further quoted the two UAW vice-presidents on the possibility of GM shipping cars from the U.S. to England. Ed Hall said a strike at GM plants in the U.S. was "likely" if GM tried to use those plants to handle any of the export business normally done by Oshawa workers. The other vice-president, Wyndham Mortimer, was unequivocal on that point: "One thing you can be sure of, that is that General Motors workers in the United States aren't going to 'scab' on those fellows in Canada." The *Star* reported that Mortimer was asked if the union would call a strike in the U.S. Mortimer replied that official action had yet to be considered, but "It all depends on how far it (the Canadian strike situation) goes—we can go further than the General Motors can."[91] In an interview with *Toronto Daily Star* reporter Frederick Griffin, Martin referred to the talks with GM officials in Detroit as "negotiations."[92]

Meanwhile, Hepburn expressed his unhappiness with the response to his request for additional RCMP troops and announced that he was going to add a further 200 recruits to his special "law-and-order" provincial police and ask the feds to withdraw their Mounties.

Martin made plans to travel to Oshawa the next day to present the results of the understanding with GM, but first he visited Windsor and gave a rousing speech to some 2,000 strike supporters. Martin predicted an early favourable end to the strike in Oshawa, referred to Hepburn as "the little Hitler" and "Canada's Pharaoh," and offered that were he to say a prayer "we would pray that this misguided, misinformed man ... would wake up suddenly and realize he is living in the middle of the 20th century."[93]

Hepburn Meets the Communist Party

Premier Hepburn's attempts to undermine the Oshawa strike through appeals to anti-communism were called out on this day—by the Communist Party. A delegation representing the Communist Party of Canada visited Hepburn to demand that he "abandon the pretext" that his obstruction of negotiations with the Oshawa strikers was because of ties between the CIO and the Communists. The delegation was headed by two Party members who held elected office in Toronto—Alderman Stewart Smith and School Board Trustee John Weir. The CPC delegation blasted Hepburn:

In your high office, you have mobilized armed forces in connection with the Oshawa strike on the basis of the entirely false charge that the Communist party was planning a disturbance. You cannot substantiate that charge. You cannot produce one shred of evidence to support it ... We have shown that you have dragged the name of our party into this matter to try to justify breaking off negotiations in violation of the democratic right of workers, and having done that ... the mobilization of armed state forces against the strike was proceeded with on the very same pretext ... Since you have decided to stand with the motor company against the demands of the Oshawa workers, say so, but do not drag the Communist Party into the matter as an excuse for your stand.[94]

Hepburn claimed in reply that, "I never had any thought of calling out the militia in the strike situation," but had taken "necessary steps to maintain law and order, in view of police reports that widespread disturbances were being planned," and had no other comment. It was a meeker response than the typical bluster from the Premier, and not very convincing. It was obvious to most by that time that the strike was remarkably peaceful, and that it was only the Premier who kept trying to raise threats of disruption.

The incident highlights a few points. One is that the Communist Party at this time had sufficient support and credibility that Hepburn felt obliged to receive their delegation. Another is that Hepburn's anti-communism was falling flat.

Friday, April 16 – Day 9

On Friday, April 16, Homer Martin made his second triumphant visit to Oshawa since the strike began. He arrived on the train from Windsor accompanied by Hugh Thompson and J. L. Cohen, who had just been retained as the union's lawyer in Canada. Thompson and Cohen had met Martin in Windsor the previous evening. They were met at the Oshawa train station by a cheering crowd, and then joined a parade through the town. The parade was led by the strikers' band, followed by the women strikers and then the rest of more than 3,000 strikers in columns of four. The *Star* called it "almost a royal welcome."

Abella's description of Martin's visit to Oshawa is so different from the contemporary news reports that it seems to be from a completely different event. He completely fails to mention the parade and cheering crowd, instead saying that Martin was due in Oshawa to "explain to the angry members of his union why he had reneged on his promises ... Martin arrived in Oshawa to face a hostile union negotiating team."[95] Abella cites no evidence at all that any member of the union or negotiating committee was hostile or angry. Media reports from the day all portray the exact opposite. As demonstrated earlier, all the workers, stewards, and union leaders who talked to reporters expressed trust in Martin and the international union, and not one accused him of breaking promises. That accusation only came from Premier Hepburn and Mayor Hall in their efforts to weaken or divide the strike.

The *Toronto Daily Star* interviewed Martin immediately on his arrival in Oshawa and reported this conversation:

> "I will confer with the committee, the stewards and with the local union."
> "Will you confer with the company?" he was asked. "I'll get in touch with C. E. Wilson (vice-president of General Motors) in Detroit, this morning by telephone."
> "With a view to what?" "To settling the strike."
> "Will you confer with the Canadian officials of General Motors here?" "I'll first call Mr. Wilson in Detroit."
> "And as a result of that?" "We hope there'll be a settlement of the strike."[96]

This clearly implied that there had been a negotiated agreement in Detroit that would lead to a settlement in Oshawa, and that Martin wanted to get confirmation from Wilson in Detroit that the Canadian officials had received their instructions.

Originally, a meeting of the stewards had been scheduled to discuss the invitation from Premier Hepburn, but that was put off once it was known that Homer Martin was arriving. Despite the Detroit understanding that negotiations would resume in Oshawa between the local union and GM of Canada, Hepburn was smarting from the

Homer Martin's second triumphant visit to Oshawa was by train from Windsor, accompanied by Hugh Thompson and J. L. Cohen, recently hired as counsel to the union. (Toronto Archives Fonds 1266, item 44181)

From the train station, there was a parade led by the strikers' band, followed by the women strikers and then the rest of more than 3,000 strikers in columns of four. The Star called it "almost a royal welcome." (Toronto Archives Fonds 1266, item 44180)

criticism of him by the Oshawa strikers and Martin, and was still trying to create obstacles. Hepburn acknowledged that he had contacted Carmichael and prevailed on him to issue a statement that there would be no resumption of negotiations unless the strikers returned to work, or the Premier sat in on the talks, "in view of the disrespectful remarks about the Premier by union leaders." Hepburn suggested Martin and Thompson should get out of Canada, calling them "a pair of braggarts, bluffers and hirelings of John L. Lewis." Hepburn the same day issued an edict to the Provincial Board of Censorship banning the showing of newsreels of the Oshawa strike anywhere in the province.[97]

The points of the Detroit understanding were discussed at meetings of the shop stewards, and then the entire membership. *The New York Times* reported that this basis for agreement was "accepted by nearly 300 shop stewards."[98] At the mass meeting of strikers later Friday evening, Martin provided more details of the discussions in Detroit between the UAW and GM. He reported that it had been agreed between GM and the UAW that the U.S. contract would serve as a framework for deals in Canada between the local unions in Oshawa, Windsor, and St. Catharines, including the provisions for seniority, and that the contracts would run concurrently with the U.S. contract.

The evening meeting was reportedly the largest mass meeting of strikers yet, with well over 3,000 workers present. While there was tremendous support from the Oshawa workers for Martin, it wasn't blind support. Martin's speech outlined that the negotiations in Detroit had reached an understanding that established the basis for a settlement of the strike, "putting it definitely on an International basis." Martin said the second point was that "your local unions should be recognized and dealt with by the plant management for the purpose of collective bargaining." Thirdly, said Martin, GM had agreed they would sign an agreement that included wages, hours, working conditions and "seniority as established in Detroit." The last and fourth point was "that the final agreement entered into shall be for exactly the same period with the agreement reached in the United States" with an expiration date of June 11, 1937. Based on GM's acceptance of these four points, Martin told the crowd, "I recommend thoroughly that you accept this proposition, return to work Monday morning, and negotiations start Monday to complete the agreement."[99]

Martin's recommendation to return to work before the workers had a signed contract was strongly rejected. The *Toronto Daily Star* reported, "the strikers first voted down thunderously," the suggestion that they return to work. The rank-and-file workers were determined on that point, and not even the International President of the union could sway them. Next, in light of the Detroit understanding, and Carmichael's new statement, the leadership recommended that the membership accept Hepburn's invitation to reconvene negotiations in his office on Saturday morning with Millard and Cohen representing the union. The members voted in favour.[100] At midnight, after the mass meeting, Martin issued a statement:

> We have always stood ready to negotiate provided negotiations were on the proper basis. A proper basis was reached last night in Detroit and confirmed today by telephone with General Motors officials in Detroit.
>
> According to the agreement reached in Detroit, negotiations were to be resumed between a local committee, guided by international representatives, including Hugh Thompson, and local plant management. With that understanding we came to Oshawa today. General Motors desires that these negotiations take place in the Premier's office.

After mentioning the telegram from Hepburn inviting Millard and Cohen to his office, Martin's statement continued:

> This invitation was dealt with at the membership meeting tonight. We are, therefore, accepting this invitation of the Premier to meet General Motors in his office, and J. L. Cohen, counsel for the international union, will attend with Mr. Millard and the committee on behalf of the union."[101]

It is noteworthy that Abella made no mention of either the stewards' meeting or the mass membership meeting. Martin's commitment to confer "with the committee, with the stewards, and with the local union" first, shows the rank-and-file democracy that was a key feature of the strike, but one that Abella did not seem to appreciate.

Significance of the Detroit Understanding Negotiated between UAW and GM

The agreement arrived at in Detroit between the top executives of General Motors and the top leadership of the international UAW was an extremely important development in the Oshawa strike. It played a critical role in the course of events from that point on, and in the final result of the strike. Nevertheless, it has been little understood in most of what has been written about the Oshawa strike. The understanding was reached after a full day of negotiations between three top GM officials and the three top officers of the UAW. This established beyond doubt that the parent company of GM of Canada was really calling the shots and working seriously to settle the strike. It also established, as Pendergest noted, "there could no longer be any question as to whether the International Union was involved in negotiations."[102] This reinforces the value of the workers in Oshawa affiliating with the UAW—they would not have had the same ability to get the U.S. executives to the table if they were operating on their own.

The details of the arrangement were not publicized by the company, most likely because they were trying to keep the balance between maintaining good relations with the international union, getting the strike in Oshawa settled, and not publicly fighting with the Premier of Ontario. Nevertheless, the basic substance of the agreement had been described to the Local 222 stewards and membership by Homer Martin. Abella stated that Martin's response to the "hostile union negotiating team" in Oshawa was to explain that he had "accepted a four-point program to settle the strike," that included opening negotiations at once, a seniority system similar to the UAW contract in Detroit, a concurrent agreement, and individual contracts with the local unions in Windsor and St. Catharines. Abella concluded, "The key point to the union of course, was the third, which meant that in future American and Canadian contracts would be negotiated at the same time to cover plants on both sides of the border."[103]

Abella's description of the Detroit understanding as a program that Martin had "accepted," rather than as an agreement that the union had negotiated with GM tends to diminish the role the international leadership played in putting pressure on GM to agree to the key provisions the union needed. Instead, his description almost makes it sound like the program had been imposed on Martin. Further, while the provision for concurrent contracts was considered a key issue for the union, the other points were also essential parts of the understanding. Seniority was probably the key substantive issue for Oshawa strikers to guarantee them job security for the future and the elimination of the debasing submission to management whims that they had experienced. The

C. H. Millard, Homer Martin, J. L. Cohen, and Hugh Thompson. Martin
is showing the others the "understanding" between the UAW and GM
that Martin had brought from Detroit to present to the union members
in Oshawa. (Toronto Archives Fonds 1266, item 44184)

agreement that contracts would be signed by the local unions for each
plant was also a key breakthrough, and one that union officials highlighted. Millard told the *Toronto Daily Star* on April 16,: "Naturally we
interpret the joint statement as victory for the international union. If
any agreement is signed with the local union, it will be a victory because
that will be recognition of the C.I.O. The local union is part of the
international union of United Automobile Workers of America which
is an affiliate of the C.I.O."

Saturday, April 17 – Day 10 – Conference Call of 45 UAW Locals

The tenth day of the strike began with an extraordinary event. At 10 a.m. Homer Martin arranged a conference call with the presidents of all forty-five UAW locals in the U.S. that represented General Motors workers. A similar call today, even with modern technology, would be seen as a significant demonstration of solidarity. In 1937, it was astonishing. It is important that Martin then issued a statement that emphasized that not just him, but the presidents of all forty-five UAW locals agreed, "that the Detroit agreement covered the Canadian plants. They unequivocally stated that General Motors must live up to the agreement and expressed themselves as unanimously behind the Canadian workers."[104] Abella stated that the call was made "to further bolster the morale of the strikers." Abella did not mention the issue of the Canadian plants being covered under the U.S. agreement. Rather than quoting from Martin's statement, Abella paraphrased it as saying "the Oshawa local had been promised all the support necessary to win the strike."[105] This shift in meaning is then portrayed by Abella as a broken promise, when he later claims "not one penny of aid came from the United States."[106] After the conference call, Homer Martin addressed another mass rally in support of the strike in Oshawa's Memorial Park.

Meanwhile, Charles Millard and J. L. Cohen headed to Toronto for the bargaining meeting with Hepburn and GM. Hugh Thompson and members of the bargaining committee accompanied Millard and Cohen to Queen's Park. When they arrived, only Cohen was admitted to the office of Hepburn's secretary, while the rest waited outside. The first issue was the disclaimer Hepburn wanted Cohen to sign that the union "was not in any way connected with the International CIO." Hepburn then went back and forth between the GM reps, who were in

Homer Martin speaks to the rally in Memorial Park, April 17, 1937.
(Toronto Archives Fonds 1266, item 44209)

Hepburn's office, and Cohen, before agreeing on a statement "that Messrs. Carmichael and Highfield represent General Motors, and Mr. Cohen and Mr. Millard, heading the employees' delegation, represent the organized workers of General Motors in Canada. Mr. Cohen and Mr. Millard specifically stated that they had no instructions from, and in no way represented the committee known as the CIO."[107] Of course, it is simply a fact that they did not represent the CIO—they represented the UAW.

According to Cohen, he then asked that the preliminary statement make clear that, "certain matters had been agreed to by General Motors in Canada through their executives in Detroit," specifically, separate agreements with the local unions at each plant, common duration of agreements with the agreement in the U.S., and seniority. Hepburn conferred with the GM executives and then told Cohen they did not agree to include those points in the preliminary statement. Cohen later told reporters that the three points were on a typed sheet that the Premier or one of his people had in his hand during the discussion. Cohen then said he would be satisfied to leave the points out as long as he had Hepburn's assurance they would be the first matters dealt with, and Hepburn gave him that assurance. Cohen then had Hepburn's approval to call Homer Martin in Oshawa, who approved the formula.

Cohen then stated that as a courtesy he wanted to discuss the statement with Millard and Thompson who had been kept waiting outside during this process. Hepburn agreed, and Cohen conferred with Thompson and Millard. The three of them decided to check some details with Martin, and Cohen was directed by reporters to a phone with a direct outside line. As Cohen was about to call Martin, Hepburn burst in and accused Cohen of entering his "private vault." Hepburn then said the talks were finished. Everyone was puzzled because the "vault" was a room commonly used by reporters to relax and make tea. It seemed Hepburn was really only looking for another excuse to prevent GM Canada and Local 222 from reaching an agreement, even though their parent organizations had already established the basis of that agreement. Hepburn falsely accused Cohen of refusing to accept the statement that had just been agreed to, and accused Millard of "identifying himself with the double-crossing treachery of the C. I. O. agents."[108] Hepburn said he would not resume negotiations with "the hirelings of Lewis," whom he accused of carrying out "remote control negotiations."[109] He tried once more to see if he could sidestep the elected leadership of the Local and pleaded for the Oshawa GM workers "to organize and send to this office men who truly represent General Motors employees."[110]

The Globe and Mail banner headline was "C. I. O. "Double-Cross" Disrupts Parley"[111] and in a front page editorial statement, "Crucifying Oshawa Workers," the *Globe* said the lesson of the aborted talks for Oshawa strikers and their wives and children, was that "They must realize at last how they are being made the dupes of self-serving and self-seeking United States agitators."[112]

Martin: Turn Back the Plane

Homer Martin drove to Toronto after the mass rally in Oshawa and, while waiting for his plane, received a report about what transpired at

Queen's Park. He then left for Flint, Michigan where he had important meetings scheduled with auto workers to attend Saturday night and Sunday. There was then one more remarkable illustration of how seriously Martin was taking the Oshawa strike. The plane was thirty miles out of Toronto, when Martin told the pilot to turn back, so he could deal with the new situation. Martin called Thompson, Cohen, Millard, and the members of the bargaining committee to meet him in his Toronto hotel room where they strategized for three hours, until 1 a.m. Martin then left for Flint Sunday morning.[113]

Sunday, April 18 – Day 11 – Ready for a Long Strike

Hepburn continued to try to ramp up hysteria about the CIO, violence, and communism. He also revealed the extent to which his motivation was protecting the mining corporations operating in the province, corporations in which he had a personal stake. Hepburn issued a statement on Sunday, April 18 that he had "definite knowledge" that CIO organizers were trying to foment strikes at Inco in Sudbury and in the Kirkland Lake and Timmins mining areas. He warned "if the programed invasion of this Province by the Lewis interests becomes any more menacing, more drastic combative action than has been instituted to date may be forthcoming from Queen's Park ... Lewis's crowd," the Premier claimed, "had only one purpose in mind—to cause strikes and close the mines ... Let me tell Lewis and his gang, here and now, that they'll never get their greedy paws on the mines of Northern Ontario as long as I am Prime Minister."[114]

Hepburn's exaggerated fearmongering about the CIO and attacks on Thompson, Martin, and Millard did not have the desired effect on the Oshawa strikers. After Hepburn sabotaged the talks on Saturday, the mood in Oshawa was calm and determined. Frederick Griffin's lead article in the *Toronto Daily Star* summed up the situation very well:

> One thing might be made as clear as it is at this moment irrefutable: the men are unshaken in their will to win peacefully. By the explosions elsewhere they are neither bewildered nor disturbed, if one may judge from the tone of scores of strikers contacted in the past week.
>
> Talk is now of a long strike and the men's executives are planning to meet it with a pacific marking-time in their tracks. "We'll stick until our belts are up to the last notch" said a chief steward Saturday night, with a north country, old country burr. "This strike has only begun. I've been through strikes in England that lasted three months, six months, nine months—and we won them. We'll win here." That is the sentiment on all sides. I might quote man after man in evidence of the morale, spirit and discipline. "We hope it lasts a while yet," said another man. "Every day gives us an education in labor-industrial matters we knew nothing about two weeks ago."[115]

This demonstration of determination and unity is remarkable. Concrete plans for a longer battle were also being put in place. The *Star* reported that the union leadership "are planning to meet and relieve the condition of enforced stalemate by a big strike dance, sports meets, boxing shows, concerts and the like, in addition to mass meetings. A protest demonstration is planned for Queen's Park Toronto, on Tuesday evening at which a large delegation of Oshawa strikers will attend."[116] The range of activities planned is very similar to the efforts made during the Flint sit-down strike to keep the union members engaged, active, and building community solidarity. The cultural and educational aspect obviously extended to the workers collectively learning about the strategy and tactics of winning the battle against GM and the provincial government; what the interviewed striker called "labor-industrial matters." All the lessons of the Flint strike were part of the immediate institutional memory of the union, most particularly the lesson that determination and boldness could overcome most obstacles.

The stewards' body continued to play an essential role. At their Sunday afternoon meeting, they set up three committees that they would need if the strike continued for a long time—a welfare committee, an entertainment committee, and a sick and benevolent committee, each chaired by one of the stewards.[117]

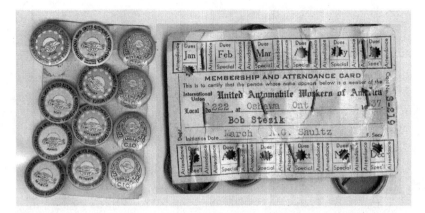

In the early years of the UAW, dues were $1 a month and were voluntary. Bob Stezik, Chairperson at Coulter Manufacturing and a member of the first Local 222 Executive Board, saved the lapel pins given when dues were paid, and pinned them to his first membership card, issued in March 1937. (Author's collection)

The stewards made another important decision at their meeting. They knew that the UAW general executive was going to discuss the Oshawa strike in Washington, DC, on Monday. Up for discussion was whether the International union leadership would call a strike of U.S. GM workers, or else raise funds to support the Oshawa strike for as long as might be required. The stewards debated the issue and came to the unanimous conclusion that **they were not in favour of a sympathy strike in the U.S.**, but that they wanted financial support.[118]

Abella does not mention any of the plans being made by the strikers, or the evident mood of determination and confidence prevailing in Oshawa. He does, however, give credence to a secret report furnished to Hepburn by an undercover police agent alleging that, "the pickets are half-hearted, most of the strikers are impatient and unhappy … and everyone around here is demanding an immediate settlement." The agent also claimed that the workers felt "betrayed by Martin's surrender."[119] Hepburn may have put some stock in the report of his agent, as Abella suggests. However, by not referencing any of the strong evidence to the contrary available in contemporary media accounts, Abella leaves the impression he also feels the report is accurate.

Monday, April 19 – Day 12 – A Most Remarkable Membership Meeting

The Monday morning *Globe and Mail* had a second front page editorial statement titled "Mayor Hall's Opportunity" that essentially called on Hall to lead a strike-breaking effort. Reminding Hall that he had promised that if the UAW refused to call a strike of U.S. GM plants, "he would call on the strikers to repudiate the Lewis emissaries and take things into their own hands," *The Globe and Mail* declared that "an agreement on wages and hours can be reached quickly with the obstacles, Martin, Thompson and Millard removed." Thus, Mayor Hall was urged to call on "the workers to repudiate the C. I. O." ... He should ask them to enlist his services, if they wish, as their representative, along with a committee of the employees, to meet the Prime Minister of the Province and officials of General Motors, in order that they may work out a square deal, and go back to their jobs respected and happy."[120] This astonishing call for Hall to personally try to displace the entire organization of Local 222 and the UAW was apparently taken seriously by the Mayor, and "it was reported that arrangements have already been made for rental of loudspeaker equipment."[121]

For their part, the strike leaders did not seem unduly worried with the prospect of the mayor winning the allegiance of the workers. If the mayor's meeting went ahead, the stewards planned to mobilize strikers to attend. In addition, *The Globe and Mail* reported, "Hugh Thompson, C.I.O. organizer, will also be present, and immediately after the Mayor finishes his speech he will get up on the platform and engage in a test of strength with Mr. Hall" for the support of the strikers.[122]

Mayor Hall met Thompson at 9:30 a.m. and said he intended to go ahead with his address to the strikers that evening. *Star* reporter

Momentous Local 222 membership meeting, April 19, 1937. The most-often reproduced photo of this meeting is from a different angle and does not show the women members, who were mostly seated at the front. (Walter P. Reuther Library)

Frederick Griffin said that "Thompson suggested that, instead of doing this, he step in where Hepburn had failed and attempt negotiations with General Motors instead."[123] Evidently this appealed to Hall's vanity, as well as offering him a way to show up Hepburn, whom he despised.[124]

GM officials must have been frustrated with the repeated obstruction from Hepburn preventing them from getting the plant back running. In any event, GM's general plants manager, J. B. Highfield, entered into "remote control" negotiations with Thompson, apparently without Hepburn's knowledge. As the *Star* reported,

> In the negotiations begun yesterday in Oshawa, with Detroit taking a hand, Mr. Highfield sat in an office and, several blocks away, Mr. Thompson sat in his room in the Genosha hotel and all day long the mayor rushed back and forth from the General Motors office to Hugh Thompson's bedroom.[125]

Apparently, Hepburn called Highfield at 2 p.m. to invite him to the premier's office, but Highfield told him he was too busy to meet.

Over the course of the day, the company agreed to the three framework issues established in Detroit and, in addition, to wage increases, hours of work and overtime, and no reprisals against union members. But the company did not agree to sign a contract before the workers returned to work. Knowing that Mayor Hall was going to try to sell this agreement when he spoke to the mass membership meeting scheduled for that evening, Thompson told Hall that it was "satisfactory enough" to be presented to the strikers. What followed was a remarkable meeting of the local union that demonstrated the determination and engagement of the members, and the interaction between the members and different levels of the union leadership. The *Star* gave an extremely detailed account by reporter Frederick Griffin that is well worth reading.[126]

Over 3,000 members attended the meeting, packing not only all the seats in the high school auditorium, but also the aisles and balcony. Griffin said the morale of the strikers was "higher than it has been yet," and judged the mood of the meeting "a fighting one." Right at the beginning some members wanted to eject reporters from papers that they considered to be unfair, but Hans McIntyre, secretary of the stewards, convinced the meeting to allow all the reporters to stay. At about 8:45 p.m., there were cheers for Hugh Thompson, who entered with the bargaining committee, but boos for Mayor Hall when he reached the platform. A gesture from Thompson quieted the booing, and Charles Millard introduced Mayor Hall.

Hall asked the crowd if they trusted and had confidence in Hugh Thompson, and when they roared their assent, he said, "Then your strike is over." Hall waved two documents that he said were signed by GM plant manager Highfield and endorsed by Thompson. One document was the basis of negotiations settled in Detroit. Hall said that the second document laid out the conditions that would prevail pending further negotiations if the strikers returned to work. There was a chorus of "no, no, no," but Hall persisted. He told the crowd:

> You'll return to work on a 44-hour week—four nine-hour days and one eight-hour day. Time and a half for overtime. Those day workers who were receiving 55 cents an hour or less obtain seven cents more an hour, and those 56 cents or over an additional five cents.

Hall said he also had GM's assurance there would be no reprisals, but the tumult of protest cut him off. According to Griffin, "above the din came shout after shout, 'What about the C.I.O.?'" Hugh Thompson told the crowd that he would address them after, but appealed to them

After 15 minutes of the meeting, reporters were asked to step out and wait in a basement classroom. Front to back, closest row: James Kingbury, *Toronto Daily Star*; J. Miller, AP; Mike Fenwick; *Clarion*. Middle row: Ivers Kelly, Canadian Press and *Globe & Mail*; Fred Griffin, *Toronto Daily Star*; no ID; Roy Greenaway, *Toronto Daily Star*; Harry Rowe, PR; William Noble, Local 222. Furthest row: H. Peterson, UP; Percy Cole, *Toronto Evening Telegram*; Ralph Hyman, *Globe & Mail*. (Walter P. Reuther Library)

to let Mayor Hall finish, saying "Don't harass anybody. Don't shout at anybody. We're all human beings." Some in the crowd yelled out "good old Hugh," and Hall was able to finish, although Griffin noted the evident strain he was experiencing, "his voice breaking, his face purple with the strain he was under, sweat dripping from his face." Hall then sat down "amidst another confused roar," and Millard said to the meeting, "I think we should look at this question very carefully and arrive at a careful decision in the light of the circumstances." At this point, fifteen minutes into the meeting, the reporters were asked to step out and were locked in a downstairs classroom while the meeting continued for some two hours.

Griffin reports that Thompson afterwards told him that he had said the agreement was acceptable because he wanted to test the membership and "prove that they are not dominated by me." Thompson had

Hugh Thompson told the April 19, 1937 meeting, "You are the organization
and the organization is you. You are one and indivisible."
(Toronto Archives Fonds 1266, item 44219)

met with the bargaining committee just before the meeting "and with
one exception, they definitely voted it down." I have found no record
of which member of the bargaining committee supported Hall's proposal. However, after Mayor Hall spoke, Millard said "I think we should
look at this question very carefully and arrive at a careful decision in
the light of the circumstances. It is a complex proposition to which it
has not been possible to give more study." The membership on the other
hand did not consider it a complex proposition at all. During the closed
portion of the meeting, there was "vociferous disagreement" with the
proposal to return to work, with speaker after speaker rising "to declare
his fighting disapproval of any such attitude."

When the reporters were readmitted to the meeting, they heard
Hugh Thompson speak. Griffin captured his remarks in detail, and they
are strong evidence of the way the strike was being conducted, and the
strength of democratic practices that were being followed:

> You have been offered something. You have refused. After a strike of 10 or
> 12 days you have decided after a unanimous or practically unanimous
> decision not to go back to work until something substantial to go back to

work for has been achieved. I am very, very happy that you are still absolutely solid, with but one thought in mind, to get the things you are after. With that spirit nothing on this earth can defeat your purpose.

We are doing our best to give you the story of the strike situation as it goes along. We report to the stewards and the stewards report to you …

This has been the greatest disciplined strike I have ever been in. You have avoided and kept out of arguments. Our own police have been responsible for this to a large extent. All the world is watching you. You have set an example by what you have done tonight. You must have known exactly what you want or you wouldn't have turned down the suggestion as you did. I am very happy …

Certain concessions you want and certain concessions you've got to get or you won't sell your labor to General Motors which is the only thing you have to sell …

No matter who says he is going to settle this strike, it will only be settled when General Motors sits down at the table and talks to your committee. No matter who sticks his finger in the pie, no matter who may try to get publicity out of it, it will be settled by General Motors and its employees.

You are the organization and the organization is you. You are one and indivisible.

Whether Thompson was setting Hall up to be shot down in flames (which Hall certainly believed, later calling it "double-crossing"[127]), or whether Thompson actually endorsed the deal, what is remarkable is that it was put to the members, who argued it out at length, and then made the decision once they had reached a clear consensus. And after the membership (over 3,000 out of 3,700 workers) had spoken—the leadership supported their decision. Thompson committed to keeping the members informed and engaged, and praised their unity and determination. It is noteworthy that the role of the stewards is also explicitly underlined.

After Thompson spoke, he said that Mayor Hall wanted to say something more. Met with boos, Hall said he intended to follow through on his ultimatum issued five days before. He accused Homer Martin of breaking his promises to the Oshawa strikers by not calling a sympathy strike in the U.S. Hall said, "You have the absolute inalienable right to join any international union you please. But what backing have you got so far?" Amidst shouts and boos, one worker shouted out, "financially." Hall asked, "What one cent have you got?" and another

Another view of women strikers at the meeting. (Walter P. Reuther Library)

striker replied, "We can show you." Despite that, Hall continued, "I'm still telling you, though, that you are being duped, you are being fooled, you are being hoodwinked." The decision by the international union to not call a sympathy strike of GM workers in the U.S. at that point was already known to the strikers, as was the reasoning behind it. And most importantly, their own stewards had already carefully considered the issue and decided unanimously that they were not in favour of a sympathy strike, but wanted financial support so they could continue the strike to a successful resolution. Mayor Hall's "ultimatum" balloon had already been deflated.

Thompson then said, "You have heard what the mayor has said ... All opposed to returning to work say 'aye'." The *Star* reported "There was a deafening roar of 'ayes'," and when Thompson asked for a show of hands "a forest of hands rose." Thompson then told the meeting, "You have gone through something in this meeting tonight that I have never experienced before. I am extremely proud of you."

The meeting next unanimously passed a resolution against Premier Hepburn's announced intention to license labour unions to restrict the rights of international unions.

Finally, to make clear the attitude of the membership towards Hugh Thompson after the events at the meeting, William Walker, a member of the bargaining committee, said that that committee wanted to ask the meeting to give Thompson another vote of confidence. "The motion passed with the men and women cheering and waving their hands." All in all, it was a remarkable demonstration of democratic rank-and-file unionism.

Mayor Hall later bitterly complained to the media that he had been betrayed and double-crossed by Thompson. Two members of the bargaining committee gave written statements to the *Oshawa Daily Times* to refute Mayor Hall. The Chair of the Bargaining Committee, George Day, had this to say:

> As a member of the bargaining committee, I wish to correct the statement issued by Mayor Hall in this morning's Globe to the effect that Hugh Thompson arranged for the Bargaining Committee to speak against the plan as outlined at the meeting by the Mayor. This is a mis-statement of facts. The members of the committee spoke on their own initiative and had no prearranged plan with Hugh Thompson. The proposition had been put to them in the same manner as all members at the meeting and the way they answered is a matter of record.[128]

The statement from William Walker was even blunter:

> As a member of the Bargaining Committee, I have read with great astonishment the absurd and preposterous statements of Mayor Alex Hall. He claims he was double-crossed by Hugh Thompson. He states that the Bargaining Committee was deliberately told to speak against his proposal that we go back to work and come to an agreement afterwards. He states that men were placed in strategic positions in the hall to shout him down.
>
> I can assure Mr. Hall that all these statements of his are simple figments of a fertile imagination, and have no foundation in fact whatsoever.

International UAW Executive Meets, Supports Oshawa

While the striking members of Local 222 were taking their fate into their own hands in a high school auditorium in Oshawa, their battle was being seriously discussed across the border in Washington, DC, where the UAW General Executive Board was meeting. UAW President

Homer Martin opened the discussion by stating, "The most acute situation that the International Union is faced with at the present moment is the Oshawa, Ontario strike." That shows remarkable support for Oshawa, considering everything else the UAW leadership was dealing with at the time. Martin reported that the General Officers of the union (Martin and the two Vice-Presidents) had urged General Motors to agree to 1) a signed agreement; 2) recognition of the union; and 3) that the signed agreement run concurrently with the U.S. agreement. Martin then reported on his trip to Oshawa and the intransigence of Premier Hepburn.[129]

The Executive Board considered both sympathy strikes and financial support for the Oshawa strikers. After the forty-four-day sit-down strike in Flint, and a series of other strikes and sit-downs, there was reluctance to call GM workers back out on strike. Homer Martin made it clear that he believed an agreement was close. He had previously stated that a sympathy strike would be a violation of the UAW contract with GM,[130] and in his report to the Board, he stated he was "personally against a sympathetic strike" because "we would be jeopardizing our entire union." According to a *New York Times* article bylined April 20:

> The union's executive board discussed the possibility of sympathetic assistance by General Motors units in the United States to assist the Oshawa strikers but no conclusion was reached. It was decided to give financial support to the strikers and a substantial sum would be voted by the board tomorrow it was said.[131]

Walter Reuther made a motion that the General Officers "endeavor to have Local Unions terminate the General Motors strike on the basis of a temporary agreement and that said temporary Canadian agreement be in effect until the termination of the U.S. General Motors Agreement, and when a U.S. General Motors Agreement is negotiated, all Canadian General Motors plants be included in this agreement."[132] Reuther's motion was discussed, but it was not adopted. It was tabled, and since it was never brought back, in effect it was defeated. The next motion before the Executive Board was "that we give our full sanction to the Oshawa Strike." This motion carried. Finally, a motion was made "that the General Executive Board go on record as authorizing the General Officers to give financial support to the Canadian Strike, and to do everything within their power to negotiate an amicable settlement as soon as possible, even though the International Union is not recognized in the final settlement." There is no record in the minutes that this motion was voted on, but there is the statement that "the consensus of opinion was that this strike be handled in the same manner as other strikes within the International Union."[133] Before the session was done, Martin was absent for a time, and on his return he "explained that he had been conferring with the officials of General Motors (long distance) in regard to the Oshawa strike. He stated, too, that he was of the opinion that the strike would be settled very shortly."[134] The acceptance of an agreement that did not explicitly recognize the International Union was not a new concession. This had already been agreed to as part of the 4-point understanding between the Detroit GM executives and the UAW Officers on April 14 that called for contracts between GM of Canada and each of the Canadian Local unions.

It is clear from the minutes that the UAW Executive Board gave serious consideration to the Oshawa strike, and were committed to supporting it, both through intervention with the Detroit GM officials and through financial support. The commitment of financial aid was communicated in a telegram from Martin to Thompson the next day that was made public. The UAW leaders were open with the Oshawa members, and also the media, that financial support would come from members of GM plants in the U.S. and then be transferred from the Executive to Oshawa. The *Toronto Daily Star*, for example, reported on April 21:

> Yesterday in Washington, Mr. Martin wired, the executive "unanimously voted necessary financial aid for the striking automobile workers." He explained that the money would be collected through the union locals in the General Motors plants of the United States but would be handled through the general executive.[135]

The *Oshawa Daily Times* reported that the intention was to raise money through a levy of $1 per member from GM workers in the U.S., which would amount to $100,000.[136] Obviously, this procedure would take at least some days to carry out, but there was no dire financial need on the part of most of the Oshawa strikers. They had received their regular pay on April 7, the day before the strike started. They were due to get their next pay on April 21, although it would not be for a full two weeks. In fact, the union advised members "not to call for your pay at the General Motors until we give you further instructions," because they were concerned GM might include quit slips in the pay packets.[137] We also know that many strikers had been conserving their resources since the strike began.

Abella provided an incomplete and misleading account of the UAW Executive Board meeting. Abella quoted Reuther's motion but neglected to say that it was not adopted. He noted that Martin advocated against a sympathy strike but gave Martin's statement the most negative possible interpretation as "reneging on his promise to the strikers." Abella omitted the crucial fact that the stewards in Oshawa had already voted (unanimously) that they were not in favour of a sympathy strike in the U.S. In addition, Martin had told the Oshawa strikers as early as April 15 that there would not be a sympathy strike. He still received a hero's welcome that day and an endorsement at the mass membership meeting. On this point, Abella's unwarranted criticism of Martin and the international union lined up with that of Mayor Hall and Premier Hepburn. Abella went further and stated, "The board also agreed that it would be impossible to support the strike financially as the union's treasury was empty. Nonetheless, for purposes of publicity, Martin wired Thompson that the executive had "unanimously voted necessary financial aid."[138] The first part of this statement is very problematic— nowhere in the Executive Board minutes is there a statement that it was impossible to support the strike financially, or that the union's treasury was empty. For Abella to claim "the board also agreed," when there is no record of that in the Board minutes is troubling, especially since Abella gives no other source for that claim. It is also patently untrue to say the Board decided it was impossible to support the Oshawa strike, because the Board explicitly discussed providing financial support to Oshawa, and agreed that they would do so—on the same basis as for any other UAW strike. The second half of Abella's statement, that the statement promising financial assistance was only "for the purposes of publicity," is an unwarranted accusation of dishonesty that is unsupported by any source.

Tuesday, April 20 – Day 13 – Hepburn Tries to Incite Strikebreaking

Hugh Thompson continued to try to find ways to sidestep Hepburn and encourage direct negotiations between GM of Canada officials and the union. On Tuesday morning, Thompson suggested to Millard that he call GM Oshawa plant manager J. B. Highfield to see "if the company has any wish to go on with it." Highfield told Millard he was willing to meet, and GM issued the following statement:

> The company, at the request of C. H. Millard, has agreed to meet the nego-tiating committee to discuss a basis of negotiations which would follow a return of the men to work. The committee will be the same as the com-mittee which negotiated with the company prior to the calling of the strike. The meeting will be held in the board room at 2 o'clock.

Highfield told Millard that these would be preliminary negotiations, prior to the real negotiations, and "it is understood that before these are started, the men will go back to work." The *Star* reported that Millard replied, "That would be a matter for discussion." Millard also asked "if it is necessary, outside advice will be acceptable?" and Highfield answered, "On the same basis as before," leaving the door open for the involvement of Thompson or other international union representatives. The *Star* also reported that, "It is further understood that Harry J. Carmichael, vice-president of General Motors in Canada, is driving from St. Catharines to take part in this afternoon's meeting. It is reported that he has been in touch with Detroit and that the con-versations may have a bearing on the result of the conference which has been initiated through a direct contact basis."[139]

This development was significant, because it set up a meeting between the company and the union in which Hepburn was not

Support for the strike was strong enough that Leo Gabourie celebrated his wedding on the picket line, April 20, 1937. (Walter P. Reuther Library)

involved at all. Further, it was clear that the Detroit headquarters of GM was continuing to play a role in working to resolve the strike. This was further highlighted by *The New York Times* report that "Renewal of peace talk in the Oshawa strike kept Mr. Martin busy on the telephone all day, conferring alternately with General Motors officials in Detroit and union spokesmen in Canada."[140] Local union officials asked for a postponement of the 2 p.m. meeting so that they could discuss matters with the bargaining committee, and it was agreed to move the talks to the next morning, Wednesday, April 21.[141]

Hepburn, however, was still determined to prevent any agreement that he did not control, and wanted to prevent the union and GM settling the strike between themselves. Hepburn arranged for Carmichael to stop at his office instead of heading to the conference in Oshawa, and they had a lengthy discussion. Hepburn also sent the following somewhat frantic wireless message to R. S. McLaughlin,

President of General Motors of Canada, who was aboard his yacht, the *Queen of Bermuda*, and homeward bound from a holiday:

> Would urgently request that you advise Carmichael to suspend any negotia-
> tions with strikers until your return Thursday morning. Would also ask you
> to give no statements regarding situation until I have had a chance to confer
> with you. Confidential reports indicate total collapse of strike imminent."[142]

Hepburn also notified the press that he met with eleven or twelve employees of GM Oshawa who wanted to accept GM's offer as presented by Mayor Hall and go back to work.[143] It is not clear who arranged this meeting, and it is even less clear who was in the delegation. All of them declined to give their names, but they did admit they had not been at the union meeting addressed by Mayor Hall, and that they spoke mainly for "non-union workers." Since almost all hourly workers had signed up with the union, it's possible this group included office workers, supervisors, or non-GM employees. The *Star* reported that: "They declined to state what went on in their interview with the premier."[144] Thompson told *The Globe and Mail* that he was not concerned by the group, stating, "I don't think there were any union men among them. Our men are holding solidly together. I am not worried in the slightest."[145]

Newspaper reporters were skeptical of this group that would not reveal who they were, but Abella accepted their claims without ques- tion. Abella stated, "Hepburn had met a secret delegation of strikers who told him that most of the men wished to return to work."[146] Abella provided no critical analysis of who was in the delegation, whether or not they were really strikers, and how likely it was they had significant support from the Oshawa GM workers, especially after the incredible display of determination and unity at the April 19 mass meeting. Abella may have not questioned the claims about this group because they bolstered his claim that the union was in trouble at this point.

Hepburn made use of the anti-strike delegation to make an open pitch for strike breaking. *The New York Times* reported that, based on the group claiming to speak for 1,500 GM workers, Hepburn "expected enough of the strikers to agree to return to work without recognition of the C. I. O. or any 'international' labor union affiliated with it to make it possible for the company to resume production under the protection of the Provincial government." He said he would "guarantee to maintain

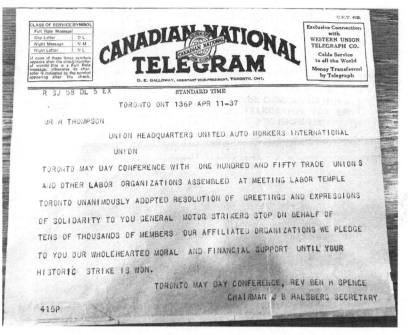

Telegram sent to Hugh Thompson in Oshawa from the Toronto May Day Conference, which planned the Toronto May 1 rally of 20,000 at Queen's Park. J. B. Halsberg on the telegram is almost certainly meant to be J. B. Salsberg. (Walter P. Reuther Library)

absolute law and order in Oshawa if the plants are reopened."[147] General Motors was not eager to accept Hepburn's invitation to invite confrontations on the picket lines in Oshawa, indicating informally "it did not believe it would be wise to try to reopen the plant as yet, in view of the temper of last night's [April 19] mass meeting."[148]

While Hepburn wanted to convince people that support for the strike was waning, there were a series of statements of solidarity with the Oshawa GM workers. An editorial in the *New Outlook*, the publication of the United Church of Canada, opposed Hepburn's appeal to anti-communism and resort to "recruiting of a little army." The editorial supported "the right of the workers of Canada to insist on collective bargaining and to conduct such bargaining under leaders of their own choice." To attacks on the CIO as a foreign organization, the *New Outlook* noted, "In the past, virtually all Canadian unions have had international affiliations. So long as they remained ineffective nobody objected." The editorial was reprinted on page 1 of the *Toronto Daily Star*.[149]

Another article in the *Star* reported support for the Oshawa strikers from U.K. political leaders and newspaper editors, including Clement Attlee, leader of the Labour Party who invoked the memory of the Tolpuddle martyrs, and the editor of the *Daily Herald*, who stated, "I wish the Ontario workers success in their efforts to secure their share of the profits being made by manufacturers in the present capitalist boom, and to win the right won long ago by workers to organize in their own defence."[150]

The Oshawa strike had received unqualified support from the beginning from the AFL-affiliated Toronto Trades and Labour Council. Other labour support included a resolution sent to Premier Hepburn from a conference of railway unions taking place in Sioux Lookout. The strongly worded resolution condemned Hepburn's provocative mobilization of police, and stated, "It is our studied opinion that your actions stamp you as being hostile to organized labor. We believe that in the struggle of organized labor for the social improvement of the lot of the working class, the opposition offered by you to the Oshawa strikers can be classified as being the most reactionary in the political history of Canada."[151] Meanwhile, the Fellowship for a Christian Social Order (FCSO) was making arrangements for a large rally in support of the Oshawa strikers to be held at Queen's Park.[152] Local 222 had been planning on sending fifty carloads of strikers, but cancelled due to breaking developments. The FCSO believed that "the teachings of Jesus Christ, applied in an age of machine production and financial control, mean Christian Socialism."[153] Eric Havelock and other members of the FCSO spoke at one of the earlier mass meetings of Local 222 during the strike, and Havelock described the occasion memorably in an article in *Labour/ Le Travail*.[154]

Wednesday, April 21 – Day 14 – Hepburn Vows Not to Deal with the Local Union

Hepburn had another meeting with Carmichael on Wednesday morning.[155] Hepburn's efforts with Carmichael and McLaughlin produced the results he desired. When Millard phoned Highfield several times regarding the follow-up meeting for the morning of April 21, he was told Highfield was not available. Then at about 11 a.m., Carmichael called Millard and gave him this statement, as reported by the *Star*:

> I can only reiterate my statement of Friday night: There can be no meeting between officials of General Motors of Canada and representatives of their employees until the men first go back to work or unless the premier of Ontario, Mr. Hepburn, meets Canadian executives of General Motors in joint conference with shop committee of the workers.[156]

In response, the union agreed to once again meet company executives in Hepburn's office. J. L. Cohen called Hepburn and made an appointment to meet him that afternoon. Hepburn tried to portray this development as vindication, but it merely reverted the situation to exactly as it was the previous Saturday, when his "vault" tantrum derailed the talks.[157]

After meeting with Carmichael the previous day, Hepburn laid out his goals to *The New York Times*:

> I will sit in on any conferences and there will be no recognition of the C. I. O., positively no recognition of that organization. **We will not deal with the local union of the U. A. W. We will deal with the men as General Motors employes, not as members of the local.** There will be no negotiations whatever carried on with paid organizers of the C. I. O.[158] (our emphasis)

Hepburn's vow that he would not "deal with the local union" is very significant. It goes beyond refusing to meet with representatives of the CIO to rejecting any formal negotiations at all with the local union, UAW Local 222.

The Premier met separately with Cohen and GM executives over four hours on the afternoon of Wednesday, April 21, and then issued this statement to the press:

> Mr. Carmichael and Mr. Millard conferred this morning and agreed upon the holding of a conference in the office of Premier Hepburn. Mr. Cohen visited the premier requesting that such a conference be arranged and stating that he and Mr. Millard represented the employees of General Motors at Oshawa and that the company would be represented by H. J. Carmichael and J. B. Highfield. Mr. Cohen stated that neither he nor Mr. Millard were instructed by or represented the committee known as C.I.O. Mr. Cohen further stated he had definite word from Mr. Martin that neither he nor Mr. Thompson would be returning to Toronto or Oshawa during the negotiations.[159]

Recognition or Repudiation of the CIO?

It was well understood that the issue of recognition of the union, and in particular the affiliation with the CIO, had been a central issue of the strike from the beginning. As a result, the press paid close attention to the exact wording in the Premier's statement, and its implications for the resolution of this key matter. The *Toronto Daily Star* asked Hepburn the key question: "Will Millard represent the Oshawa U.A.W. as well as the employees?" Hepburn's answer was, "I'm not concerned with that. He will not be representing the C.I.O. That's the line of demarcation."[160] This is a significant climb down in Hepburn's position from his statement just the evening before that "we will not deal with the local union of the U. A. W." Now, Hepburn had conceded that if Millard represented the local union, he was not going to object. He also was willing to meet with Millard knowing that he was a full-time paid representative of the UAW (affiliated to the CIO), and no longer a GM Oshawa employee. Thus, the statement that Cohen and Millard were not "instructed by or represented the committee known as C.I.O." was, in the words of the *Toronto S Daily tar*, "the simple truth, as neither has been at any time, being merely representatives of the U.A.W.A."[161] The *Star* further noted that "the document carefully avoided any exclusion of the status of the local union as one of the main points of further discussion."[162]

The New York Times report stated that, "The agreement was interpreted as a victory for the Premier" who insisted against formal recognition of the CIO, but also acknowledged that, "At the same time it was pointed out that even if the final agreement should not be signed by C. I. O. leaders or 'international' representatives of the U. A. W. A., the negotiators for the employes are duly accredited agents for the Oshawa local of the union, which in turn is affiliated to the C. I. O."[163] In fact, Hepburn told *The New York Times* that Cohen had used the telephone in the premier's office to check with Martin in Washington. "Hepburn said that he was not concerned with the question of whether Messrs. Cohen or Millard represented the U. A. W. A. in negotiations or any other group other than the C. I. O."[164]

As Thompson bluntly put it, "There can be no repudiation [of the CIO] when the representatives of the international union are sitting in on the conference with the premier."[165] *The New York Times* noted that the union officials believed "that the mere signing of a contract with their local representatives, regardless of how they were designated, was de facto recognition of the U. A. W. A., and through it, the C. I. O."[166] Whether or not the CIO would be in fact "repudiated" in the final contract with GM of Canada would depend on the exact wording of that document, but it was not the case that the CIO was repudiated in the April 21 preliminary document setting out the basis for re-opening formal negotiations.

The other aspect of the April 21 statement worth commenting on is the understanding that Martin and Thompson would not be in either Oshawa or Toronto for the duration of negotiations. Thompson clearly saw this as a diplomatic gesture to help reach a negotiated settlement to the strike. He told the *Star*, "I guess it would be just as well if I slid out of the picture for a bit; then there'll be no excuse for saying I'm gumming up the works."[167] Thompson expressed confidence in the union leadership in Oshawa to see that, "the strike will be carried on in an orderly and efficient manner" in his absence. "Certainly I have the welfare of the citizens of Oshawa at heart because I have stepped out of the picture three times to satisfy the premier's ego," he told the *Star*.[168] Also, as had been asserted earlier, when the union accepted Hepburn's invitation to meet with J. L. Cohen and Charlie Millard, "international union officials did not need to be Americans at any time. Canadians may be equally effective representatives" of the international union.[169]

Hepburn also accepted the union's firm position "that the strikers will not return to work until an agreement satisfactory to them has been signed by their representatives and approved by them."[170] As the *Toronto Daily Star* reported, Hepburn stated, "The men will go back to work when an agreement has been consummated between the company and the bargaining committee."[171] The stage was now set for formal negotiations between GM and the union to take place in Premier Hepburn's office the next day, with the Premier acting as mediator.

During the four hours that Cohen was conferring with the Premier, four strikers kept vigil. Two of them said they were interested in looking over the anti-strike delegation that was rumoured to be heading back to Queen's Park. "We just want to get a look at their faces and see who they are—shake hands with them," one striker told the *Star*.[172] As it turns out, "the back to work delegation failed to appear."[173] It was also reported that on this day the first installment of funds from the international union had arrived in Oshawa. Hugh Thompson announced that, "Mrs. Cohen, a Toronto social worker and wife of the union lawyer, would distribute the money as relief where necessary."[174]

Abella claimed that **before** the meeting of Hepburn and Cohen on April 21, "the negotiating committee however, was ready to sign an agreement **on almost any terms**."[175] In *On Strike*, Abella went further and stated that "Hepburn now had the upper hand."[176] These statements are unsupported, and furthermore they are not logical. If the negotiating committee was ready to agree to "almost any terms," and if Hepburn had the upper hand, then the result would have been the union agreeing to cede some ground in the negotiations. But in fact, the union maintained exactly the same position as they had taken on April 15 and that had been agreed to by the Detroit GM executives. It was not the union that retreated—it was Hepburn. The premier had vowed that he would not negotiate or recognize the local union, but by the time of the meeting with Millard and Cohen he had agreed that he wouldn't raise the issue of them representing the local union as long as they agreed they were not acting on behalf of the CIO. On April 17, before the vault incident, Millard and Cohen had agreed to essentially the same statement agreed to on April 21, when "Mr. Cohen stated that neither he nor Mr. Millard were instructed by or represented the committee known as C.I.O." Both of these statements are also in line with the April 15 understanding between GM's top U.S. executives and the UAW Executive Board that GM of Canada would sign agreements with the local unions in Canada that were based on the framework of the GM-UAW contract in the U.S.

Abella concluded, "It seemed that Hepburn had finally achieved his goal. The agreement would be signed by the local union only, and the CIO had been effectively excluded."[177] Abella fails to mention that just the day before, Hepburn had vowed that he would NOT negotiate with the local union. It was not Hepburn who had achieved his goal—it was the union.

Thursday, April 22 – Day 15 – Tentative Agreement

On the morning of the 15th day of the strike, the *Toronto Daily Star* reported that "Everyone was cheerful."[178] The strikers were hopeful about the talks to take place in Toronto, and in addition it was pay day—GM was distributing a deferred week's pay that they owed for the beginning of April. General Motors had announced that the pay envelopes would not include "quit slips" (notices of dismissal), so that removed any anxiety by strikers about collecting their pay.[179]

Far from making them feel financial pressure to abandon the strike, the pay was "enough, without any strike relief of any kind, to enable them to stay out striking for another two weeks at least," in the opinion of *Toronto Daily Star* reporter, Frederick Griffin, who added, "One thing has been forgotten in the many arguments of the past two weeks and that is this: The strikers were not suffering in pocket or stomach any more than they would have been had they been at work. Had they been at work, their next pay day would not have come until today—as it did come today, when they were paid."[180]

Men and women strikers line up to collect their pay from GM on April 22, the 15th day of the strike. This was a regular pay day— they had previously been paid on April 7, the day before the strike. (Oshawa Museum A016.12.3)

On the morning of April 22, the bargaining committee met in the office of the union's counsel, J. L. Cohen, and then proceeded to Queen's Park to meet the Premier and GM officials. From left to right: Pat Murphy, William Walker, Gertrude Gillard, George Day, C. H. Millard, George Frise, E. E. Bathe, F. P. Palmer, J. L. Cohen. (Toronto Archives Fonds 1266, item 44248)

In the morning, the Local 222 bargaining committee drove to confer with Cohen at his office in Toronto.[181] According to *The New York Times*, the committee included a shop committee of seven men and one woman.[182] They then all went to the Premier's office in Queen's Park where negotiations began in the afternoon.[183] When the union bargaining committee finally met GM of Canada officials, it was their first face-to-face negotiations since the strike began. Amazingly, Premier Hepburn's repeated obstructions had prevented the two principal parties from talking directly to each other for the entire 14 days of the strike. Once started, the talks proceeded smoothly, except for one snag when Hepburn was informed that a UAW representative, Claude Kramer, had arrived in Oshawa to advise the strikers in the absence of Hugh Thompson. Hepburn asked for, and was given, a signed statement from Cohen that he had "no intention of discussing with Mr. Kramer any features of the agreement now being worked out."[184] With that final obstacle out of the way agreement was quickly reached, and Hepburn released a statement to the press stating that, "a complete agreement was arrived at and, at this moment, only the approval of the employes, to whom the matter will be referred at a mass meeting to be called for tomorrow, is required."[185] As union representatives had said from the beginning—Hepburn had been the main obstacle, and once the union was able to negotiate directly with Canadian GM officials, an agreement was reached in a few hours.

Of course, although not mentioned by Hepburn, it was also essential for the stewards to discuss and vote on the tentative agreement. The 300 stewards met at union headquarters late Thursday evening. The atmosphere is captured by this *Toronto Daily Star* article:

> The cheers that came at intervals through the green baize doors of the assembly room, strictly tiled by a union policeman, soon spread to the 75 to 100 of the rank and file who crowded into the waiting room between the assembly hall and the little private offices.
>
> C. H. Millard spoke first. When J. H. Cohen [*sic*], labor solicitor, arrived about 10 p.m., he was greeted by cheers as he pushed up the three flights of crowded stairs to the waiting room.[186]
>
> The stewards discussed the details of the agreement for more than an hour before voting orally. "They shouted "Aye," and a joyous pandemonium broke loose for a few minutes."[187]

Cohen then issued this official statement:

The agreement negotiated by the bargaining committee was enthusiastically and unanimously endorsed as a basis of settlement to be recommended to the mass meeting.[188]

It was now up to the strikers themselves.

Friday, April 23 – Day 16 – Victory

April 23, 1937, was a day of celebration in Oshawa. The first order of business was to vote on the tentative agreement. The meeting was scheduled for 10 a.m. at the Oshawa Armoury. The building was secured and ballot boxes were brought in. By 9:30 a.m. at least 1,000 strikers were waiting, standing four abreast in a line that was a block long. As the strikers entered, they were identified by the chief stewards and showed proof of payment of union dues. They were handed blank ballots as they went in. The *Toronto Daily Star* reported that "Girl strikers, decked out in their Sunday best, marched up Simcoe St. in twos and fours, smiling happily. 'We've won,' two of them called across the street to a friend." Apparently, the women strikers were allowed to bypass the line-up and enter directly. Delegations from the Windsor GM plant and the McKinnon's plant in St. Catharines were issued credentials and also allowed to enter the meeting. Strikers on picket duty were relieved by UAW members from Windsor, St. Catharines, and two Oshawa feeder plants so that they could vote. The total Oshawa police presence amounted to one officer directing traffic.

The doors were tiled at 10:50 a.m. Each member of the bargaining committee addressed the meeting. Millard went over the terms of the settlement in greater detail than the others. Cohen summed up. Balloting

Voting on the tentative contract was scheduled for 10 a.m. April 23 at the Oshawa Armoury. By 9:30 at least 1,000 strikers were waiting, standing four abreast in a line that was a block long. (Toronto Archives Fonds 1266, item 44264)

"Long lines of stewards behind trestle tables separatèd the 'yeas' from the'nays.' They threw the overwhelming 'yea' ballots back into boxes, and held out in their hands the 'nay' slips."—*Toronto Daily Star* (Oshawa Museum A016.12.2)

did not start until 12 noon.[189] Despite some speculation in the press that there would be dissent, none was evident either at the stewards, meeting the evening before, or at the mass meeting in the Armories.

Hepburn had earlier complained that he believed a secret ballot vote would have resulted in acceptance of the deal presented by Mayor Hall. Perhaps in response, photographers and reporters were allowed to watch the ballot count. The *Star* noted that, "Long lines of stewards behind trestle tables separated the 'yeas' from the 'nays.' They threw the overwhelming 'yea' ballots back into boxes, and held out in their hands the 'nay' slips." While the ballots were being counted the crowd was cheering and singing. Continuing from the *Toronto Daily Star* account:

> Long lines of women strikers swayed in opposite directions while they sang songs. It looked like a practice drill. The whole of the crowd, which was too big to get entirely into the armories, was in a jubilant mood. Cheers broke out from time to time.[190]

Only fifteen minutes into the count, Millard went to the microphone and announced, "From the whisper I hear from those counting the ballots, there is not a doubt of the result. In fact, I am so sure of it I am instructing the pickets to return to their posts in order to remove the tents and other equipment."[191] The final tally was announced at 12:48 p.m.—2,205 in favour of the agreement and only 36 opposed.

The response to the vote was joyous. Even *The Globe and Mail* reporter noted that the "city is celebrating. Gaily, jubilantly." "General Motors employees tossed their hats in the air." Boxing matches were staged in the Armoury and a dance was held in the evening.[192]

The contract was signed in the Premier's office in the afternoon. Carmichael and Highfield signed for GM. Signing for the union were George Day (head of the stewards and chair of the bargaining committee), E. E. Bathe (Vice-President of Local 222), and Charlie Millard (Local 222 President). J. L. Cohen was with them. At that point both Millard and Cohen were employees of the UAW. A meeting was arranged for the next day in Windsor, where Carmichael and Cohen would take part in negotiations to achieve a contract based on the Oshawa agreement.

But as soon as the strike ended, the debate over who won it began.

Union counsel J. L. Cohen announcing the result of the vote—2,205 in favour of the agreement and only 36 opposed. (Toronto Archives Fonds 1266, item 44268)

The contract was signed in Premier Hepburn's office in the afternoon of April 23. Seated, from the left: H. J. Carmichael, VP and General Manager of GM Canada; Premier Mitch Hepburn; Charles Millard, Local 222 President; Louis Fine, Department of Labour. Sanding, from the left: J. B. Highfield, GM Oshawa Plant Manager, E. E. Bathe, Local 222 Vice-President; J. L. Cohen, union counsel; George Day, GM Shop Committee Chairperson. (Toronto Archives Fonds 1266, item 44274)

Chapter 6

Winners, Losers, and Lessons

> The agreement reached is a victory
> for those opposed to Lewisism.
>
> *The Globe and Mail*, editorial, April 24, 1937, page 6.

> Yesterday's shift, the first since the strike closed the plants 19
> days ago, saw union members working under considerably
> improved conditions. They could look forward, among other
> things, to a larger pay envelope next pay day.
>
> Older hands were back on the job with confidence that
> their seniority rights would be maintained, that the company
> no longer has the right to fire older workers and
> hire new men without consulting the union.
>
> More than that, they saw their first day with unionism
> on the job, with shop stewards watching assembly
> lines and checking up with the foremen on maintenance
> of all clauses in the agreement.
>
> The *Daily Clarion*, April 27, 1937, page 3.

The first winners of the Oshawa 1937 strike were the workers. As the *Daily Clarion* highlighted, the biggest immediate change as a result of the strike was a transformation of the workplace from one where management wielded total power, to one where the workers had collective strength to enforce negotiated rights. This was best represented by the presence of stewards, who performed their union functions despite not having explicit recognition in the contract. This was certainly not a victory for the forces "opposed to Lewisism."

In the longer term, we know today that the contract that settled the Oshawa strike was a clear defeat for the forces that wanted to stop militant industrial unionism from crossing the Canadian border. If not immediately, over the next several years industrial unions were successful in organizing Canadian workers in basic manufacturing and resource industries, and most were affiliated with the CIO. But even at the time of the contract settlement, the reality of the achievements of the union clearly contradicted the anti-CIO pronouncements of Premier Hepburn and most media outlets, particularly *The Globe and Mail*. To assess the contract signed by General Motors of Canada and the union, we should look at the contemporary assessments of that contract, as well as the actual wording of the document signed on April 23, 1937.

The Globe and Mail, and its editor, George McCullagh, had been either Mitch Hepburn's loudest supporter, or perhaps the main instigator urging him to take a firm stand against any incursion by the CIO. After the deal was finally signed, *The Globe and Mail* claimed that the battle in Oshawa had been "Canadianism fighting warfare imposed by foreign agitators":

> The agreement reached is a victory for those opposed to Lewisism. The C.I.O. is not mentioned in the settlement … We are certain Canadian workers will not submit to remote control by, or contribute to the success of, an organization built on sit-down strikes, bloodshed and law defiance. The C.I.O. cannot live down a record which marks it as a sponsor of gangdom. When its agents come here it is this background the Canadian people have in mind. Canadian workers will resent compulsion by gangsters. No matter what false and flimsy claims may be put forth by Lewis agents and their comrades the Reds, the C.I.O. is repudiated.[1]

The Globe and Mail already knew that workers in Oshawa had embraced the policies and organization of the CIO and its auto industry affiliate, the UAW. Many workers in Canada were responding enthusiastically to the idea of militant industrial unionism and believed that they were most likely to advance their own interests by being part of an organization that could unite workers on both sides of the border against their common employers. The vain attempt by *The Globe and*

Mail to claim that the CIO was "repudiated" because those three initials did not appear in the final text of the agreement was vigorously countered by union representatives.

Immediately after the signatures were on the agreement, Local 222 President C. H. Millard had declared, "The agreement is with the local union. I know and they know and the world knows the union has been recognized. All this business of trying to avoid saying so in so many words is just child's play." The *Toronto Daily Star* reported that "Neither Premier Hepburn nor General Motors heads disputed his assertion."[2]

Homer Martin and Hugh Thompson returned to Oshawa for the "Victory Rally" held in Oshawa on Saturday evening, April 24. Premier Hepburn again tried and failed to have them barred from entering Canada.[3] Martin declared to the crowd of 2,000:

> The settlement is a complete victory for the C.I.O. and provides you with advances in wages and improved working conditions. It was made by and for you as members of the United Automobile Workers of America. The U.A.W.A. would not stand in the way of you getting better hours and wages and so because of the antipathy felt toward it, we moved a few miles out so that the agreement we had already settled upon could be signed.[4]

Martin made it clear that he and Thompson had been out of the country to allow Hepburn to save face, but that the agreement that was finally signed was the one that had already been agreed to. In fact, Martin argued that if not for the Premier's meddling, "You men could have been back at work ten days ago."[5] Thompson reinforced Martin's assertion that the points of the agreement had been agreed to sometime before, and that the international union had played the major role in getting General Motors to accept the terms of the contract. *The Globe and Mail* quoted Thompson:

> "The strike was not settled at Queen's Park," Thompson told some 2,000 automobile workers. "It was settled at Grand Boulevard and Woodward Avenue, Detroit, between a foreign corporation and 'foreign agitators'. Martin conferred there with General Motors Corporation, and we used 'remote control' from Washington while the conference was under way in Toronto," the C.I.O. man claimed.[6]

Thompson clearly enjoyed throwing Hepburn's accusation of "remote control" back in his face.

Saturday, April 24, workers held a victory parade through the streets of Oshawa.
(Toronto Archives Fonds 1266, item 44296)

Some women members in the victory parade.
(Toronto Archives Fonds 1266, item 44297)

At the victory rally—Hugh Thompson, Homer Martin, and Claude Kramer.
(Toronto Archives Fonds 1266, item 44299)

Victory rally - Saturday, April 24, 1937.
(Toronto Archives Fonds 1266, item 44304)

The mass membership meeting the day after the contract was ratified left no doubt about the opinion of the GM workers in Oshawa. In response to Thompson's claim that, "Two Toronto newspapers had not told the truth concerning the strike and their editorials had tried to mislead the people," the meeting adopted a resolution to censure *The Globe and Mail* and the *Toronto Evening Telegram*.[7] The members then adopted a resolution reaffirming the allegiance of the workers to the UAW and the CIO. Finally, they voted to express their trust in Hugh Thompson and Homer Martin.[8]

Hepburn later admitted to the *Financial Post* that despite hoping to demolish the CIO, he had at best only succeeded in "holding it at arm's length."[9] The *Toronto Daily Star*, the only mainstream paper to be critical of Hepburn's anti-CIO crusade, mocked attempts to claim that Hepburn had succeeded because the agreement did not include an explicit reference to the CIO:

> Why was it Mr. C. H. Millard who signed first for the men when their agreement with General Motors was consummated? Obviously because he is head of the men's organization. What is the organization for which he signed as "President"? He is president of only one thing: Local 222 of the United Automobile Workers of America. And what is the United Automobile Workers of America? It is the C.I.O. union in the automobile industry.[10]

The Text of the 1937 Contract

The fact that the local union was recognized is very clear in a careful review of the text of the contract.[11] There are repeated references in the agreement to "a Shop Committee." The key section is Paragraph 4 (a) which states:

> The Management of the Oshawa Factory recognizes a Shop Committee consisting of nine members who shall be variously elected from fellow employees who are members of the local union. The Factory Manager shall be advised of the personnel of the Shop Committee and any changes made from time to time.

The key here is that the members of the Shop Committee are elected by employees "**who are members of the local union**," which can only mean Local 222 of the UAW. The agreement provides that it is the Shop Committee that has the authority to investigate grievances and meet with management to adjust grievances. Any dispute over any terms of the contract is dealt with through the grievance procedure, so this paragraph makes clear that it is the representatives of the local union, elected by the members, who are recognized by General Motors management to represent the members and to bargain with management.

In addition, the contract makes two other explicit references to the authority of the Shop Committee. It is stated that "the question of a suitable minimum wage" will be "later discussed and negotiated by shop committee and management." It is also noted that the issue of overtime work and pay for workers classified as maintenance will also "be later dealt with between shop committee and management."

Near the end of the short contract is the statement that "this agreement shall continue in force until and so long as and concurrent with the agreement between General Motors Corporation in the United States, dated February 11th, and the United Automobile Workers of America." This is one of the "four points" of the Detroit understanding. This contract term reinforces the connection between the local union in Oshawa and the international UAW. It is also an explicit mention of the name of the international union.

The contract concludes, "This agreement covering the Oshawa Factory of the company is signed by the union employees hereunder who signed on behalf of themselves and their successors in office representing the employees of the company who are **members of the local union**." [our emphasis] Since all parties understood that the local union was UAW Local 222, this is, as Millard asserted, recognition of the union. To underscore this fact, the union signatories, as the *Toronto Daily Star* pointed out, signed with their names and the titles of their elected offices in Local 222: C. H. Millard, President; George Day, Chairman; E. E. Bathe, Vice-President.

Contract Patterned on the U.S. Agreement

The Oshawa agreement contains all the key provisions of the UAW contract with General Motors in the United States, as well as some provisions that went beyond that agreement. If the two contracts are compared, it is clear that GM lived up to the commitment given to the UAW during their meetings in Detroit, to extend the provisions of the U.S. contract to Oshawa. The fact that the Oshawa contract goes even further is strong evidence that the leadership of the strike was not "ready to sign an agreement on almost any terms," as Abella claimed.

The March 12, 1937, agreement covering GM plants in the United States was "supplemental to and a part of the agreement dated February, 11, 1937."[12] This agreement was achieved after four weeks of negotiations between the top leadership of the international UAW and top GM executives following the end of the Flint sit-down strike. While it is somewhat more detailed than the Oshawa contract, the bulk of the agreement deals with the grievance procedure, and seniority (lay-off, transfer and rehiring procedure). These are two items that were most important to the Oshawa workers. In both cases, it is obvious that the language of the U.S. contract provided the template for the Oshawa agreement.

Grievance Procedure: Establishing a grievance procedure was one of the two basic building blocks necessary to having a real union—a collective organization that could protect the rights of workers on the job. The right to file a grievance, and to have a union representative meet with management to attempt to resolve it, challenged the previous system where supervisors had total power and workers risked their jobs if they raised a complaint. Wyndham Mortimer pointed out that this was one of the hardest items to negotiate in the March 12 agreement because "the corporation's legal advisers argued that for the foreman to deal with the shop steward was tantamount to giving up one of the employer's age-old prerogatives, namely the right to discipline, to run his own business."[13]

The grievance procedure agreed to in the U.S. recognized a shop committee of between five and nine members for each plant, depending on the number of workers in the plant. The shop committee handled grievances through several steps, which could eventually reach the top of the corporation and then be referred to an impartial umpire if not resolved. Fine points out that this grievance procedure "accorded the UAW effective recognition in all of GM's automotive plants."[14] However, this gain was short of the UAW's starting objective of having management give explicit recognition of the vast steward system that the union championed.[15]

The grievance procedure in the Oshawa contract is modelled very closely on the U.S. March 12 agreement. There is recognition of a shop committee of nine members elected by members of the local union. The steps of the grievance procedure are basically the same, and some paragraphs of the Oshawa agreement are word-for-word identical to the U.S. agreement. Both contracts end with the provision that unsettled grievances "may be referred to an impartial umpire by mutual agreement of both parties." The Oshawa contract also did not provide explicit recognition of stewards, but stewards continued to be elected and play an important role in the GM unit of Local 222 for many years after 1937.

Seniority: The seniority section of the Oshawa agreement is almost word-for-word a reproduction of the first six paragraphs of the corresponding section of the U.S. agreement. The only substantive difference is that in the U.S. agreement an employee notified to report for work has three days to report or provide an acceptable explanation for not reporting, or they are considered to have voluntarily quit. In the Oshawa agreement, they have one day to report. Homer Martin had explained this difference when he addressed the Local 222 members on April 16, and said it was because Oshawa was a smaller town.[16] Following those six paragraphs, the U.S. agreement had a few provisions that were not in the Canadian agreement. One provision allowed management to maintain a list of people who could be kept at work out of line of seniority. The U.S. agreement also noted that existing rules requiring the layoff of married women were maintained (unless altered in a manner satisfactory to the employees), and that when there were layoffs for an extended period of time "creating a social problem in the community," the rules would be modified to give preference to employees with dependents. The fundamental purpose of seniority is to reduce the power of management to arbitrarily decide who works and who does not, and replace that with an objective and fair measure—length of service with the company. The U.S. contract allowed GM management greater power to circumvent seniority, and by that important measure, the seniority section of the Oshawa contract is significantly stronger than the corresponding section in the U.S. agreement. Sidney Fine noted that in the March 12, 1937, agreement, "The

UAW was unsuccessful in its efforts to have seniority determined on the basis of service alone, as it had requested in its January 4 demands," but did make some progress towards this goal. [17]

No Discrimination: The no discrimination clause in the Oshawa contract closely followed similar provisions in the February 11, 1937, agreement in the U.S., and provided that "no discrimination of any sort will be practiced either by the Company or the employees, by reason of any activity, past or future, of any employees with, or in respect to, trade union activity or trade union membership." The U.S. contract had stated that "no discrimination shall be made or prejudices exercised by the Corporation against any employee because of his former affiliation with, or activities in, the Union or the present strike."[18]

Additional Gains for Oshawa

In addition to the key contract building blocks of seniority and a grievance procedure, the Oshawa agreement achieved a number of other basic improvements for GM workers, some of which go beyond what was in the U.S. agreement.

Hours of Work: The first paragraph of the Oshawa contract provided that the hours of work would be forty-four hours per week, comprised of four nine-hour days and eight hours on Friday, with all overtime paid at the rate of time and one-half.[19] This meant an immediate significant reduction in hours for Oshawa workers who, before the strike, had been working ten hours per day, fifty hours per week, and often more, all at straight time rates. The U.S. agreement stated that "The present policy of the Corporation is an eight-hour day and a forty-hour week with time and one half for all overtime after eight hours per day or forty hours per week."[20] This did not constitute a change or an improvement, but codified the existing practice. The UAW had initially demanded a thirty-hour week and a six-hour day.[21]

Wages: The U.S. contract did not include any general wage increases. GM had announced a five-cent increase in hourly pay just before signing the February 11 agreement ending the sit-down strike, but it was not one of the terms of the agreement. The five cents was considered by the union to be a gain of the strike, but it also may have been a response to Chrysler's announcement of a 10 percent increase the previous day.[22] The U.S. March 12 agreement did provide that, "Any wage complaints which cannot be settled by the local plant management will be dealt with further according to the grievance procedure."[23] In contrast, the Oshawa agreement provided a five cent per hour increase for all day workers earning over fifty-five cents per hour, and for all female bonus group workers; and seven cents per hour for all day workers being paid fifty-five cents per hour or less. The U.S. agreement stated that it was not possible to establish a uniform minimum wage in all GM plants due to "the variety of businesses and conditions under which General Motors operates its various plants."[24] However, GM agreed that minimum wage rates within a plant could be dealt with through the grievance procedure. The Oshawa contract included this commitment: "The question of a suitable minimum wage to be later discussed and negotiated by shop committee and management."[25] According to *The New York Times*, the Oshawa contract "gives to the workers concessions on wages and hours which the American contract did not include, but still does not give to the Canadian workers as good wages or hours as the American workers.[26] The article stated that both parties agreed the differential was justified "in view of lower living costs and different standards of living in the two countries." The UAW was finally successful in achieving wage parity between autoworkers in the U.S. and Canada in 1970.

Group Bonus Production Basis: The negotiated changes to the group bonus system in the Oshawa contract are even more significant. General Motors agreed to reduce the group bonus target from 140 to 120 percent starting with the production of the 1938 model, and to accomplish this by hiring more workers in proportion. They further agreed that, "the Company will co-operate to bring it down to one hundred per cent.[27]

This amounted to a massive improvement in working conditions for the large majority of workers who were part of the group bonus system, by significantly reducing the amount of production they had to accomplish to meet minimum wage rates, and an equivalent increase in wages if they exceeded the objective. It is also very significant that

GM agreed to accomplish this by hiring additional workers in proportion to the reduction of the production bonus objective. There were no equivalent gains in the U.S. agreement. There the UAW had demanded mutual determination by the union and management of the speed of production but fell short of its goal. The final language stated that time studies would "be made on the basis of fairness and equity consistent with quality of workmanship, efficiency of operations and the reasonable working capacities of normal operations. The local management of each plant has full authority to settle such matters." If there was a dispute, "the job will be restudied and if found to be unfair an adjustment in the time will be made." This language gave the union a voice, but left decision-making authority in the hands of management.[28]

The settlement in Oshawa thus meant shorter hours, at a better pace of work, and an increase of pay, all very significant improvements to the lives of assembly workers (and their families).

No Strikes or Work Stoppages: Remarkably, the Oshawa contract had no prohibition or restrictions on walkouts or strikes during the term of the contract. In contrast, the U.S. agreement stated, "Should any difference arise over grievances there shall be no suspensions or stoppages of work until every effort has been exhausted to adjust them through the regular grievance procedure, and in no case without the approval of the International officers of the Union."[29]

Rest periods and specified pay day: The Oshawa contract had two other provisions that were not in the U.S. March 12 agreement. The company agreed to provide five-minute rest periods in the morning and afternoon. GM Oshawa also agreed to pay workers every other Friday—a real improvement for Oshawa workers over GM's previous policy of issuing pay "on two days of the month decided by the company."[30] Neither provision was in the U.S. contract.

Windsor and St. Catharines

Another confirmation that the framework of settlement negotiated by the UAW international officers and U.S. executives of GM was implemented, was the speedy conclusion of agreements with the UAW locals representing GM workers in Windsor and St. Catharines. The Windsor agreement, in fact, was negotiated, signed, and ratified in one day—on April 24, 1937—the day after the Oshawa agreement was signed. The St. Catharines contract was settled on April 27. This fulfilled the commitment to sign agreements based on the U.S. contract with each Canadian plant.

The Windsor agreement[31] mirrored Oshawa's on hours of work, wage increases, seniority, grievance procedure, reducing the production basis to 100 percent through increased hiring, rest periods, regular pay days, and no discrimination. It also was concurrent with the February 11, 1937, U.S. contract. The Windsor contract referred to a "Plant Negotiating Committee" rather than a shop committee, but the role was the same. It provided for that committee to be represented in grievance discussions with the plant general manager "by a duly accredited representative or counsel of the Union, or they may act jointly."[32] The *Daily Clarion* reported that, "the agreement was endorsed by the union membership with only two dissenters at a meeting in the Hungarian Labor Temple." The *Daily Clarion* added that Andrew Hinding, a union member who had been fired by the plant management "and who had been called some uncomplimentary names by F. M. Church, plant manager, in the bargain, was reinstated."[33] Because there were no women among the 550 Windsor GM workers, there was no reference to a wage increase for women workers, and also no provision for separate seniority groups for men and women.

The *Daily Clarion* reported that on April 27, GM employees and management "arrived at a tentative agreement to be submitted to a mass meeting of Local 199, United Automobile Workers of America. The agreement is similar to that signed by Oshawa Local 222 of the U.A.W.A. Representing the St. Catharines GM workers were R. Lawrie, business agent of the U.A.W.A., J. Crozier, president of the union, Bert Hillier, Alex Beard, Miss Jean Blair, and Clinton Liptrott. J. L. Cohen acted as legal counsel for the union."[34] It is significant that the St. Catharines bargaining committee included a woman to represent women workers, as was done in Oshawa.[35]

There are three key take-aways from reviewing the Oshawa contract between General Motors of Canada and the local union. Firstly, it is very clear that on the most important points, seniority and the grievance procedure, the Oshawa contract not only maintains the framework of the March 12, 1937 agreement in the U.S., but in numerous paragraphs uses the exact same wording. This strongly supports the claims made by Thompson, Martin, and other union leaders that this framework had been agreed to in Detroit on April 15. There is no question that the "four points" announced at that time had all been fulfilled—1) the resumption of negotiations (once Hepburn's obstructions were overcome), 2) seniority, 3) contracts with the different local unions in Canada, and 4) contracts concurrent with the February 11, 1937, contract in the U.S.

Secondly, the workers in Oshawa were strong enough to achieve gains that went significantly beyond what had been achieved in the United States on March 12. The seniority language in the Oshawa agreement was stronger and allowed far less discretion to management to skirt seniority rules. The Oshawa contract achieved specified wage increases, shortened the hours of work that had been in place prior to the strike, and forced the corporation to commit to a very significant reduction in the pace of work—a reduction that management agreed would be achieved by hiring more workers in proportion. The workers in Oshawa also established a regular pay day and two five-minute rest periods.

Finally, despite claims to the contrary, General Motors had agreed to recognize the local union through recognition of a shop committee elected by the members of the local union. The contract was signed by a full-time representative of the international union (C. H. Millard, who was also President of Local 222) and two other officers of the Local (Vice-President E. E. Bathe and Chairperson of the GM Bargaining Committee George Day).

The achievements of the workers in Oshawa were the result of the incredible solidarity and mobilization of the rank and file members, the establishment of radically democratic structures of decision-making, the broad support from workers and the community, and the significant benefits of being part of the radically disruptive international UAW which had demonstrated that its commitment to workers in the auto industry extended to pushing the limits of the law, confronting corporations without compromise, and relying on the members to fight and win battles. In light of all this, claims that the union was "bankrupt" and "ready to sign an agreement on almost any terms"[36] must be seen to be ludicrous.

The Oshawa Workers Were Never "On Their Own"?

> In fact, the strikers were totally on their own. They had no savings, nor was there any strike pay to tide them over. Their earlier jubilation had worn off, and they were becoming increasingly desperate.[37]

In a literal sense, this assertion by Abella that the strikers were "totally on their own" is nonsense. Attention and support from the leadership of the international UAW could be seen from before the beginning of the strike through to its successful conclusion, and played a critical role in its success. A bigger problem is that Abella seems to think of support only in terms of cash transfers. Abella views unions as external servicing organizations, not as organic participatory organizations of workers. After all, there was no strike pay for the workers who occupied GM plants in Flint for forty-four days, fought off the police, withstood periods of time with no heat or water, and found ways to fend off injunctions. Does this mean the Flint workers were "on their own" because the international union didn't send them a bank transfer? If we see the union as a real, radically democratic organization of the workers themselves then it is obvious that the Oshawa strikers had willingly and enthusiastically joined an organization whose principles and actions they wanted to be a part of. They were like any other group of workers in any city who had decided to take up the battle to improve their lives by becoming part of the UAW. They supported industrial unionism and the mobilizing strategy and tactics that they saw being carried out by the UAW as part of the CIO. This also included having a vision of a democratic union run by the workers themselves with maximum participation, and building a union that had a strong, militant presence in the workplace that could organize workers to fight for their own interests. The successful tactics and strategies of the UAW, including building a mass stewards' body, ensuring the active participation of women workers and women relatives, building working class solidarity, and focusing on achieving seniority rights, a grievance procedure, and shorter hours of work, were central features of UAW organizing everywhere. Joining the UAW meant they would be adopted successfully in Oshawa.

The remarkable level of rank-and-file engagement in building the strike, and the impressive level of engagement and support from the top UAW leadership are evident in the strike calendar for April 1937 shown in Figure 1.

Strike Calendar - April 1937

Sunday	Monday	Tuesday	Wednesday	Thursday	Friday	Saturday
				1 STEWARDS	2	3
4	5 STEWARDS	6	7 STEWARDS (300) decision to strike	8 **STRIKE** MASS MEETING (3000)	9 UAW-GM STEWARDS (200-300)	10 HOMER MARTIN PARADE (3000) MASS MEETING (3000)
11 RALLY (7000)	12 Organizing meeting STEWARDS (300)	13 UAW-GM	14 UAW-GM STEWARDS MASS MEETING (3000)	15 UAW-GM (Detroit)	16 STEWARDS HOMER MARTIN PARADE (3000) MASS MEETING (3000+)	17 HOMER MARTIN - Conference Call RALLY HOMER MARTIN - Toronto mtg.
18 STEWARDS	19 UAW GEB (Washington) MASS MEETING (3000+)	20 UAW-GM (Detroit)	21	22 Tentative Contract STEWARDS	23 MASS MEETING Vote	24 VICTORY PARADE HOMER MARTIN
25	26	27	28	29	30	

Figure 3. Key: STEWARDS - Meetings of the stewards body. MASS MEETING - Local 222 membership meetings. PARADE/RALLY - Public Rallies. HOMER MARTIN - Homer Martin's meetings and speeches in Oshawa and Toronto. UAW-GM - Negotiations between GM & UAW. UAW GEB - UAW General Executive Board.

During the sixteen days of the strike, there were regular mass meetings of the Local 222 membership. There are newspaper accounts of six meetings, but there could well have been more. Some of these meetings had an attendance of over 3,000 workers. The meetings heard reports from local and international leaders, and the membership of the local made key decisions there, such as rejecting Mayor Hall's proposal to return to work without a signed contract based on promises from GM management. In addition, the stewards had been holding regular meetings even before the strike, and these continued throughout the strike. Several of the meetings were reported to have 300 or more stewards in attendance. The most important of these stewards' meetings also were reported in the major media, and that includes six meetings during the course of the strike, plus the meeting on April 7, where the decision was made to strike the following morning. With rapidly changing developments, threats from the Premier, negotiations that were on-again, off-again, the possibility of deployment of Hepburn's private militia, an outpouring of attacks from much of the media, and a steady stream of conflicting information, the stewards' meetings played a critical role in keeping the members informed and united. The stewards were able to have thorough discussions, make decisions, and then share information and help mobilize the members they represented. Having one steward for approximately every fifteen workers made this process more personal and qualitatively different than just having bulletins from the leadership to the members.

The union also built substantial support for the strike from the community and broader labour movement. During the strike, there were at least four mass public rallies and parades. Both times that Homer Martin visited Oshawa in the midst of the strike, there were cavalcades and parades with upwards of 3,000 people, and there were at least two large public gatherings in Memorial Park in central Oshawa, with up to 7,000 in attendance.

Ed Hall, UAW Vice-President, had visited Oshawa and spoken to a Local 222 membership meeting on March 25. Of course, the assignment of Hugh Thompson, with his deep experience as a UAW organizer, was vitally important support for the Oshawa local. In addition, other UAW or CIO representatives helped out at various times, including Sam Kraisman of the International Garment Workers, who spoke at a packed meeting at the Legion Hall on February 25,[38] Paul Brokaw, CIO publicity rep, who was in Oshawa briefly,[39] and C.R. Kramer, of the CIO education department, who was in Oshawa at the strike headquarters at the end of the strike when Thompson was in Washington.[40] Over the period of the strike, the international union also put Millard on staff and hired J. L. Cohen as the union's counsel, which meant they were paying the salaries of three staff primarily devoted to winning the strike and organizing General Motors. Homer Martin visited twice during the strike—a considerable commitment from the President of the international union during a period when sit-down strikes were exploding in number, and the international union was dealing with an almost overwhelming number of negotiations and legal challenges. On April 17, during his second visit to Oshawa, Martin arranged the unprecedented conference call with forty-five local presidents from GM plants in the United States to update them about the situation in Oshawa and gain their support and commitment of solidarity. Martin even had his plane turn around later on April 17 to return to Toronto, where he had additional discussions with Millard, Cohen, and the bargaining committee to plan how to deal with the latest obstruction from Hepburn. When Homer Martin took part in the victory parade on April 24, it was his third visit to Oshawa within two weeks.

One of the most important contributions to the Oshawa strike by the international union leadership, and also one of the most neglected in writing about the strike, is the serious pressure that the top UAW leaders were able to bring to bear on GM's top executives, who were in a position of authority over their wholly owned Canadian subsidiary. The UAW had just prevailed in one of the toughest, longest and most significant battles in U.S. labour history, and had wrestled union recognition, seniority, and a grievance procedure out of the worlds' wealthiest corporation. When the top officers of the international union let GM know they were serious about settling the strike in Oshawa, GM executives were listening. Ed Hall had told the Oshawa members on March 25 that he had already had discussions about their issues with C. E. Wilson, GM Executive Vice-President. Homer Martin had been in touch with William S. Knudsen, Executive Vice-President of General Motors, the day after the strike began, and there were more top-level discussions between GM and the UAW on April 13, 14, and 15. While these discussions were going on, GM executives were warned by the top UAW leaders that if they attempted to use vehicles assembled in the U.S. to ship to Canada or to replace Canadian-assembled vehicles for export that there would be a strike in the U.S. plants. The international UAW leadership also strenuously argued the legal point that the February 11 contract included Canada, because the first point of that agreement was that "the Corporation hereby recognized the Union as the collective bargaining agency for those employes of the Corporation who are members of the Union." There was no exemption for Canadian workers in the text of that provision. At the end of the lengthy discussions on April 15, GM and the UAW arrived at an arrangement that was intended to be the basis for a settlement in Oshawa, and the strike likely would have been resolved the next day when Homer Martin arrived in Oshawa but for the interference of Premier Hepburn.

Homer Martin took a break from the UAW Executive Board meeting on April 19 to speak to GM executives in Detroit, and the press reported that there were more U.S. GM-UAW discussions on April 20. The international leadership was closely following the final negotiations that led to a tentative agreement on April 22. Homer Martin was conferring with General Motors while talks were under way in Toronto, and was apparently aware of what the final terms of settlement would be in advance.[41] All of this effort had a major influence in the final resolution of the Oshawa strike: the U.S. agreement of March 12, and the understanding of April 15 clearly provided the basis for much of the final Oshawa contract. The fact that the Oshawa agreement not only incorporated the key provisions of the U.S. contract, but went beyond it, is testament to the solidarity and strength of the Oshawa local, and their determination and willingness to continue the strike until they achieved their objectives.

As far as financial support for the Oshawa strike was concerned, this was the topic of serious discussion at the UAW General Executive Board meetings the week of April 19 in Washington, DC. Despite Abella's misrepresentation, it is clear the international leadership of the UAW was committed to supporting the Oshawa strikers, and had made plans to raise money from U.S. locals. There is no reason to believe that this plan would not have been carried out if the strike continued for any length of time. The UAW leadership had already demonstrated over and over their commitment to workers who were on strike or occupying plants. Meanwhile, most Oshawa strikers were not "desperate," because they had just been paid. Some strikers also spoke up to Mayor Hall to say they had already received financial support when he claimed they had received nothing, and this was reported by the press.

Abella stated that, "The question of who had won the strike now became as prickly as the issues of the strike themselves."[42] His answer to the question is oddly contradictory. Abella said that it was "anything but a victory for Hepburn," and noted that the strike achieved its key objectives, that the strikers affirmed their affiliation with the UAW and CIO, and that by "defeating both the power of big business and the provincial government [it] inspired workers throughout the country, and gave the CIO the impetus it so badly needed to begin organization in the mass production industries."[43] But at the same time, Abella claimed that Millard and Thompson believed that "the union was lucky to get any type of settlement." According to Abella, "Thompson had told Millard to agree to any proposal the company made since the union was totally bankrupt and the men now realized that they had been "bamboozled" by Martin's lavish promises." Abella further argued, "Had Hepburn been able to keep the company away from the bargaining table for several more days, he would likely have achieved a complete victory, totally crushed the strike and, perhaps with it, the CIO in Canada."[44] Abella provided as a source for these statements his interview with Millard and a letter to Abella from Thompson. However, there is no quotation given from either the interview or the letter, so it is not clear if this assessment came from either Millard or Thompson (or both, or maybe neither). There is no reference, either, to support the assertion that the strikers felt "bamboozled," but lots of evidence that the strikers were ready to continue the strike if necessary and had confidence in their leadership. It is also hard to maintain that Martin had bamboozled anyone when the understanding between the UAW leadership and GM that Martin explained to the strikers' mass meeting on April 16 was delivered in full in the final agreement. Abella's claim that there had also been a promise of a sympathy strike that was reneged on, also does not stand up to scrutiny. The Oshawa stewards themselves had voted that they did not want a sympathy strike called in the U.S.. And why would the union strike against GM plants in the States when they had already negotiated with the top GM executives and been given a commitment that the Oshawa strike would be settled on favourable terms?

None of Abella's contradictory remarks make sense. He admitted that the Oshawa strike was a historic breakthrough for the CIO and industrial unionism, but didn't want to admit that the success was due to the principles and strategies that were followed. Abella did not believe that ordinary workers play an important role in unions or the strikes, so he only paid attention to statements from sources he considered more "important"—political leaders, media, and union leaders. Abella ignored the stewards and their meetings completely, for example, and paid scant attention to the mass meetings of the strikers. He never made any effort to find out what the rank-and-file strikers were saying or doing during the strike. It is likely Abella was strongly influenced by the views of Millard, who certainly had an axe to grind. Millard may have wanted to play down the 1937 accomplishments of the Oshawa members and the Local and International union leadership because he was removed from leadership by the left wing in Local 222 and the Canadian UAW a few years later, and then carried out a bitter fight against the left for years.

History's Judgement – the Oshawa Strikers Won

The best measure of who won and who lost the Oshawa strike is, of course, the results that followed. Local 222 survived and prospered, and still represents over 3,000 GM workers in the Oshawa assembly plant. There were certainly ups and downs, and the union faced a particularly difficult period later in 1937 and over the next year or two. An economic slowdown and internal division in the international UAW were factors in this. However, as Laurel Sefton MacDowell demonstrated, the activists of Local 222 were able to hang on, and use their commitment to an activist and working-class-based unionism to carry out a successful "reorganization campaign" in which stewards played a central role.[45] They also built support for the union through the Ladies' Auxiliary, a Rod and Gun Club, and community initiatives that included co-op stores, the formation of a workers credit union, organizing supplier plants, and the creation of an Oshawa labour council. Thus, despite a decline in union membership in 1938 and 1939, the UAW in Oshawa "laid its organizational groundwork which later provided a solid basis for dramatic union growth during the war."[46]

By the 1940s, the CIO unions had conquered the mass industries of Canada as convincingly as they had in the U.S. Auto, steel, rubber, electrical, forestry, and other workers joined CIO-affiliated unions in Canada by the millions over the ensuing decades, and played a predominant role in improving the working and living conditions of the working class in profound ways—improving wages, negotiating and then bringing into legislation medical coverage, establishing pensions, and achieving the forty-hour work week. The commitment to democratic and militant unionism also survived for a long time, both in Oshawa and in the broader Canadian labour movement, but was eventually undermined and largely destroyed by the adoption of anti-communism by most of the union leadership during the Cold War years. The destruction of left leadership in much of the labour movement was followed by the era of concessions, team concept, and subservience to the corporate capitalist class, as the gains of workers came under increasing attack by corporations and governments starting in the late 1970s.

The story of the Oshawa 1937 strike, and the victory it represented for militant, rank-and-file, class-struggle unionism should serve as an example for new generations of working class and union activists who desire to revitalize a fighting labour movement that is willing and able to fight for major improvements in the work and lives of the working class.

Lessons and Legacy

A close examination of the Oshawa 1937 strike is inspiring because it reveals a battle where rank and file workers and shop floor militants were in charge, and were a major factor in its success. Many details of the strike would likely be surprising to members and leaders of unions today. They were certainly surprising to me as an engaged member of Local 222 from 1980 to the present. They may also be surprising to researchers and labour historians because so much of the story has remained untold or has been misrepresented. Perhaps the most astonishing detail to learn is that in the short organizing period before the strike, a stewards' body was created with one steward for every company supervisor—a group of approximately 300 union activists that provided information, education, and organization to the workforce of 3,700, and provided leadership in worker resistance on the shop floor. From today's vantage point, it may be hard to envisage the meeting on April 7, 1937, where the stewards convened for over five hours until 1:05 a.m., took the decision to call a strike, and made all the arrangements to see that it came off successfully. They coordinated a walkout of all the workers five minutes after they clocked in, organized picketing, and set up picket line support. The ratio of stewards to workers was better than 1 to 15 in 1937. In contrast, since the 1950s the ratio of front-line union reps to workers in the unionized auto plants (both in the U.S. and Canada) has been 1 to 250.

The level of engagement and support from Oshawa GM workers was also remarkable, with regular mass membership meetings during the strike with attendance topping 3,000 at key junctures. The packed meeting that listened to Mayor Hall's passionate entreaty and rejected it resoundingly is a great example. The Local membership developed enough self-confidence that they were willing and able to vote down the request of UAW President Homer Martin to return to work before they had a signed contract.

The engagement of members extended to involving women workers (some 300 or more of them) who played a prominent role that was also noticed by the contemporary media. Several women were stewards or chief stewards, and there was a woman on the eight-member union bargaining committee. (There was also a woman on the bargaining committee of the McKinnon Plant in St. Catharines, the only other GM of Canada plant that had women workers.) A women's auxiliary was formed to carry out support activities, and there was significant solidarity organizing in the Oshawa community and beyond.

These features of the strike did not come about accidentally. They were part of the organizing strategy of the newly founded UAW, and all had been prominently used during the epic Flint Sit-down Strike and other battles in the U.S. auto industry. They were also all aspects of the class-struggle approach to union organizing that had been championed by the left (primarily the Communist parties of the U.S. and Canada and their allies) since the early 1920s. In Oshawa, there had been a legacy of attempts to form unions on an industrial model as far back as the 1880s with the Knights of Labor. But, the building of a solid foundation for successful industrial unionism didn't begin in earnest until after the defeat of the 1928 strike and was primarily led by Communists who organized shop units, united front organizations of the unemployed, ethnic communities, and civil rights groups, and established the Workers' Unity League and the Auto Workers Industrial Union. While their strategic considerations changed with changing circumstances, the Communists consistently aimed at advancing the interests of workers as a class. This principle is the explanation for their policies of advocating industrial unionism, and working for the unity of men and women workers, workers of different ethnic backgrounds, and employed and unemployed workers—all of which were important to the eventual successful organizing campaign in Oshawa. It also explains the consistent emphasis Communists placed on organizing workers in the workplace, where they directly confront corporate management. The determination to have the most democratic forms of union structure, with the deepest engagement of rank-and-file workers, and the biggest possible "army of stewards"[1] to take on management directly, all flow from this ideological understanding. Many of these policies are also key components of what is often termed "rank-and-file unionism," but they go beyond membership engagement and democracy to an understanding of class relations in capitalist society and a clear commitment to the interests of workers as a class.

The events of the strike provide very strong evidence that organizing as part of the UAW (and CIO) was beneficial to the GM workers in Oshawa. Canadian nationalism—portraying the CIO as "foreign invaders"—was used in the attempts to defeat the strike by both Hepburn and Mayor Hall, but was successfully combatted in 1937. The nationalist, and anti-communist, outlook of Irving Abella and others has since served to distort and downplay the important lessons of the Oshawa strike. The UAW was a better choice not because it was an international union, but because of **the type** of international union that it was. The UAW commitment to industrial unionism, rank and file democracy, shop-floor militancy, and mobilizing working class solidarity was what was needed. The boldness, creativity, and determination shown during the Flint sit-down strike and the rest of the explosive organizing going on in the U.S. auto industry also made the UAW the obvious choice of auto workers in Canada. In addition to being the kind of union Oshawa GM workers needed, the UAW was also best positioned to unite workers on both sides of the border against their common employers. The UAW was able to take on the top GM management in Detroit on behalf of GM workers in Canada. International solidarity on that basis was essential to the Oshawa victory.

Of course, ideological leadership was contested, in Local 222, in the UAW, and in the CIO. Unlike some CIO unions, like the Farm Equipment Workers and United Electrical Workers, the left didn't hold overall leadership in the international UAW, although it had significant influence before Walter Reuther and his slate swept the 1947 UAW election. There was no open conflict in the UAW leadership at the time of the Oshawa strike, but undoubtedly there were tensions between Homer Martin and others that later led to deep factional battles. In Local 222, there were clearly some strains between Millard and others in the Oshawa strike leadership, and this may have reflected some divisions between support-ers of the CCF and the Communists. The Communists chose to play a low-profile role during the Oshawa organizing and strike in the interest of unity, especially since Hepburn aimed so much of his rhetorical fire-works against Communists, claiming they were running the CIO and the strike. This policy was in line with the strategic orientation at the time of the Red International of Labour Unions, and the international Communist movement. Judged by its results, the United Front approach could not have been more successful. The victory in Oshawa was just one episode in the triumph of the CIO and industrial unionism that trans-formed the labour movement in Canada and the U.S.[2]

Following the 1937 Oshawa strike, and the later unionization of Chrysler and Ford in Canada, the left maintained substantial influence and support in Local 222 and more generally in the Canadian Region of the UAW. One indication of that support was the defeat of Charlie Millard as District Director in 1939 by George Burt, who was supported by the left. The election of Burt overturned the recommendation of the CIO leadership for Millard.[3] In the years following the victory in 1937, left and right contended for leadership of Local 222, and leadership positions alternated between them for the next two decades. The influence of the left went beyond elections though. For example, Local 222 sponsored a weekly Open Forum on Sunday evenings. In the fall of 1943, this forum featured a well-attended series of discussions on the Soviet Union. The Local paper reported that, "specific discussions to date have been on Labor in the USSR, Agriculture and the Constitution of the Soviet Union ... It is hoped in this way to give those interested at least a glimpse of the varied life existing among the people of the USSR. Future subjects to be dealt with concern the matters of Health, Science, Education and other related topics."[4] At that time, of course, support for the Soviet Union, our wartime ally against Nazi Germany, extended beyond progressive unionists to most Canadians.

Another indicator of the influence of the left and a class-struggle approach was the persistence of shop-floor stewards' positions in many workplaces. Stewards at GM continued to play a role on the shop floor through the 1940s and also held regular bi-weekly meetings with a varied agenda. These meetings were reported on in the Local paper. GM stewards were still functioning until the mid-1950s, although they

GM stewards who resisted speedup in 1949 were fired, which resulted in a twenty-one-day strike that was supported by the Local 222 membership and leadership, and by the Canadian District Council of the UAW, but not by the International union. This picture shows the "UAWA Police" who were mobilized to support the strike. (Local 222)

were never recognized in the collective agreement. Another measure of the strength of the left in Local 222 and the Canadian section of the UAW at that time was the major wildcat strike against GM Oshawa in 1949 that was sparked by the firing of stewards who resisted company speed-up. The Local 222 membership voted to strike over the firings and stayed out on strike for twenty-one days, defying pressure from the Union's international leadership. The District Council (representing Canadian UAW Locals) not only voted to publicly support the wildcat, they donated $1,000 to the Local's strike fund to bolster the battle.[5]

The strength and effectiveness of unions with red or red-influenced leadership in winning gains for workers made them a target of the capitalist ruling class. Part of the motivation of the anti-communism of the Cold War and McCarthyism was to weaken unions by eliminating leaders who fought for the working class without compromise. The Taft-Hartley legislation in the U.S. in 1947 combined loyalty oaths that required all union officials to swear they were not Communists with provisions to gut the effectiveness of unions by outlawing solidarity strikes and secondary boycotts, and by introducing "right-to-work" laws allowing states to ban union shops. Right-wing leaders in the labour movement failed to fight Taft-Hartley, choosing instead to take advantage of it to advance themselves by eliminating their opposition. Unions like UE, Mine-Mill, the Longshore and Warehouse Union

(ILWU), and a dozen others, who refused to eliminate left leaders or to endorse Cold War policies were expelled from the CIO and viciously raided by other unions. In Canada, the Canadian Seamen's Union (CSU) shared a similar fate.

Walter Reuther consolidated his control of the UAW starting in 1947 through a purge of left-wing staff, and an effort to remove Local leadership that did not toe the line. In Oshawa, that included visits from Reuther to try to sway the results of Local elections, and the laying of charges to expel members who were accused of meeting with Communists, notably Local 222 President Cliff Pilkey and staffer Paul Siren.[6]

The purge of the left was a major setback for the labour movement, which became largely dominated by leaders who endorsed the ideology of "partnership" with corporate management and class collaboration. This was true in the UAW in both the U.S. and Canada, including in Local 222. This didn't mean the end of resistance, but it certainly made it more difficult. In the auto industry, resistance to corporate demands for concessions was a factor in the 1985 split of the Canadian section of the union to form the Canadian Auto Workers (now Unifor), which further fragmented opposition to the corporate agenda. Contract gains were made in Canada over the next twenty years that were not matched by the UAW in the U.S., but by the early years of the 2000s, both unions had fully bought into partnership with the auto manufacturers and were accepting major concessions such as two-tiered wages and the elimination of defined benefit pensions for new hires. Conversely, when opposition to the concessions and corruption in the union led to a successful movement for "one member one vote" in the U.S. and the election of dramatically more militant leadership, there was no corresponding movement for reform in Unifor.

There are important lessons for both labour activists and labour researchers to be learned from the Oshawa 1937 strike. The labour movement in Canada and the United States has been in retreat for many years but is showing some signs of resurgence. Future progress will depend on transforming unions into organizations that are based on the interests of their members as part of the working class—on class struggle, not class collaboration. This requires more than ever reaching and engaging rank and file workers and leading them to find ways to exercise their power in their workplaces. The Oshawa 1937 strike can serve as a guidepost in this necessary effort to revitalize the labour movement. We should look for ways to translate the example of the Oshawa stewards into deeper and denser representation structures in today's workplaces. Oshawa showed that this can be done even without formal recognition in a collective agreement. We need to learn how to ensure that union democracy is real engagement, and not just a formality.

The strikers in Oshawa in 1937 proved the benefits of a real commitment to equality and challenging divisions and discrimination; of building solidarity with workers in the community; and of building meaningful solidarity with workers across the country and internationally. Radical industrial unionism requires radicals—people who understand that capitalism is a system designed to rob us and needs to be replaced. The successes of 1937 would not have been possible without the contribution of this outlook, and it is the "missing ingredient" we need in the labour movement today.

Notes on Sources and Bibliography

There has been a lot of historical research focusing on the early days of the UAW, but much of it focuses on developments in the United States. *Walter Reuther: The Most Dangerous Man in Detroit* by Nelson Lichtenstein covers this period in great detail and provides a good overview of the forces at play in the establishment of industrial unionism in the auto industry. Lichtenstein's work tells the story with a focus on Reuther, who was UAW President from 1946 until his death in 1970, but also provides a comprehensive account of the internal and external struggles during the period when the union's success was still uncertain.[1] The pivotal 1937 sit-down strike in Flint that established the UAW is described in detail by key participant Henry Kraus in two books (*The Many and the Few*, and *Heroes of Unwritten Story*), and by academic Sidney Fine (*Sit-down: The General Motors Strike of 1936-1937*).[2] Important insights also come from other sit-down strike participants, Wyndham Mortimer (*Organize! My Life as a Union Man*) and Len De Caux (*Labor Radical: From the Wobblies to CIO, A Personal History*).[3] Union and Communist activist Walter Linder highlighted the importance of Communists in the organizing that led up to the Flint sit-down, and the radically democratic organization of the workers during it in *How Industrial Unionism Was Won: The Great Flint Sit-down Strike Against General Motors 1936-1937.*[4] The official Communist assessment of the successes and failures of the Flint sit-down was provided in the contemporary pamphlet by William Weinstone, Secretary of the Michigan Branch of the CPUSA, *The Great Sit-Down Strike.*[5]

Roger Keeran's book, *The Communist Party and the Auto Workers' Unions*, documents that in the United States "in the 1920s and 1930s Communists in auto were the main voices on behalf of industrial unionism and class struggle," and played a role in "building the UAW that could not have been easily duplicated by others."[6] John Manley's article, "Communists and Autoworkers: The Struggle for Industrial Unionism in the Canadian Automobile Industry, 1925-36" shows that the same was true on this side of the border.[7] Manley concluded, "While it is an exaggeration to argue that Communists alone built the UAW in Canada, they can be credited with laying most of its foundation."[8] The first Canadian worker to join the UAW, James Napier, provides a first-hand account of that foundational work in *Memories of Building the UAW.*[9]

Communist organizing efforts in the Canadian auto industry in the 1920s and 1930s were part of a broader strategy of organizing the working class through international organizations like the Red International of Labour Unions (RILU), and its Canadian affiliate from 1930 to 1936, the Workers' Unity League (WUL). *Raising the Workers' Flag* by Stephen Endicott provides a well-documented study of the contributions of the WUL to the intense class conflict of the Depression years and the efforts to unionize workers in those difficult circumstances.[10] John Manley's article on the WUL, "Canadian Communists, Revolutionary Unionism, and the "Third Period": The Workers' Unity League, 1929-1935," reviews the work of WUL leaders and concludes they modified and adapted the Communist line to local realities and "led the majority of all strikes and established union bases in a host of hitherto unorganized or weakly organised industries" in 1933-1934.[11] Tom McEwen's autobiography, *The Forge Glows Red*, includes many details about the key events and personalities he was involved with as first general secretary of the WUL.[12] Other details from the perspective of one of the leaders of the Canadian Communists can be found in *Yours in the Struggle: Reminiscences of Tim Buck*.[13] Parallel developments in the U.S. are well documented in *American Trade Unionism: Principles and Organization Strategy and Tactics*, a collection of contemporary writings about the U.S. labour movement from the early 1900s to the mid-1940s by William Z. Foster, a prominent leader of the CPUSA and the head of the Trade Union Unity League (TUUL), the equivalent of the WUL in the U.S.[14]

Robert Dunn's book, *Labor and Automobiles*, published in 1929, has extensive information about the state of the auto industry in North America on the eve of the Great Depression, including detailed sections on wages, hours of work, speedup, and health and safety. Dunn surveys early efforts to unionize the auto industry in the U.S., and also includes an account of the Oshawa strike of 1928 and developments in Canada.[15]

Gender, race, and ethnicity, are important factors in understanding divisions within the working class, as are conflicts between skilled trades and production workers. These demographic issues all had relevance in the efforts to unionize the auto industry in the 1930s. Achieving working class unity depended on how divisions and discrimination were dealt with, and the extent to which they were overcome.

The role of women workers in the early years of auto industry unionism in Ontario and the contradictions faced by women union members are the subject of *Labour's Dilemma: The Gender Politics of Auto Workers in Canada, 1937-1979*, by Pamela Sugiman. Sugiman draws on oral histories to provide important insight into the lives of women at home, at work, and in their union activities.[16]

August Meier and Elliott Rudwick showed that combatting racism against Black workers was fundamental in establishing the UAW, in their book *Black Detroit and the Rise of the UAW*. Meier and Rudwick also discuss conflicts over how to deal with racism between different groups and individuals contending for union leadership at that time.[17]

Steve Babson's groundbreaking book, *Building the Union: Skilled Workers and Anglo-Gaelic Immigrants in the Rise of the UAW*, showed that there was substantial overlap between three strategic groups that made major contributions to the success of the UAW—skilled workers, the left, and immigrants from England, Scotland, and Ireland.[18] Babson noted that in seeking the pivotal organizations and events that determined the broader sweep of history, "the evidence indicates that factories, like neighborhoods and nation-states, each represent the unique crystallization of their particular history, even as they also represent the prevailing dynamics of the surrounding world."[19]

The historic 1937 strike in Oshawa took place within this broader context, but despite its acknowledged groundbreaking nature, it has been the subject of relatively few academic studies. Perhaps the lack of detailed research on the Oshawa strike is because Irving Abella's publications have been so widely accepted as authoritative.[20]

The most detailed and informative account of the day-to-day events of the Oshawa strike is found in the MA thesis by James Pendergest,

Labour and Politics in Oshawa and District 1928-1943.[21] Pendergest's work is carefully sourced, and includes important information about the views and roles of many of the key union activists and leaders, as well as the political background of the Oshawa community, particularly the growth, influence, and conflicts between the Communist Party and the CCF, and their impact on the labour movement. Pendergest's research material, including tapes of his interviews of key figures, and detailed notes from newspapers, has been deposited with the Oshawa Museum. Unfortunately, Pendergest's work has received insufficient attention from historians, perhaps because it was never published and was overshadowed by Abella's articles and books that came out at about the same time.

Much of the other research on the early period of the UAW in Canada focuses on developments after 1937, and refers to the strike only briefly. Nonetheless, examining how conflicts and trends developed in the union afterwards may make clearer what the key issues were during the strike that marked its beginning. Particularly useful is Don Wells' article examining the early history of UAW Local 200, representing Ford workers in Windsor. In "Origins of Canada's Wagner Model of Industrial Relations: The United Auto Workers in Canada and the Suppression of 'Rank and File' Unionism, 1936-1953," Wells described the evolution of a local union from one based on the rank and file and centred on workplace direct action, into one following a top-down model based on collective bargaining by leadership and acceptance of stability in labour-management relations.[22] This evolution was anything but peaceful, and some of the forces that contested it are foreshadowed in the Oshawa strike. Charlotte Yates, in her book *From Plant to Politics*, focussed on the period from the formation of the first UAW locals in Canada in 1936 up to 1984.[23] Yates largely accepted Irving Abella's analysis of the Oshawa strike, but provided much useful material about the internal struggles between left and right in the union after that date.

Laurel Sefton MacDowell's work, "After the Strike – Labour Relations in Oshawa, 1937-1939" showed that the Oshawa strike had important effects in the community as well as in the workplace. [24] MacDowell detailed the gains made as a result of the "class conscious-ness" that developed in industrial workers in Oshawa during the period following the strike, even though they were not reflected in immediate growth in union membership. This included learning to deal with local management and the grievance procedure, formalizing the structure of a ladies' auxiliary, and cultural activities such as sports leagues, a theatre troupe, and a rod and gun club. The strike and establishment of Local 222 also had impacts on working-class community life, such as the launch of a workers' credit union, growth of a co-op society, the creation of a labour press, and labour influence in municipal politics.[25] The roots of all these later advances can be seen as growing from the strategies and tactics followed by the Oshawa strikers.

Christine McLaughlin demonstrated the value of seeking out the voices of rank-and-file workers and union activists in two pieces that investigate the establishment of the UAW in Oshawa.[26] Her oral history interviews powerfully evoke what it was like at work and in the community before the union was established, and the transformational changes that resulted from its success. Carole Condé and Karl Beveridge also relied on extensive interviews with more than two dozen union pioneers in Oshawa in the production of their multi-media history of the birth of the union in Oshawa, and its history up to the beginning of the 1980s.[27] Transcripts of key interviews are available from Library and Archives Canada, and several were a valuable resource for this book in understanding the early drive for unionization, the events of the strike, and the reasons for its success—all told in the words of the workers involved.[28]

Contemporary daily newspapers provided a rich source of material, because the Oshawa strike was a major news story that was given extensive coverage. A modern reader would probably be astounded by the breadth and detail of coverage of the events, including long interviews with many of the key figures on all sides, detailed accounts of union membership and stewards' meetings, and photos and interviews of strikers. I reviewed the coverage of the *Toronto Daily Star*, *The Globe and Mail*, the *Toronto Evening Telegram*, and *The New York Times*, who all had reporters on the scene in Oshawa providing daily coverage, as did the local newspaper, the *Oshawa Daily Times*. The Communist Party publication, the *Daily Clarion* is a valuable source because of the role that Communists and their supporters played before and during the strike.[29] As Abella and others pointed out, during the strike "Every day, a truck from Toronto arrived at the picket line, carrying that day's edition of the *Daily Clarion*, which was handed out free to the strikers."[30] Every single day of the strike, the front page of the *Toronto Daily Star* featured a banner headline about the strike. On the first day of the strike, April 8, 1937, the *Star* had seven separate articles about the strike that started on page 1 and another article and five photos on pages 2 and 3.

I also used some of the archival resources of Unifor Local 222, which include minute books of membership and executive meetings back to 1937, most issues of the Local Union publication *The Oshaworker* back to 1943, and other publications, documents, and memorabilia.[31] On the occasion of George Burt's retirement as Canadian Director of the UAW in 1968, the Education Department of the Canadian section of the union published *Where Was George Burt?*, which includes Burt's recollections of working at GM Oshawa in the years prior to the strike, and the events of the strike.[32] Burt's accounts were valuable, since he played an important role in the organization of Local 222. The most extensive archival resource on the early history of the UAW, including the Canadian section of the union, is housed at the Walter P. Reuther Library (WRL) at Wayne State University in Detroit. I reviewed WRL records including minutes of UAW Executive Board meetings and the records of UAW Region 7 (the Canadian Region). The WRL also has collections of the papers of Hugh Thompson, the UAW organizer assigned to Oshawa before and during the strike; George Burt; and Art Shultz, the first Financial Secretary of Local 222. The Archives of Ontario has extensive material relating to the Oshawa strike in the Mitchell Hepburn Fonds.

Bibliography

Archives
Library and Archives Canada - Carole Condé and Karl Beveridge Fonds
Walter P. Reuther Library, Archives of Labor and Urban Affairs, Wayne State University.
Local 222 (UAW, CAW, Unifor)

Newspapers
Toronto Daily Star
The Globe and Mail
The Evening Telegram
Financial Post
Daily Clarion
The New York Times

Publications of Local 222
Official Opening U.A.W. Hall November 17, 1951. UAW Local 222 Education Committee,
   1951.
Forty Years of Progress: 40ᵗʰ Anniversary 1937-1977. UAW Local 222, 1977.
50th Anniversary Book. CAW Local 222, 1987. Untitled.
A 75-Year Retrospective "In Our Own Words." Toronto: National Automobile, Aerospace,
   Transportation and General Workers Union of Canada, 2012. Sarnovsky, Joe, editor.
The War Worker. Published biweekly in 1943.
The Oshaworker. Published biweekly starting in January 1944.

Interview
Interview with Don Nicholls, December 1, 2021.

Books and Articles
Abella, Irving. "The CIO, the Communist Party and the Formation of the Canadian
   Congress of Labour 1936-1941," *Historical Papers/Communications historiques 4(1)*
   (1969) 112-128.
Abella, Irving. "The CIO: Reluctant Invaders," *Canadian Dimension* Vol. 8, No. 6
   (March-April 1972).

Abella, Irving. *Nationalism, Communism and Canadian Labour: The CIO, the Communist Party, and the Canadian Congress of Labour 1935-1956.* Toronto and Buffalo: University of Toronto Press, 1973.

Abella, Irving. "Oshawa 1937" in Abella, Irving ed., *On Strike: Six Key Labour Struggles in Canada, 1919-1949.* Toronto: James Lewis & Samuel, 1975.

Babson, Steve. *Building the Union: Skilled Workers and Anglo-Gaelic Immigrants in the Rise of the UAW.* New Brunswick and London: Rutgers University Press, 1991.

Baldwin, Neil. *Henry Ford and the Jews: The Mass Production of Hate.* New York: Public Affairs, 2001.

Benedict, Daniel. "Good-bye to Homer Martin," *Labour/Le Travail,* 29 (Spring 1992), 117-155.

Betcherman, Lita-Rose. *The Little Band: The clashes between the Communists and the political and legal establishment in Canada, 1928-1932.* Ottawa: Deneau, 1982.

Buck, Tim. *Steps to Power.* Toronto: Trade Union Educational League, 1925.

Buck, Tim. *Thirty Years, 1922-1952: The Story of the Communist Movement in Canada.* Toronto: Progress Books, 1952.

Buck, Tim. *Yours in the Struggle: Reminiscences of Tim Buck.* Toronto: NC Press, 1977.

Canadian Auto Workers. *No Power Greater.* Toronto: Canadian Auto Workers, 2003. Multimedia DVD.

Condé, Carole and Beveridge, Karl. *Oshawa—A History of CAW Local 222 (1982-83)* Multimedia installation.

De Caux, Len. *Labor Radical: From the Wobblies to CIO, A Personal History.* Boston: Beacon Press, 1970.

Dunn, Robert W. *Labor and Automobiles.* New York: International Publishers, 1929.

Endicott, Stephen. *Raising the Workers' Flag: The Workers' Unity League of Canada, 1930-1936.* Toronto Buffalo London: University of Toronto Press, 2012.

Fine, Sidney. *Sit-down: The General Motors Strike of 1936-1937.* Ann Arbor: University of Michigan Press, 1969.

Foner, Philip S. *History of the Labor Movement in the United States: Volume II.* New York: International Publishers, 1955.

Foster. William Z. *American Trade Unionism: Principles and Organization Strategy and Tactics.* New York: International Publishers, 1947.

Frank, David. *J. B. McLachlan: A Biography.* Toronto: James Lorimer & Company, 1999.

Gilpin, Toni. *The Long Deep Grudge: A Story of Big Capital, Radical Labor, and Class War in the American Heartland.* Chicago: Haymarket Books, 2020.

Gindin, Sam. *The Canadian Auto Workers: The Birth and Transformation of a Union.* Toronto: James Lorimer & Company Publishers, 1995.

Gonick, Cy. *A Very RED Life: The Story of Bill Walsh.* St. John's: Canadian Committee on Labour History, 2001.

Halpern, Rick. *Down on the Killing Floor: Black and White Workers in Chicago Packinghouses, 1904-54.* Urbana and Chicago: University of Illinois Press, 1997.

Havelock, Eric. "Forty-Five Years Ago: The Oshawa Strike," *Labour/Le Travail* 11, 1983, 119-124.

Kealey, Gregory S. and Palmer, Bryan D. *Dreaming of What Might Be: The Knights of Labor in Ontario, 1880-1900.* Toronto: New Hogtown Press, 1987.

Keeran, Roger. *The Communists and the Auto Workers' Unions.* New York: International Publishers, 1980.

Kraus, Henry. *The Many and the Few: A Chronicle of the Dynamic Auto Workers*. Los Angeles: The Plantin Press, 1947.

Kraus, Henry. *Heroes of Unwritten Story: The UAW 1934-39*. Urbana and Chicago: University of Illinois Press, 1993.

Lichtenstein, Nelson. *Walter Reuther: The Most Dangerous Man in Detroit*. Urbana and Chicago: University of Illinois Press, 1995.

Linder, Walter. *How Industrial Unionism Was Won: The Great Flint Sit-down Strike Against General Motors 1936-1937*. Brooklyn: Progressive Labor Party, 1970.

Logan, H. A. *Trade Unions in Canada: Their Development and Functioning*. Toronto: MacMillan Company of Canada, 1948.

Losovsky, A. *Program of Action of the Red International of Labour Unions*. Quebec: Red Flag Publications, 1978.

MacDowell, Laurel Sefton. "After the Strike: Labour Relations in Oshawa, 1937-1939." *Relations Industrielle/Industrial Relations*, 48 (4) (1993); 691-711.

MacDowell, Laurel Sefton. "The Career of a Canadian Trade Union Leader: C. H. Millard 1937-1946," *Relations Industrielles/Industrial Relations*, 43 (3) (Autumn 1988), 609-632.

Manley, John. "Communists and Autoworkers: The Struggle for Industrial Unionism in the Canadian Automobile Industry, 1925-36," *Labour/Le Travail*, 17 (Spring 1986) 105-133.

Manley, John. "Canadian Communists, Revolutionary Unionism, and the "Third Period": The Workers' Unity League, 1929-1935," *Journal of the Canadian Historical Association* 5 (1994) 167-194.

Marquart, Frank. *An Auto Worker's Journal: The UAW from Crusade to One-Party Union*. University Park and London: The Pennsylvania University Press, 1975.

Matles, James J. and Higgins, James. *Them and Us: Struggles of a Rank-and-File Union*. Boston: Beacon Press, 1974.

McEwen, Tom. *The Forge Glows Red: From Blacksmith to Revolutionary*. Toronto: Progress Books, 1974.

McLaughlin, Christine. *The McLaughlin Legacy and the Struggle for Labour Organization: Community, Class, and Oshawa's UAW Local 222, 1944-49* (unpublished MA thesis, 2008).

McLaughlin, Christine. "Producing Memory: Public History and Resistance in a Canadian Auto Town," *Oral History Forum d'histoire*, 33 (2013) 1-31.

Meier, August and Rudwick, Elliot. *Black Detroit and the Rise of the UAW*. New York Oxford: Oxford University Press, 1979.

Meyer, Stephen. *"Stalin Over Wisconsin": The Making and Unmaking of Militant Unionism, 1900-1950*. New Brunswick, New Jersey: Rutgers University Press, 1992.

Mortimer, Wyndham. *Organize! My Life as a Union Man*. Boston: Beacon Press, 1971.

Morton, Desmond. *Working People*. Ottawa: Deneau, 1980.

Napier, James. *Memories of Building the UAW*. Toronto: Canadian Party of Labour, 1975.

Palmer, Bryan. *Working-Class Experience: The Rise and Reconstitution of Canadian Labour, 1800-1980*. Toronto and Vancouver: Butterworth & Co. Canada, 1983.

Pendergest, James A. *Labour and Politics in Oshawa and District, 1928-1943*. Unpublished MA thesis. Kingston: Queen's University, April 1973.

Pendergest, James A. "The Attempt at Unionization in the Automobile Industry in Canada, 1928," *Ontario History*, 70, 4 (1978), 245-262.

Petryshyn, J. «Class Conflict and Civil Liberties: The Origins and Activities of the Canadian Labour Defense League. 1925-1940,» *Labour/Le Travailleur*, 10 (Autumn 1982), 39-63.

Roberts, Barbara Ann. Whence They Came: Deportation from Canada, 1900-1935. Ottawa: University of Ottawa Press, 1988.

Robertson, Heather. *Driving Force: the McLaughlin Family and the Age of the Car.* Toronto: McClelland & Stewart, 1995.

Sinclair, Upton. *The Flivver King: A Story of Ford-America.* Detroit: United Automobile Workers of America, 1937.

Jack Skeels oral history interview of Hugh Thompson, March 28, 1963, Walter P Reuther Library.

Stepan-Norris, Judith and Zeitlin, Maurice. *Left Out: Reds and America's Industrial Unions.* Cambridge: Cambridge University Press, 2003.

Stunden, Nancy. "Oshawa Knights of Labor Demonstration Medal", *Canadian Labour History: Newsletter of the Committee on Canadian Labour History* 4 (1974) inside front cover.

Sugiman, Pamela. *Labour's Dilemma: The Gender Politics of Auto Workers in Canada, 1937-1979.* Toronto Buffalo London: University of Toronto Press, 1994

UAW International Union Education Department, *Where Was George Burt?* Windsor, 1968.

Veres, Louis Joseph. *History of the United Automobile Workers in Windsor 1936-1955.* Unpublished MA thesis, University of Western Ontario, 1956.

Verzuh, Ron. "Proletarian Cromwell: Two Found Poems Offer Insights into One of Canada's Long-Forgotten Communist Labour Leaders," *Labour/Le Travail* 79 (Spring 2017) 185-227.

Weinstone, William. *The Great Sit-Down Strike.* New York: Workers Library Publishers, 1937.

Wells, Donald M. "Origins of Canada's Wagner Model of Industrial Relations: The United Auto Workers in Canada and the Suppression of "Rank and File" Unionism, 1936-1953," *Canadian Journal of Sociology/Cahiers canadiens de sociologie* 20(2) 1995. 193-225.

Yates, Charlotte. *From Plant to Politics: The Autoworkers Union in Postwar Canada.* Philadelphia: Temple University Press, 1993.

No author. *The Bosses' Boy: A Documentary Record of Walter P. Reuther,* undated but 1947. Published by a Rank and File Committee.

No author, "The Knights of Labour Medallion," *Numismatica Canada* 1,. 2 (June 2002) 74-77.

Online Resources

R.C.M.P. Security Bulletins, a unique, static collection of primary documents digitised for the University of New Brunswick's History Department. https://journals.lib.unb.ca/index.php/RCMP/issue/archive

Appendices

Appendix A: GM of Canada – Oshawa Agreement, April 23, 1937[1]

APPENDIX C

COPY OF AGREEMENT BETWEEN GENERAL MOTORS OF CANADA
AND ITS EMPLOYEES AT OSHAWA, APRIL, 1937

MEMORANDUM OF AGREEMENT entered into this day between

GENERAL MOTORS OF CANADA, hereinafter
referred to as The Company

—and—

The Employees of the Company at Oshawa,
hereinafter referred to as The Employees,

1. Hours of Work

The hours of work of employees shall be forty-four (44) hours per week, composed of nine (9) hours per day of the first four (4) days of the week and eight (8) hours on Friday. With the exception of maintenance men, a list of whom will later to agreed upon between the employees and the Company, and with the exception of the service parts department employees, all overtime shall be paid for at the rate of time and one-half. The question of overtime work of maintenance men so listed to be later dealt with between shop committee and management.

2. Wages

(a) Wages of female group bonus workers shall be increased by five cents per hour on base rate.

(b) Wages of all day workers now being paid fifty-five cents per hour or under shall be increased by seven cents per hour.

(c) Wages of all day workers now receiving over fifty-five cents per hour shall be increased by five cents per hour.

The question of a suitable minimum wage to be later discussed and negotiated by shop committee and management.

3. Seniority

Lay-Off, Transfer and Rehiring Procedure.

Employees shall be regarded as temporary employees for the first six months of their employment. There shall be no responsibility for the reemployment of temporary employees if they are discharged or laid off during this period.

After six months continuous employment, the names of such employees shall then be placed on the seniority list for their respective departments or occupational groups, in order of date of hiring. In any department in which both men and women are employed they should be divided into separate non-interchangeable occupational groups. Seniority shall start from the time of hiring and shall be by departments, or non-interchangeable occupa-

378

tional groups within departments by agreement, except where changes in
methods, products, or policies would otherwise require the permanent laying off of employees, in which case seniority shall become plant-wide for
the employees involved and they shall be transferred to other departments
on work they are capable of doing and at the standard rate for such work.
Up-to-date seniority lists for each department or occupational group shall
be maintained by the supervisor of such department or group and shall be
available to any affected employee.

When an employee is transferred from one department or occupational
group to another for any reason, there shall be no loss of seniority.
However, in case of temporary transfers not exceeding sixty days, an
employee will retain his seniority in the Department or occupational group
from which he was transferred and not in the new department.

Twelve (12) consecutive months of unemployment or a voluntary
quit or discharge breaks seniority.

If an employee is notified to report for work and does not report
within one day, or give a satisfactory explanation for not reporting, he
shall be considered as having voluntarily quit.

4. Grievance Procedure

(a) The Management of the Oshawa Factory recognizes a Shop Committee consisting of nine members who shall be variously elected from their
fellow employees who are members of the local union. The Factory Manager
shall be advised of the personnel of the Shop Committee and any changes
made from time to time.

(b) Any employee having a grievance in connection with his work,
or any group of employees having a joint grievance in connection with
their work, should first take up the matter with the Foreman of the Department. The Foreman will attempt to make a satisfactory settlement.

(c) If the employee or group of employees is not satisfied with
the Foreman's decision they may then take it up with the Superintendent
or such convenient higher authority. If further action is desired, they
may refer the case in writing to be considered by a meeting of the Shop
Committee. The members of the Shop Committee may, upon receipt of such
written request, investigate the circumstances of the complaint.

(d) If the Committee is unable to adjust the grievance the matter
will then be taken up with the Factory Manager or such higher authority
as in the opinion of the Committee is deemed necessary to deal with the
case.

(e) Any cases not satisfactorily settled between the Shop Committee and the Factory Manager may be referred by a delegation from the
Committee to the highest officers of the Company, when, if the matter is
of such importance that it still remains unsettled, the case may be referred to an impartial umpire by mutual agreement of both parties.

5. Rest Period

379

It is agreed that the employees shall be allowed a five minute rest period after the first two hours in the morning and after the first two hours in the afternoon.

6. Pay Day

Commencing May 7th all employees shall be paid every other Friday.

7. Production Basis

Beginning the production season of 1938 models, the objective of 140 will be reduced to 120, thereby increasing the base hiring rate in proportion.

The Company will co-operate to bring it down to one hundred per cent.

8. No Discrimination Clause

Both parties agree that no discrimination of any sort will be practised either by the Company or the employees, by reason of any activity, past or future, of any employee with, or in respect to, trade union activity or trade union membership.

Neither the company nor the employees shall intimidate employees either against or in favour of trade union membership.

This agreement shall continue in force until and so long as and concurrent with the agreement between General Motors Corporation in the United States, dated February 11th, and the United Automobile Workers of America.

This agreement covering the Oshawa Factory of the company is signed by the union employees hereunder who signed on behalf of themselves and their successors in office representing the employees of the company who are members of the local union.

C.H. Millard,   H.J. Carmichael, Vice Pres.
President   General Motors of Canada Ltd.

E.E. Bathe,   James B. Highfield
Vice President   General Factory Manager

G.H. Day
Chairman

Witnessed: Louis Fine, Department of Labor, Ontario.

SOURCE: P.A.O., Hepburn Papers, Copy of agreement with General Motors, Apr., 1937.

Appendix B: GM-UAW Agreements, February 11, 1936[2]

AGREEMENT ENTERED INTO ON THIS 11 DAY OF FEBRUARY,
1937, BETWEEN THE GENERAL MOTORS CORPORATION (Hereinafter
referred to as the "Corporation"), AND THE INTERNATIONAL
UNION, UNITED AUTOMOBILE WORKERS OF AMERICA (Hereinafter
referred to as the "Union ").

1. The Corporation hereby recognized the Union as the collective
    bargaining agency for those employes of the Corporation who are
    members of the Union. The Corporation recognizes and will not
    interfere with the right of its employes to be members of the
    Union. There shall be no discrimination, interference, rest-
    raint, or coercion by the Corporation or any of its agents
    against any employes because of membership in the Union.

2. The Corporation and the Union agree to commence collective bar-
    gaining negotiations on February sixteenth with regard to the
    issues specified in the letter of January fourth, 1937, from the
    Union to the Corporation, for the purpose of entering into a
    collective bargaining agreement, or agreements, covering such
    issues, looking to a final and complete settlement of all
    matters in dispute.

3. The Union agrees to forthwith terminate the present strike again-
    st the Corporation, and to evacuate all plants now occupied by
    strikers.

4. The Corporation agrees that all of its plants, which are on
    strike or otherwise idle shall resume operations as rapidly as
    possible.

5. It is understood that all employes now on strike or otherwise
    idle will return to their usual work when called and that no
    discrimination shall be made or prejudices exercised by the
    Corporation against any employee because of his former affiliat-
    ion with, or activities in, the Union or the present strike.

6. The Union agrees that pending the negotiations referred to in
    paragraph two, there shall be no strikes called or any other
    interruption to or interference with production, by the Union or
    its members.

7. During the existence of the collective bargaining agreement
    contemplated pursuant to paragraph two, all opportunities to
    achieve a satisfactory settlement of any grievance or the en-
    forcement of any demands by negotiations shall be exhausted, be-
    fore there shall be any strikes or other interruption to or in-
    terference with production by the Union or its members. There
    shall be no attempts to intimidate or coerce any employes by the
    Union and there shall not be any solicitation or signing up of
    members by the Union on the premises of the company. This is
    not to proclude individual discussion.

8. After the evacuation of its plants and termination of the strike
    the Corporation agrees to consent to the entry of orders, dis-
    missing the injunction proceedings which have been started by
    the Corporation against the Union, or any of its locals, or
    officers or any of its locals, including those pending in Flint,
    Michigan and Cleveland, Ohio, and subject to the approval of the
    Court to discontinue all contempt proceedings which it has in-
    stituted thereunder.

UNITED AUTOMOBILE WORKERS	GENERAL MOTORS CORP.
Wyndham Mortimer	W.S.Knudsen
1st Vice. Pres.	
Lee Pressman	J. T. Smith
Gen. Counsel C.I.O.	
John L. Lewis	D. Brown
Chairman C.I.O.	

Frank Murphy

James F. Dewey

-2-

February 11, 1937

The Honorable Frank Murphy
Governor of Michigan
Lansing, Michigan

Dear Governor:

We have been told that the United Automobile Workers of America, in justifying its demand for the bargaining privilege, state that they fear that without protection of some kind we might deliberately proceed to bargain with other groups for the purpose of undermining the position of this particular Union. We have said that we have no such intention.

On the other hand, we cannot enter into any agreement with anyone which can have the effect of denying to any group of our employes the rights of collective bargaining to which it is entitled, and which fails to protect them in the exercise of these rights.

On our part therefore we undertake not to seek or to inspire such activities on the part of other groups, for the purpose of weakening this particular union.

This undertaking we assume on condition that the Union refrain from coercion and intimidation inside and outside of the shop in its efforts to increase its membership.

As evidence of our intention to do all we can to hasten the resumption of work in our plants and to promote peace, we hereby agree with you that within a period of six months from the resumption of work we will not bargain with or enter into agreements with any other union or representative or employes of plants on strike in respect to such matters of general corporate policy as referred to in letter of January fourth, without first submitting to you the facts of the situation and gaining from you the sanction of any such contemplated procedure as being justified by law, equity or justice towards the group of employes so represented.

Yours respectfully,

W. S. Knudsen (signed)

Dear Governor:

Following is a list of plants on strike which we mentioned to you in our letter of February tenth:

Atlanta	Georgia	Fisher Body
"	"	Chevrolet Motor Co.
Kansas City	Missouri	Fisher Body
Cleveland	Ohio	Fisher Body
Janesville	Wisconsin	Chevrolet Motor Co.
"	"	Fisher Body
Norwood	Ohio	Chevrolet Motor Co.
"	"	Fisher Body
St. Louis	Missouri	Chevrolet Motor Co.
"	"	Fisher Body
Flint	Michigan	Fisher #1
"	"	Fisher #2
"	"	Chevrolet Motor Co.
Toledo	Ohio	Chevrolet Motor Co.
Detroit	Michigan	Cadillac Motor Co.
"	"	Fleetwood Fisher Body
Anderson	Indiana	Guide Lamp

Yours respectfully,

uopwa26cio
F

Appendix C: GM-UAW Agreement, March 12, 1937[3]

AGREEMENT ENTERED INTO THIS   DAY OF MARCH 1937
BETWEEN GENERAL MOTORS CORPORATION (HEREINAFTER REFERRED
TO AS THE "CORPORATION") and THE INTERNATIONAL UNION,
UNITED AUTOMOBILE WORKERS OF AMERICA (HEREINAFTER REFERRED
TO AS THE "UNION") IS SUPPLEMENTAL TO AND A PART OF THE
AGREEMENT DATED FEBRUARY 11, 1937, BETWEEN THE PARTIES.

The parties have been negotiating in regard to the issues specified in the letter of the Union to the Corporation dated January 4th,
1937, and referred to in the Agreement of February 11th, 1937, between
the parties, and have reached the following settlement:-

1.- A Grievance Procedure. In line with the general policy of the
    Corporation and as applied in those plants where the plant
management by mutual understanding with the Union, recognizes the
Union shop committee as hereinafter referred to, the procedure in dealing with grievances of its members will be as follows:-

1. Any employee having a grievance in connection with his work, or
    any group of employes having a joint grievance in connection with
their work, should first take up the matter with the foreman of the
department. The foreman will attempt to make a satisfactory settlement of the matter.

2. If the employee or group of employes is not satisfied with the
    foreman's decision, they may then take it up with higher author-
ity, or they may refer the case in writing to a member of a shop
committee which represents said employes provided there be such a
committee. The members of shop committees shall be permitted to leave
their work to investigate or adjust grievances in any department after
duly notifying their foreman and punching their time cards out. Upon
entering a department other than their own in the fulfillment of their
duties, they shall notify the foreman of that department of their
presence and purpose and give the foreman a copy of the complaint, if
the foreman has not already received one, before taking the case up
with the employee or employes involved at their work. If the committeeman is unable to adjust the grievance in the department with the foreman, he may then take it up with the superintendent or employment
manager.

3. The membership of shop committees shall be not less than five,
    nor more than nine members in each plant who are employes of the
company. The shop committee's jurisdiction shall be limited to the
plant or plants located in one group, which are under the supervision
of the local plant management with which they deal. The plant management shall be advised of the personnel of the shop committee and any
changes thereof.

4. If a committeeman does not succeed in adjusting the grievance
    satisfactorily with the foreman, superintendent or employment
manager, the case should then be referred to his shop committee as a
whole, which will decide whether or not the matter should be taken up
with the local management. If the committee decides to take the matter
up with the management, the management will meet with the committee
and attempt to settle the matter.

5. Any cases not satisfactorily settled with the local management
    by a committee representing employes, may be referred by the
committee to the proper higher officers of their organization, who, if
they see fit, will take the cases up with the General Manager of the
Division or Executives designated by the Corporation to deal with such
cases, if the General Manager has already dealt with the shop committee
on the matter.

6. Any cases not satisfactorily settled at this point will be
    reviewed jointly by the Vice President of the corporation in
charge and the highest officer of their organization, with such
additional representatives as either party may desire. If the matter
is not satisfactorily settled by them the case may be referred to an
impartial umpire by mutual agreement of both parties.

B. Lay-Off, Transfer and Rehiring Procedure. Employes shall be
    regarded as temporary employes for the first six months of their
employment. There shall be no responsibility for the reemployment of
temporary employes if they are discharged or laid off during this
period.

-2-

After six months' continuous employment, the names of such employes shall then be placed on the seniority list for their respective departments or occupational groups, in order of date of hiring. In any department in which both men and women are employed, they should be divided into separate non-interchangeable occupational groups.

Seniority shall start from the time of hiring and shall be by departments, or non-interchangeable occupational groups within departments by plant agreement, except where changes in methods, products, or policies would otherwise require the permanent laying off of employes, in which case seniority shall become plant-wide for the employes involved and they shall be transferred to other departments on work they are capable of doing and at the standard rate for such work. Up to date seniority lists for each department or occupational group shall be maintained by the supervisor of such department or group and shall be available to any affected employee.

When an employee is transferred from one department or occupational group to another for any reason, there shall be no loss of seniority. However, in case of temporary transfer not exceeding sixty (60) days, an employee will retain his seniority in the department or occupational group from which he was transferred and not in the new department.

Twelve (12) consecutive months of unemployment or a voluntary quit or a discharge breaks seniority.

If an employee is notified to report for work and does not report within three days, or give a satisfactory explanation for not reporting, he shall be considered as having voluntarily quit.

Upon application, leaves of absence may be granted employes, without loss of seniority, at the discretion of the local plant management.

Any employee being elected to a permanent office in, or as a delegate to any labor activity necessitating a temporary leave of absence, shall be granted such leave of absence and shall at the end of the term in the first instance or at the end of the mission in the second instance, be guaranteed reemployment with the seniority standing which he had when the leave of absence was granted, if there is sufficient work for which he is in line at the then current rate of pay.

The management in each plant will prepare a separate list of employes, who in the judgment of the management should be retained or recalled to work, regardless of any other provisions, in order to facilitate tooling or rearrangement of the plant, the taking of inventory and the starting of production and similar situations. In the selection of this list, length of service shall be secondary to other qualifications, but should be given reasonable consideration.

The list of such employes will be maintained in the Employment Department and be available to the accredited representatives of employes. Any changes therein will be listed promptly.

The members of shop committees who have been designated to represent other employes shall be included in this list.

For temporary reductions in production, the work week may be reduced before any employes are laid off.

For extended periods of reduced production, temporary employes will be laid off, and thereafter the work week will be reduced before employes with seniority are laid off.

In a reduction of the working force in any department or occupational group affecting employes with seniority, employes with less service shall be laid off before employes with longer service according to the seniority list, except employes on the special list provided above. If, in the judgment of the management, production in the plant must be materially reduced for an extensive period, thus creating a social problem in the community, this rule will be modified in a manner satisfactory to the employes to give preference in the available employment to employes with dependents as against employees without dependents.

-3-

In increasing the working force in any department or occupational group, employes will be called back in the reverse order in which they were laid off. Temporary employes will not be called back until all employes with seniority have been called back.

The present local rules regarding laying off married women are to apply unless changed in a manner satisfactory to the employes.

C. **Timing Operations.** The policy regarding speed of operations is that time studies shall be made on a basis of fairness and equity consistent with quality of workmanship, efficiency of operations and reasonable working capacities of normal operators. The local management of each plant has full authority to settle such matters. If an employee or group of employes claim the timing of their work is too fast and the foreman is unable to adjust the matter, the job will be restudied and if found to be unfair an adjustment in the time will be made.

D. **Wage Payment Plans.** The Corporation has no preference in regard to wage payment plans. Wage Payment plans may be adopted, changed or modified as desired by the employes directly involved and the local management in each plant has the full authority to settle such matters.

E. **Working Hours.** The policy of the Corporation with respect to the normal work week is subject to such national and state legislation which may apply. The present policy of the Corporation is an eight-hour day and a forty-hour week with time and one half for all overtime after eight hours per day or forty hours per week.

F. **Discharge Complaints.** It is important that complaints regarding unjust or discriminatory discharges be handled promptly according to the grievance procedure herein provided. Such complaints must be filed within three days of the discharge and the local plant management must review and render a decision on the case within five days of its receipt. In the event of appeal from the decision of the local plant management a final decision will be made as promptly as possible and in any event not more than four weeks from the original filing of the case.

An employee who is reinstated after discharge shall be returned to work of a similar class, at the same rate of pay.

G. **Wages.** General Motors believes in high wages and will continue to pay high wages in the future as it has in the past.

General Motors operates a number of plants in may communities throughout the United States, producing a wide variety of products sold in highly competitive markets, some of which are seasonal. It employs thousands of skilled men of practically every trade in metal manufacturing and many others. Accordingly, the question of local wage rates is a matter which must be determined by the local plant management for each plant in the light of these facts.

Any wage complaints which cannot be settled by the local plant management will be dealt with further according to the grievance procedure.

2. All cases of alleged discriminatory discharge raised by the Union during negotiations, have been reviewed and such cases as have been mutually agreed upon have been referred to the plant in which they occurred, to be handled thereafter in accordance with the grievance procedure.

3. Any claims of discrimination against temporary employes may be reviewed by the shop committees with the local plant management. Such individual cases shall not be further appealed to the higher authority provided in the procedure for adjusting grievances, but the right is reserved to the shop committees to appeal any general charge of discrimination by the plant managements as so provided.

-4-

4.   Minimum Wages. The general trend of industry is toward higher minimum wage levels to establish an American standard of living for all workers. This is a national problem. Due to the variety of businesses and conditions under which General Motors operates its various plants, it has been impossible to establish a uniform minimum wage rate in all General Motors plants. However, in plants where the minimum wage rates become a matter of dispute, the matter will be dealt with promptly and if not settled satisfactorily by the local management, will be speedily dealt with according to the grievance procedure.

5.   Should any difference arise over grievances there shall be no suspensions or stoppages of work until every effort has been been exhausted to adjust them through the regular grievance procedure, and in no case without the approval of the International officers of the Union.

6.   This agreement shall continue in full force and effect until terminated by either party or changed by consent of both parties. Either party may terminate this agreement, by giving sixty days notice in writing to the other on or after June 11, 1937. If either party desires to modify or change this agreement it shall, at least sixty days prior to the date when it proposes that such change or modification becomes effective, give notice in writing of the proposed change or modification. The other party, within ten days after receipt of said notice, shall either accept or reject the proposal or request a conference to negotiate the proposal. No notice to modify or change this agreement shall be given by either party prior to June 11, 1937.

uopwa26cio
F

Appendix D: GM of Canada–Walkerville Agreement, April 24, 1937[4]

126

MEMORANDUM OF AGREEMENT: entered into this Twenty-fourth day of April, 1937, between

GENERAL MOTORS OF CANADA LTD., hereinafter referred to as the Company,

—and—

The Employees at the Company at Walkerville, hereinafter referred to as the Employees.

1. HOURS OF WORK:

The hours of work of employees shall be forty-four (44) hours per week, composed of nine (9) hours per day of the first four (4) days of the week, and eight (8) hours on Friday, with the exception of maintenance men, a list of whom will be later agreed upon between the employees and the company, and with the exception of the service parts department employees, all overtime shall be paid for at the rate of time and one-half. The question of overtime work of maintenance men so listed, to be later dealt with between shop-committee and management.

2. WAGES:

(a) Wages of all day workers now being paid fifty-five (55) cents per hour or under shall be increased by seven (7) cents per hour.

(b) Wages of all day workers now receiving over fifty-five (55) cents per hour shall be increased by five (5) cents per hour.

(c) The question of suitable minimum wage to be later discussed and negotiated by shop committee.

3. SENIORITY:

(a) After six months' employment within any period of twenty-four months, an employee shall be entitled to be placed on a seniority list for the department or occupational group in which he is employed. The order of employees on the seniority list shall be according to the respective dates of hiring. If an employee is placed on the seniority list after six months of intermittent rather than continuous employment, the date of hiring of such employees shall be considered to have been six months prior to the final day upon which he attained seniority.

127

(b) A copy of the seniority list showing the name and the date of each employee shall from time to time be posted on the Bulletin Board.

(c) Seniority shall be by departments or non-interchangeable groups within a department. However, if necessary to avoid a protracted lay-off of employees in any such department or group, seniority shall become plant wide for the employees involved and they may be transferred to other departments or groups.

(d) When an employee is for any reason transferred from one department or occupational group to another, he shall incur no loss of seniority.

(e) Lay-off and re-hiring shall be according to seniority. Employees last on the seniority list shall be laid off first. Employees shall be re-hired in the reverse order in which they were laid off.

(f) If a seniority list is exhausted and additional men are needed, any laid-off employee, capable of doing such work, shall be hired unless it is probable that he will be recalled to his regular department or group within the month.

(g) Twelve consecutive months of unemployment, unless due to illness or plant lay-off, a voluntary quit, or discharges, breaks seniority. If an employee is notified to report to work and does not report within three days or give satisfactory explanation for not reporting, he shall be considered as having voluntarily quit.

(h) Any employee on the seniority list who is elected to a permanent position in any labour activity, may obtain leave of absence and shall thereafter be re-employed without affecting his place on the seniority list.

(i) Overtime shall be evenly distributed among all those normally performing the work.

4. GRIEVANCE PROCEDURE:

All grievance between the parties hereto shall be handled according to the following procedure:

(a) A grievance shall be first taken up directly with the foreman concerned. If a grievance affects more than one employee, those affected shall designate one of their number as a representative to take the matter up with the foreman.

128

(b) If the employee or representative is not satisfied with the decision of the foreman, he may within two days, appeal in writing to the superintendent of the department concerned and may be represented before the superintendent by a member of the plant negotiation committee, elected by and composed of Union members who are employees of the Company in the Walkerville plant. The superintendent, shall, within two days after the hearing of the appeal, render a written decision.

(c) If the employee or representative is not satisfied with the decision of the superintendent, he may, within two days, appeal in writing to the plant manager, before whom he shall be represented by the Plant Negotiating Committee. The matter shall be heard at the next regular conference between the Plant Manager and the Plant Negotiating Committee and the Plant Management shall, within two days, render a written decision of the controversy.

(d) If the Plant Negotiating Committee is not satisfied with the decision of the Plant Management, it may, within two days, appeal in writing to the General Manager of the Company. The matter shall be heard by the General Manager within seven days after receiving notice of the appeal. The General Manager shall render a written decision within two days after hearing the appeal. In proceedings or negotiations with the General Manager, the plant negotiating committee may be represented by a duly accredited representative or counsel of the Union, or they may act jointly.

(e) If the representative in the proceedings with the General Manager is not satisfied with the decision of the General Manager, the parties hereto shall agree upon an arbitrator to whom the matter shall immediately be referred for arbitration to be held forthwith.

(f) At any conference with the Plant Manager or with the General Manager, as aforesaid, the Plant Negotiating Committee may have present any employee involved in the matter being negotiated.

(g) Both parties will attempt to settle grievances under the foregoing procedure as speedily and effectively as possible. Until the completion of all the foregoing steps, there shall be no strikes, or lock-outs, nor shall the Union cause or permit any stoppage, reduction in the rate of production or any other act calculated to penalize the Company.

5. REST PERIOD:

It is agreed that the employees shall be allowed a five (5) minutes rest period after the first two (2) hours in the morning and after the first two (2) hours in the afternoon.

129

6. PAY DAY:

Commencing May 7, all employees shall be paid every other Friday.

7. PRODUCTION BASIS:

Beginning with the production season of 1938 models, the objective of 140 will be reduced to 120, thereby increasing base hiring rate in proportion. The company will co-operate to bring it down to 100 per cent.

8. NO DISCRIMINATION CLAUSE:

Both parties agree that no discrimination of any sort will be practiced by either the company or the employees, by reason of any activity, past or future, of any employee with, or in respect to, trade union activity or trade union membership.

Neither the company nor the employees shall intimidate employees either against or in favour of trade union membership.

This agreement shall continue in force until and so long as and concurrent with the agreement between General Motors Corporation in the United States, dated February 11th, and the United Automobile Workers of America.

This agreement covering the Walkerville factory of the company is signed by the Union employees hereunder, who signed on behalf of themselves and their successors in office, representing the employees of the company, who are members of the Union.

Martin J. McKeon
   President

Robert McCartney
   Chairman Negotiating Committee

H. J. Carmichael
Vice-President
General Motors of Canada Ltd.

F. M. Church
Plant Manager.

WITNESSES: Louis Fine, Ontario Department of Labour.

From a copy of agreement supplied by UAW regional office - Windsor.

Appendix E: McKinnon–St. Catharines Agreement, April 27, 1937[5]

MEMORANDUM OF AGREEMENT entered into this 27th day of April, 1937,
between

The McKinnon Industries, Limited hereinafter
referred to as The Company

-and-

The Employees of the Company at St. Catharines
hereinafter referred to as The Employees.

1.   HOURS OF WORK

The hours of work for moulders and core makers
shall be forty-five (45) hours per week composed of five (5) days
of nine (9) hours each commencing with Monday and no work on
Saturday. All time above nine (9) hours on one day or on any day
except said five (5) days shall be overtime work and shall be paid
for at the rate of time and one-half.

The hours of work for other employees shall be
agreed upon between the Company and the Committee herein provided
for and when so agreed shall form a part of this agreement. In
the event of failure to agree by Wednesday, May 5th., the matter
shall be referred for decision to a committee composed of a representative of the Company. Mr. J. L. Cohen representing the
Employees and Mr. Louis Fine Chief Conciliation Officer, Ontario
Department of Labor.

The question of overtime work of power house
employees, malleable iron and annealing furnaces, continuous furnace
operations and policemen, shall be dealt with by the Company and
the said Committee and in the event of no agreement by Wednesday.
May 5th., shall be decided by the three above mentioned. All
other overtime, including overtime by piece workers, shall be paid
for at the rate of time and one half effective from the date of
this agreement.

2.   WAGES

(a) Wages of all female bonus workers and of
male bonus workers twenty-one (21) years or under to be increased
by five (5) cents per hour on base rate.

(b) Day workers - five (5) cents per hour increase.

(c) The wage increases to male bonus workers
over twenty-one (21) and of piece workers to be agreed upon between

--2--

The Company and the Committee herein provided for and when so agreed shall form a part of this agreement. In the event of failure to agree by Wednesday, May 5th. the matter shall be decided by the three above mentioned.

(d) All wage increases to be effective as of April 30th.

3. SENIORITY

Lay-Off. Transfer and Rehiring Procedure.

Employees shall be regarded as temporary employees for the first six months of their employment. There shall be no responsibility for the reemployment of temporary employees if they are discharaged or laid off during this period.

After six months continuous employment, the name of such employee shall then be placed on the seniority list for their respective departments or occupational groups, in order of date of hiring. In any department in which both men and women are employed they should be divided into separate non-interchangeable occupational groups. Seniority shall start from the time of hiring and shall be by departments, or non-interchangeable occupational groups within departments by agreement, except where changes in methods, products, or policies would otherwise require the permanent laying off of employees, in which case seniority shall become plant-wide for the employees involved and they shall be transferred to other departments on work they are capable of doing and at the standard rate for such work. Up-to-date seniority lists for each department or occupational group shall be maintained by the supervisor of such department or group and shall be available to any affected employee.

In the case of the facilitating of tooling or the starting of production or similar situations the employees length of service as determined above will be given first consideration, but the employees ski l and training and the requirements of the job are also factors to be taken into consideration. With the

-- 3 --

consent of the Committee herein provided for, the family
~~status of such employees may also be~~ taken into consideration.

When an employee is transferred from one
department or occupation group to another for any reason, there
shall be no loss of seniority. However, in case of temporary
transfers not exceeding sixty days, an employee will retain his
seniority in the Department or occupational group from which he
was transferred and not in the new department.

Twelve (12) consecutive months of unemployment
or a voluntary quit or discharge br aks seniority.

If an employee is notified to report for work
and does not report within one day, or give a satisfactory
explanation for not reporting, he shall be considered as having
voluntarily quit.

4. GRIEVANCE PROCEDURE

(a) The management recovnizes a Shop Committee
consisting of sevne membe s who shall be variously elected from
their fellow employees who are members of the local union. The
Factory Manager shall be advised of the personnel of the Shop
Committee and any changes made from time to time.

(b) Any employee having a grievance in con-
nection with his work, or any group of employees having a joint
grievance in connection with their work, should first take up
the matter with the Foreman of the Department. The Foreman
will atemp to make a satisfactory settlement.

(c) If the employee or group of employees is
not satisfied with the Foreman's decision they may then take it
up with the Superintendent or such convenient higher authority.
If further action is desired, they may refer the case in writing
to be considered by a meeting of the Shop Committee. The members
of the Shop Committee may, upon receipt of such written request,
investigate the circumstances of the complaint.

(d) If the Committee is unable to adjust the
grievance, the matter will then be taken up with the Factory

-- 4 --

Manager or such higher authority as in the opinion of the
Committee is deemed necessary to deal with the case.

(e) Any cases not satisfactorily settled between
the Shop Committee and the Factory Manager may be referred by a
delegation from the Committee to the highest officers of the
Company, when, if the matter is of such importance that it still
remains unsettled, the case may be referred to an impartial umpire
by mutual agreement of both parties.

5. PAY DAY

Commencing May 7th. all employees shall be paid every
other Friday.

6. PRODUCTION BASIS

Commencing with the productive season of 1938 models
the base of seventy-five 975) points will be increased to ninety (90)
and the hiring rate increased correspondingly.

7. NO DISCRIMINATION CLAUSE

Both parties agree that no discrimination of any
sort will be practised either by the Company or the employees, by
reason of any activity, past or future, of any employee with, or
in respect to, trade union activity or trade union membership.

Neither the Company nor the employee shall intimidate
employees either against or in favour of trade union membership.

The agreement shall continue in force until and so
long as and concurrent with the agreement between General Motors
Corporation in the United States, dated February 11th, and the
United Automobile Workers of America.

--5--

       This agreement covering the St. Catharines
Factory of the company is signed by the union employees
hereunder who signed on behalf of themselves and their
successors in office representing the employees of the
company who are members of the local union.

    "John W. Crozier"   "H. J. Carmichael"
      President   Pres.

    "George Compbell"
      Treasurer
                             "Wm. A. Wecker"
                                 Gen. Mgr.
    "Robt. A. Lawrie"
      Chairman Negotiating Committee

Approved
"J. L. Cohen"

                        Witnessed "Louis Fine"
                          Ontario Dept. of Labor

Notes

Introduction

1. *Toronto Daily Star*, April 19, 1937, 2.
2. Ibid., April 19, 1937, 2.
3. Ibid., April 13, 1937, 3.
4. Irving Abella, "The CIO: Reluctant Invaders," *Canadian Dimension* Vol. 8 No. 6 (March-April 1972) 20-23.
5. Tony Leah, *Building Blocks of Victory in Oshawa 1937: The Left, The Rank and File, & The International Union*. Unpublished MA thesis, Hamilton, McMaster University School of Labour Studies, October 2023. Available at https://solinet.ca/building-blocks-of-victory-in-oshawa-1937/
6. *Toronto Daily Star*, April 14, 1937, 2.
7. Philip S. Foner, *History of the Labor Movement in the United States: Volume II* (New York: International Publishers, 1955), 158.
8. R. Emmett Murray, *The Lexicon of Labor* (New York: The New Press, 1998), 152.
9. For example, see Judith Stepan-Norris and Maurice Zeitlin, *Left Out: Reds and America's Industrial Unions* (Cambridge: Cambridge University Press, 2003); James J. Matles and James Higgins, *Them and Us: Struggles of a Rank-and-File Union* (Boston: Beacon Press, 1974); Toni Gilpin, *The Long Deep Grudge: A Story of Big Capital, Radical Labor, and Class War in the American Heartland* (Chicago: Haymarket Books, 2020); Stephen Meyer, *"Stalin Over Wisconsin": The Making and Unmaking of Militant Unionism, 1900-1950* (New Brunswick, New Jersey: Rutgers University Press, 1992). Rick Halpern, *Down on the Killing Floor: Black and White Workers in Chicago's Packinghouses*, 1904-54 (Urbana and Chicago: University of Illinois Press, 1997).
10. Irving Abella, *Nationalism, Communism and Canadian Labour: The CIO, the Communist Party, and the Canadian Congress of Labour 1935-1956* (Toronto and Buffalo: University of Toronto Press, 1973).
11. Irving Abella, "Oshawa 1937" in *On Strike: Six Key Labour Struggles in Canada 1919-1949*, edited by Irving Abella (Toronto: James Lewis and Samuel, 1974).
12. Irving Abella, "The CIO, the Communist Party and the Formation of the Canadian Congress of Labour 1936-1941," *Historical Papers / Communications historiques 4(1)* (1969) 112-128.
13. Abella, *Reluctant Invaders*.
14. Abella, *Nationalism, Communism and Canadian Labour*, 23.
15. Abella, *On Strike*, 120.
16. Abella, *Nationalism, Communism and Canadian Labour*, 23.
17. Ibid.
18. Ibid., 20.

19. Ibid., 4.

20. Abella, *Reluctant Invaders*, 20.

21. Abella, *Nationalism, Communism and Canadian Labour*, v.

22. Ibid.

23. Ibid., vi.

24. Ibid., vi.

25. Ibid., 221-222.

26. Bryan Palmer, *Working-Class Experience: The Rise and Reconstitution of Canadian Labour, 1800-1980* (Toronto and Vancouver: Butterworth & Co. Canada, 1983) 220.

27. Ibid., 219.

28. Ibid., 219.

29. Desmond Morton, *Working People* (Ottawa: Deneau, 1980) 160.

30. The use of the word 'bankrupt'—which implies something significantly more serious than having no funds available—is taken from Abella: *On Strike*, 120.

31. Charlotte Yates, *From Plant to Politics: The Autoworkers Union in Postwar Canada* (Philadelphia: Temple University Press, 1993), 25-26.

32. Laurel Sefton MacDowell, "After the Strike - Labour Relations in Oshawa, 1937-1939," *Relations Industrielles* (Québec, Québec) 48 (4) (1993), 692.

33. Ibid., 694.

34. Sam Gindin, *The Canadian Auto Workers: The Birth and Transformation of a Union* (Toronto: James Lorimer & Company Publishers, 1995), 63.

35. Ibid., 67.

36. *No Power Greater*, multimedia DVD, (Toronto: Canadian Auto Workers 2003), "The GM Oshawa Strike, 1937" screen 9, no author listed.

Chapter 1: The McLaughlins vs. The Workers

1. Karl Marx and Friedrich Engels, *Manifesto of the Communist Party* (Peking: Foreign Languages Press, 1968), 30.

2. Heather Robertson, *Driving Force: the McLaughlin Family and the Age of the Car* (Toronto: McClelland & Stewart, 1995) 87-88.

3. Robertson, 90.

4. Robertson, 313. Sam McLaughlin was appointed as an honorary colonel of the 34th Ontario Regiment in 1931. He had been an honorary lieutenant-colonel since 1921.

5. Robertson, 112-113.

6. Robertson, 165.

7. Christine McLaughlin, "Producing Memory: Public History and Resistance in a Canadian Auto Town," *Oral History Forum d'histoire*, 33 (2013), 13-14.

8. Gregory S. Kealey, and Bryan D. Palmer. *Dreaming of What Might Be: The Knights of Labor in Ontario, 1880-1900*, (Toronto: New Hogtown Press, 1987) 43.

9. E. P. Thompson, *The Making of the English Working Class* (London: Victor Gollancz, 1963), 9.

10. Kealey and Palmer.

11. Knights of Labor memorabilia were widespread enough in Oshawa that I was able to purchase some from a local collector in the early 2000s.

12. Foner.

13. "The Knights of Labor Medallion," *Numismatica Canada*, 1 no. 2 (June 2002): 74. No author.

14. Nancy Stunden, "Oshawa Knights of Labor Demonstration Medal," *Canadian Labour History: Newsletter of the Committee on Canadian Labour History* 4 (1974) inside front cover.

15. Ibid.

16. "The Knights of Labour Medallion," *Numismatica Canada* 1, 2 (June 2002), 76.

17. Roger Keeran, *The Communist Party and the Auto Workers' Unions*, (New York: International Publishers, 1980) 33.

18. Robertson, 229.

19. Keeran, 32-37.

20. Condé and Beveridge Interviews, Art Shultz, Library and Archives Canada–Carole Condé and Karl Beveridge Fonds.

21. Ibid., 5.

22. Robertson, 226.

23. John Manley, "Communists and Autoworkers: The Struggle for Industrial Unionism in the Canadian Automobile Industry, 1925-36," *Labour/Le Travail*, 17 (Spring 1986). 108-109, Robertson, 226, McLaughlin 28-29.

24. *The Worker*, April 7, 1928, quoted in Pendergest, 20.

25. Manley, "Communists and Autoworkers," 109.

26. Ibid., 111.

27. Ibid., 112.

28. Ibid., 112. The term "Border Cities" was commonly used in the 1920s and 1930s to refer to the cities and towns near Windsor, Ontario that were close to the U.S. border. This included Walkerville, Sandwich, Windsor, and Ford City (later East Windsor) that were incorporated into Windsor in 1935. Ford City was a company town built around a Ford Motor company factory.

29. Ibid., 112.

30. *Oshawa Daily Times*, quoted in Robertson, 225.

31. Slim Phillips later ran on the 1939 Oshawa Labour Council Slate for municipal office. MacDowell, After the Strike, 706.

32. James A. Pendergest, *Labour and Politics in Oshawa and District, 1928-1943*. Unpublished MA thesis. Kingston: Queen's University, April 1973, 25.

33. Robertson, 226.

34. *The Worker*, April 7, 1928, quoted in Pendergest 32-33.

35. Pendergest, 25.

36. Ibid., 30.

37. *The Steering Wheel*, International Auto Workers' Union Local 18011, (June 15, 1928) 1. WRL: Robt. W. Dunn Collection, Box Number 2, Folder 2-10.

38. Manley, "Communists and Autoworkers," 115.

39. Pendergest, 32-33.

40. Ibid., 30.

41. Manley, "Communists and Autoworkers," 116.

42. Ibid., 116.

43. "To All Automobile Workers in the Border Cities," leaflet, Communist Party of Canada, District No. 3, Ontario, June 1928, WRL: Robt. W. Dunn Collection, Box Number 2, Folder 2-10.

Chapter 2: 1928-1936: Communists Build a Foundation

1. Keeran, 13.

2. Ibid., 7.

3. Tim Buck, *Yours in the Struggle: Reminiscences of Tim Buck*. Toronto: NC Press, 1977, 119-121.

4. Stephen Endicott, *Raising the Workers' Flag: The Workers' Unity League of Canada, 1930-1936*. Toronto Buffalo London: University of Toronto Press, 2012, 22.

5. William Z. Foster, *American Trade Unionism: Principles and Organization Strategy and Tactics*. New York: International Publishers, 1947, 178.

6. Buck, *Yours in the Struggle*, 148; Endicott, 31, 144.

7. Keeran, 7-8.

8. Ibid., 128.

9. Endicott, 300, 318-319.

10. Foster, 7.

11. Ibid., 364-369.

12. Ibid., 364-365.

13. Ibid., 365.

14. A. Losovsky, *Program of Action of the Red International of Labour Unions* (Quebec: Red Flag Publications, 1978). The RILU General Secretary has been identified variously as Solomon Lozovsky, Solomon Abramovich (or Alexandr) Lozovsky, and A. Losovsky.

15. Endicott, 20-21.

16. Tim Buck, *Steps to Power* (Toronto: Trade Union Educational League, 1925).

17. Ibid., 39.

18. *Canadian Unionist*, August 1928, 21, quoted in Pendergest, 34.

19. *The Evening Telegram*, November 2, 1928, 1.

20. Ibid., November 2, 1928, 2.

21. Ibid., November 3, 1928, 2.

22. Pendergest, 39.

23. Manley, "Communists and Autoworkers," 117.

24. Pendergest, 39.

25. Ibid., 40.

26. Ibid.

27. Leaflet in the author's possession. Archived at: https://solinet.ca/wp-content/uploads/2022/12/AWIU-Leaflet-Oshawa-March-4-1929.pdf

28. Ibid.

29. Manley, "Communists and Autoworkers," 119. Manley states that a "Comrade Giles" was at the centre of the Oshawa strike, perhaps the Alfred Giles whose name was on the AWIU leaflet issued advertising the March 4 meeting.

30. Ibid., 117.

31. Ibid., 119, Robert W. Dunn, *Labor and Automobiles*. New York: International Publishers, 1929, 175.

32. Ibid., 23.

33. Endicott, 55. McEwen was sometimes known as Tom Ewen, which is how Endicott refers to him.

34. Foster, 178-179.

35. WUL Charter for the British Columbia Relief Camp Workers' Union. Archived at: https://upload.wikimedia.org/wikipedia/commons/b/b2/Charter-saskatchewan-archives-board-r-255c8.jpg

36. Tom McEwen, *The Forge Glows Red: From Blacksmith to Revolutionary* (Toronto: Progress Books, 1974), 248. McEwen's book reproduced the 1933 Constitution of the WUL as reprinted by the Stratford *Beacon-Herald*. That paper had been caught out printing false quotes attributed to the WUL during the militant furniture workers strike in 1933, and printed the full Constitution as a remedy.

37. Ibid., 256.

38. Endicott, 273, 276. Endicott has an organizational chart of the WUL on page 335.

39. Endicott, 272-299.

40. Manley, "Communists and Autoworkers," 120.

41. Ibid.

42. Dunn, 203, 211.

43. Frank Marquart, *An Auto Worker's Journal: The UAW from Crusade to One-Party Union* (University Park and London: The Pennsylvania University Press, 1975) 33-34.

44. Pendergest, 46.

45. Manley, "Communists and Autoworkers," 122-123.

46. Ron Verzuh, "Proletarian Cromwell: Two Found Poems Offer Insights into One of Canada's Long-Forgotten Communist Labour Leaders," *Labour/Le Travail* 79 (Spring 2017) 213. Ron Verzuh obtained the RCMP record on Harvey Murphy, dated December 7, 1930. The report notes "Present locality of activities: Toronto, Oshawa and Windsor, chiefly amongst Auto Workers' Industrial Union in interests of C.P. of C. General Remarks: Murphy first came to prominent attention during the Oshawa strike in April 1929. Later he interested himself in the formation of the auto Workers Industrial Union in Windsor, Oshawa and Toronto. He was again active in the Steel Workers' Strike at Hamilton and also took an active part in the Free Speech Demonstrations at Toronto."

47. Condé and Beveridge Interviews, J. B. Salsberg 1-2.

48. Manley, "Communists and Autoworkers," 121.

49. Ibid., 122.

50. Pendergest, 73.

51. Pendergest, 78. "The fact that Farkas was a Hungarian was stressed in the *Oshawa Daily Times*, which described the literature he had distributed prior to the fight as "of such a description to raise the anger of any loyal citizen of the British Empire."

52. *Oshawa Daily Times*, July 24, 1931.

53. Pendergest, 79.

54. Ibid., 84.

55. Ibid., 74-84.

56. Ibid., 84.

57. Ibid., 85.

58. Ibid., 93-94

59. Ibid., 94-95.

60. Manley, "Communists and Autoworkers," 112.

61. Pendergest, 78.

62. Condé and Beveridge Interviews, J. B. Salsberg, 3.

63. Condé and Beveridge Interviews, J. B. Salsberg, 3, *A 75-Year Retrospective "In Our Own Words."* Toronto: National Automobile, Aerospace, Transportation and General Workers Union of Canada, 2012. Sarnovsky, Joe, editor, 16.

64. Barbara Ann Roberts, *Whence They Came: Deportation from Canada, 1900-1935* (Ottawa: University of Ottawa Press, 1988) 127-129.

65. Roberts, 140.

66. Quoted in Pendergest, 85.

67. Roberts, 143.

68. J. Petryshyn. "Class Conflict and Civil Liberties: The Origins and Activities of the Canadian Labour Defense League. 1925-1940" *Labour/Le Travailleur*, 10 (Autumn 1982), 40-41.

69. Ibid., 40.

70. Ibid., 51.

71. Ibid., 53.

72. Pendergest, 80-81.

73. Lita-Rose Betcherman, *The Little Band: The Clashes Between the Communists and the Political and Legal Establishment in Canada, 1928-1932.* (Ottawa: Deneau, 1982), 23-28.

74. Manley, "Communists and Autoworkers," 123.

75. Keeran, 111-114.

76. John Manley, "Canadian Communists, Revolutionary Unionism, and the 'Third Period': The Workers' Unity League, 1929-1935," *Journal of the Canadian Historical Association* 5 (1994), 167.

77. Ibid., 123.

78. Manley, "Communists and Autoworkers," 124-126. The Auto Workers Union was resuming activity but had dropped "Industrial" from its name.

79. Public Archives of Canada, Strikes and Lockouts Files Volume 361, File 71, *Border Cities Star* March 26, 1934, quoted in Manley, "Communists and Autoworkers," 125.

80. Manley, "Communists and Autoworkers," 126-128.

81. Keeran, 128.

82. Manley, "Communists and Autoworkers," 128.

Chapter 3: Setting the Stage

1. *The New York Times*, April 9, 1937, 1.

2. Abella, *On Strike*, 110.

3. James Napier, *Memories of Building the UAW*. Toronto: Canadian Party of Labour, 1975, 127.

4. Cy Gonick, *A Very RED Life: The Story of Bill Walsh* (St. John's: Canadian Committee on Labour History, 2001) 37-52.

5. Napier, 47.

6. Nelson Lichtenstein, *Walter Reuther: The Most Dangerous Man in Detroit*. Urbana and Chicago: University of Illinois Press, 1995, 31. The Reuthers wrote of "the atmosphere of freedom and security, shop meetings with their proletarian industrial democracy; all these things make an inspiring contrast to what we know as Ford wage slaves in Detroit."

7. Ibid., 37-44.

8. David Frank, *J. B. McLachlan: A Biography* (Toronto: James Lorimer & Company, 1999), 453-457.

9. Endicott, 146, 301.

10. See for example Neil Baldwin, *Henry Ford and the Jews: The Mass Production of Hate* (New York: Public Affairs, 2001).

11. Upton Sinclair, *The Flivver King: A Story of Ford-America* (Detroit: United Automobile Workers of America, 1937).

12. For example: http://www.autolife.umd.umich.edu/Labor/L_Overview/1941 Strike_Rouge.htm.

13. Endicott, 305.

14. Ibid., 311.

15. Ibid., 314.

16. Ibid., 316-318.

17. Ibid., 319.

18. Serge M. Durflinger, "'Six Thousand Tons of Fighting Apparatus'": Canadian Reactions to the Visit of the German Cruiser Karlsruhe to Vancouver, March 1935," *The Northern Mariner/Le marin du nord*, XVI No. 2, (April 2006) 1-13.

19. Tim Buck, *Thirty Years, 1922-1952; the Story of the Communist Movement in Canada*. (Toronto: Progress Books, 1952), 116-130. The CCF later joined with the Canadian Labour Congress to found the New Democratic Party (NDP) in 1961.

20. Keeran, 118-119. The IWW influence waned after the failure of an ill-timed strike at the Murray Body plant.

21. Babson, 164.

22. Keeran, 125, 131.

23. Keeran, 115-116. In building the local, Mortimer was assisted by the CP nucleus in the plant which published a shop paper called *Red Motor*, and the CP's Hungarian-language paper *Uj Elore*.

24. Keeran, 123.

25. Ibid., 125.

26. Ibid., 125.

27. Keeran, 137-140. Len De Caux, *Labor Radical: From the Wobblies to CIO, A Personal History.* Boston: Beacon Press, 1970, 211-219.

28. Keeran, 107.

29. Ibid., 128.

30. Ibid., 142.

31. Wyndham Mortimer, *Organize! My Life as a Union Man.* Boston: Beacon Press, 1971, 103.

32. Ibid., 104.

33. Henry Kraus, *The Many and the Few: A Chronicle of the Dynamic Auto Workers* (Los Angeles: The Plantin Press, 1947), 82-89. Henry Kraus' book is a good first-hand account of the organizing in Flint and the course of the Flint sit-down strike.

34. Ibid., 127-128.

35. Walter Linder, *How Industrial Unionism Was Won: The Great Flint Sit-down Strike Against General Motors 1936-1937.* Brooklyn: Progressive Labor Party, 1970, 98.

36. Kraus, 1947.

37. *Life* (magazine) Volume 2 Number 3, January 18, 1937, "U.S. Labor Uses a Potent New Tactic—The Sit-Down Strike."

38. *Toronto Daily Star*, February 11, 1937,1.

39. The exciting events are well covered in Kraus, Linder, and Sidney Fine, *Sit-down: The General Motors Strike of 1936-1937.* Ann Arbor: University of Michigan Press, 1969.

40. Keeran, 184.

41. William Weinstone, *The Great Sit-Down Strike.* New York: Workers Library Publishers, 1937, 4, 6.

42. Ibid., 37.

43. Ibid., 38.

44. Ibid., 40.

45. Mortimer, 142-144. Mortimer was fudging a bit by linking stewards to shop committees. The latter were clearly recognized in the contract, stewards were not explicitly mentioned.

46. Dunn, 23.

47. Ibid.

48. Ibid., 18-24.

49. Manley, "The Workers Unity League," 186.

50. Ibid., 179.

51. Endicott, 310.

52. Manley, "The Workers Unity League," 187.

53. Endicott, 303.

54. Ibid., 303.

55. Ibid., 189.

56. Manley, "The Workers Unity League," 189.

57. Manley, "Communists and Autoworkers," 128.

58. Ibid., 128.

59. *Oshawa Daily Times*, October 31, 1935, 1, and November 1, 1935, 1.

60. Ibid., 129.

61. Ibid., 130.

62. *Where Was George Burt?*, 14.

63. Buck, *Yours in the Struggle*, 257-258.

64. Condé and Beveridge Interviews, Bill Rutherford, 1.

65. Don Nicholls' interview with author. Don has been an active associate member of the Local 222 Retired Workers Chapter for many years and was previously a Typographical Union Local President and an Executive Board member of the Oshawa and District Labour Council.

66. Ibid.

67. Condé and Beveridge Interviews, Joe Salsberg, 2.

68. Ibid.

69. *Oshawa Daily Times*, March 12, 1937.

70. Pendergest, 132.

71. *Where Was George Burt?*, 14, 16.

72. Logan, H. A. *Trade Unions in Canada: Their Development and Functioning*. Toronto: MacMillan Company of Canada, 1948, 342.

73. Gilpin, 80.

74. Manley, "Communists and Autoworkers," 130-131.

75. Napier, 11.

76. Napier, 11; Manley, "Communists and Autoworkers," 131.

77. Napier, 15.

78. Manley, "Communists and Autoworkers," 131.

79. Manley, "Communists and Autoworkers," 132.

80. Napier, 15.

81. Ibid., 17.

82. Louis Joseph Veres. *History of the United Automobile Workers in Windsor 1936-1955*. Unpublished MA thesis, University of Western Ontario, 1956, 27-28; Napier, 16-17. Veres seems to muddle the conclusion of the strike on December 30, with some events that did not happen until weeks later, after the conclusion of the Flint sit-down, when George Edwards of Local 174 met with Kelsey Wheel management in Windsor to demand that they rehire 5 strikers who had been fired, including Napier.

83. Ibid., 17.

84. *Oshawa Daily Times*, December 30, 1937, 1.

Chapter 4: Organizing for the Strike – Leadership and Engagement

1. Pendergest, 133. This is the inflation adjusted equivalent of over $5 billion.

2. *50th Anniversary Book*. CAW Local 222, 1987. Untitled, 16.

3. *Where Was George Burt?*, 18.

4. *Forty Years of Progress: 40th Anniversary 1937-1977* UAW Local 222, 1977, 16.

5. Pendergest, 134.

6. Gindin, 58.

7. *Toronto Daily Star* April 7, 1937, 30.

8. Ibid.

9. Ibid., April 14, 1937, 3.

10. Ibid. I suspect that the figure of $0.75 for women day-workers is a typographical error by the *Star*, and perhaps should have been $0.45.

11. Pendergest, 136. In 1951 Malcolm Smith confirmed that he "attended the first meeting I knew of to form a Union in the industrial plants of Oshawa, in November

of 1936." *Official Opening U.A.W. Hall November 17, 1951*. UAW Local 222 Education Committee, 1951, 13.

12. H. A. Logan, *Trade Unions in Canada: Their Development and Functioning* (Toronto: MacMillan Company of Canada, 1948), 341.

13. Condé and Beveridge Interviews, Bill Rutherford, 1-2.

14. Condé and Beveridge Interviews, J. B. Salsberg, 10.

15. *75-Year Retrospective*, 16.

16. In the author's collection. The list supplied to Benedict is a photocopy dated March 26, 1949.

17. Abella, *On Strike*, 95.

18. Condé and Beveridge Interviews, Bill Rutherford and Ethel Thomson.

19. Abella, *On Strike*, 95.

20. *Where Was George Burt?*, 18.

21. Pendergest, 134

22. Ibid., 134

23. Tim Buck, *Yours in the Struggle*, 258.

24. Ibid., 261-262.

25. Condé and Beveridge Interviews, Ethel Thomson, 7; Ethel Thomson and Vi Pilkey, 8.

26. Condé and Beveridge Interviews, Joe Salsberg, 3.

27. Condé and Beveridge Interviews, Art Shultz, 3.

28. Condé and Beveridge Interviews, Art Shultz, 4.

29. Condé and Beveridge Interviews, George Burt, 3. *Where Was George Burt?* 18: "In Oshawa there was a group of people who had been debating how they would get in touch with the CIO. I was not part of that group ... but I knew these people and some of them worked with us in the body shop."

30. Pendergest, 137.

31. Abella, *Nationalism, Communism and Canadian Labour*, 9.

32. Pendergest, 136.

33. Jack Skeels interview of Hugh Thompson, March 28, 1963, 23. UAW Oral Histories, Institute of Labor and Industrial Relations (University of Michigan--Wayne State University), Walter P. Reuther Library.

34. Hugh Thompson Papers, Walter P. Reuther Library..

35. Babson, 75.

36. Skeels, 3. Phil Raymond was head of the Auto Workers Union at that time.

37. Skeels, 3-4.

38. Skeels, 5-6.

39. Skeels, 9-11.

40. Fine, 212-213 and footnote 386.

41. Skeels, 22-23.

42. *Financial Post*, April 10, 1937, 1. This effectively answers Abella's later claim that the CIO were "reluctant invaders."

43. Condé and Beveridge Interviews, Salsberg, 7.

44. Ibid., 8.

45. Condé and Beveridge Interviews, Salsberg, 7-8.

46. Laurel Sefton MacDowell, "The Career of a Canadian Trade Union Leader: C. H. Millard 1937-1946," *Relations Industrielles/Industrial Relations*, 43(4) 610.

47. Pendergest, 104.

48. Ibid., 126. The CCF candidate in the 1935 federal election in Oshawa was another business owner, William Noble, the proprietor of Noble's Tire and Radiator Shop, Pendergest, 120

49. Daniel Benedict, "Goodbye to Homer Martin," *Labour/Le Travail*, 29 (Spring 1992), 154. Benedict based some of his description of Millard on his "personal knowledge and discussions with Millard and some of his associates." 152.

50. Ibid., 120-121.

51. MacDowell, C. H. Millard, 611.

52. Abella, *Nationalism, Communism and Canadian Labour*, 65.

53. Pendergest, 125.

54. MacDowell, C. H. Millard, 611.

55. Condé and Beveridge Interviews, Salsberg, 8.

56. Ibid., 10.

57. Ibid., 9.

58. Buck, *Yours in the Struggle*, 258.

59. Pendergest, 135.

60. Pendergest, 135.

61. *Official Opening U.A.W. Hall November 17, 1951* (UAW Local 222 Education Committee, 1951), 6.

62. Pendergest, 138.

63. Ibid., 139.

64. *Oshawa Daily Times*, March 16, 1937, 1.

65. Ibid., March 24, 1937, 1.

66. Ibid., 140-141.

67. Tom St. Amand, "Long forgotten street became part of Canadian labour history" in *The Sarnia Journal*, May 19, 2020, retrieved on May 28, 2024 at: https://www.thesarniajournal.ca/top-story/long-forgotten-street-was-part-of-canadian-labour-history-7970599

68. St. Amand, Pendergest, 151-152, *Toronto Daily Star*, March 4-5, 1937.

69. *Toronto Daily Star*, March 5, 1937, 2.

70. *Toronto Daily Star*, March 5, 1937, 1.

71. Ibid.

72. Ibid., 2.

73. Ibid., 139-140.

74. Local 222 Membership Meeting Minute Book p. 5, March 25, 1937.

75. Robertson, 293.

76. Condé and Beveridge Interviews, Shultz, 12.

77. Pendergest states that "each department had a head steward with several sub-stewards under his leadership. Each of the sub-stewards was responsible for 50 men," Pendergest, 143. However, none of the contemporary news accounts mention the term "sub-steward", the commonly used terms are chief steward and steward. Pendergest's estimate of a ratio of 1 to 50 does not square with the accounts of meetings of 200 or 300 stewards during the strike.

78. *The Evening Telegram*, March 27, 1937.

79. Abella, *Nationalism, Communism and Canadian Labour* 9.

80. *Oshawa Daily Times*, March 31, 1937, 1.

81. *Toronto Daily Star* April 8, 1937, 3; Abella, *On Strike* 101.

82. Pendergest, 141-143.

83. Ibid., 143-145.

84. Ibid., 145.

85. Ibid., 145-146.

86. Ibid., 12

Chapter 5: The Strike

1. *Toronto Daily Star*, April 8, 1937 p. 3. A GM management statement claimed there was no need for a strike because they had already agreed to many union demands, including: "Stewards and grievances. Steward plan has been on trial since middle of March."

2. Ibid., 2.

3. First quote, Logan, 248; second quote, Weinstone, 14.

4. Pendergest, 143.

5. Abella, *On Strike*, 99.

6. Abella, *Nationalism, Communism and Canadian Labour*, v.

7. Condé and Beveridge Interviews, Rutherford, 8. Christine McLaughlin states that Rutherford was a member of the Labor Progressive Party (the name of the Communist Party of Canada from 1943 to 1959). McLaughlin interviewed Rutherford's widow, Betty, but gives no other source confirming Rutherford's party membership, and I don't believe Rutherford every identified himself publicly as a Communist.

8. Donald M. Wells, "Origins of Canada's Wagner Model of Industrial Relations: The United Auto Workers in Canada and the Suppression of 'Rank and File' Unionism, 1936-1953," *Canadian Journal of Sociology/Cahiers canadiens de sociologie* 20(2) 1995, 201.

9. Ibid., 200. The Union was able to increase representation to 67 stewards and 14 committee members by January 11, 1944, *Agreement Between Ford Motor Company of Canada, Limited Windsor, Ontario and Local 200 U.A.W.-C.I.O. as amended on the eleventh day of January 1944.*

10. Agreement between Chrysler Corporation of Canada Limited and Local 195, of the International Union, United Automobile Aircraft and Agricultural Implement Workers of America, Affiliated with the Congress of Industrial Organizations, an Unincorporated Voluntary Association. September 1, 1942.

11. Lichtenstein, 141.

12. Weinstone, 34.

13. Matles and Higgins, *Them and Us*, 10. The preamble, adopted at the 1936 founding convention of UE states, "We, the Electrical, Radio and Machine Workers (UE), realize that the struggle to better our living and working conditions is in vain unless we are united to protect ourselves collectively against the organized forces of the employers. Realizing that the old craft form of trade union organization is unable to defend effectively the interests and improve the conditions of the wage earners, We (UE) form an organization which unites all workers in our industry on an industrial basis, and rank-and-file control, regardless of craft, age, sex, nationality, race, creed or political belief, and pursue at all times a policy of aggressive struggle to improve our conditions." Matles and Higgins, 7-8. The preamble is unchanged in the current (2021) UE constitution: https://www.ueunion.org/sites/default/files/UE_Constitution_2021_English.pdf

14. Ibid., 87.

15. Toni Gilpin, 75-76.

16. Ibid., 203.

17. Ibid., 203.

18. Ibid., 204.

19. *The Bosses' Boy: A Documentary Record of Walter P. Reuther* (Rank and File Committee, 1947), archived at: https://solinet.ca/thebossesboy/

20. Halpern, 142-143.

21. Meyer, 6.

22. Ibid., 108.

23. *Toronto Daily Star*, April 8, 1937, 1-2.

24. Ibid., 2. Charlie Millard told James Pendergest that "Hugh Thompson had been in favour of a strike and he had been the man most responsible for setting a deadline for strike action," Pendergest, 148.

25. Abella, *On Strike*, 96-97.

26. Pendergest, 152.

27. Ibid., 153.

28. *Toronto Daily Star*, April 8, 1937, 3.

29. Abella, *On Strike*, 102.

30. Ibid., 103, 105.

31. *Toronto Daily Star*, April 8, 1937, 1.

32. Ibid., April 9, 1937, 2.

33. Pendergest, 158.

34. Ibid., 156.

35. *Toronto Daily Star*, April 8, 1937.

36. *Toronto Daily Star*, January 16, 1946, 5. Griffin's features on life in the Soviet Union were later published: Frederick Griffin, *Soviet Scene, A Newspaperman's Close-ups of New Russia* (Toronto: MacMillan Co. of Canada, 1932).

37. *Toronto Daily Star*, April 8, 1937, 1. "During the Oshawa motor workers' strike the liquor store, the brewery warehouse and all beverage rooms in that city will be closed, E. G. Odette, head of the Ontario Liquor Control Board announced ... Mayor Hall said [the] request was made on advice of C. H. Millard."

38. *Toronto Daily Star*, April 9, 1937, 2.

39. *Oshawa Daily Times*, April 10, 1937, 2. Accompanying Millard were Frank Palme, a member of the bargaining committee, and George Frise, Harry James and Allie Dean, who were not. It seems that at some point after this meeting, George Frise was added to the bargaining committee.

40. *Toronto Daily Star*, April 10, 1937, 2.

41. Ibid., 2

42. Ibid., 2.

43. Ibid., April 10, 2.

44. Ibid., April 12, 2.

45. *Oshawa Daily Times*, April 10, 1937, 1.

46. Ibid., April 10, 1, 3.

47. Abella, *On Strike*, 107-108

48. Ibid., 108; Pendergest, 163.

49. *New Commonwealth*, April 17, 1937. Possibly the buttons referred to were dues pins—lapel pins issued to certify payment of the monthly dues of $1.

50. Pendergest, 164.

51. Pendergest, 164.

52. Agreement Between GM Corporation and the UAW, February 11, 1937.

53. WRL, Shultz Papers, cited by Pendergest, 164.

54. *Toronto Daily Star*, April 10, 1937, 2.

55. Ibid. April 10, 1937, 3.

56. Ibid., April 13, 1937, 9.

57. Ibid.

58. Mortimer, 144.

59. *The New York Times*, April 11, 1937, 39. These developments were also reported on page 1 of the *Toronto Daily Star* April 12, 1937.

60. Mortimer, 145.

61. *Toronto Daily Star*, April 12, 1937, 9.

62. Ibid. April 13, 1937, 2.

63. Ibid., April 13, 1937, 1.

64. Ibid. April 13, 1937 p. 2

65. Provincial Archives of Ontario, Hepburn Papers, cited by Pendergest p. 169.

66. *Toronto Daily Star*, April 13, 1937, 3.

67. Ibid., April 13, 1937, 3.

68. Ibid., April 12, 1937, 1.

69. Ibid., April 13, 1937, 2.

70. Ibid., April 13, 1937, 1.

71. Pendergest, 167.

72. *Toronto Daily Star*, April 14, 1937, 1.

73. Ibid., April 14, 1937, 2.

74. Ibid., April 14, 1937, 2.

75. Ibid., April 15, 1937, 1. Reverend R. J. Irwin, Donlands United Church, is quoted as saying Hepburn Hussars are worse than "Iron Heel."

76. Ibid., April 14, 1937, 1.

77. Ibid., April 14, 1937, 3.

78. Ibid,. April 14, 1937, 1.

79. Ibid., April 14, 1937, 1.

80. Ibid., April 15, 1937, 2.

81. Ibid., April 15, 1937, 1.

82. Ibid., April 14, 1937, 1, 2.

83. Ibid., April 15, 1937, 2.

84. *The New York Times*, April 16, 1937, 1.

85. Ibid., April 16, 1937, 13.

86. Ibid., April 16, 1937, 1.

87. Abella, *On Strike*, 114.

88. *The Globe and Mail*, April 16, 1937, 1.

89. *The Globe and Mail*, April 16, 1937, 1, 3.

90. *The New York Times*, April 17, 1937, 3.

91. *Toronto Star*, April 15, 1937, 2.

92. Ibid., April 15, 1937, 2.

93. Ibid., April 16, 1937, 3.

94. *Toronto Daily Star*, April 16, 1937, 4.

95. Abella, *Nationalism, Communism and Canadian Labour*, 17.

96. *Toronto Star*, April 16, 1937, 1.

97. *The New York Times*, April 17, 1937, 3.

98. Ibid.,1.

99. Homer Martin Speech at Oshawa, Ontario, April 16, 1937, in the Walter P. Reuther Library, Homer Martin Collection Box 3 Folder 11.

100. *Toronto Daily Star*, April 17, 1937, 1, 2; *The New York Times*, April 17, 1937, 1, 3.

101. *The New York Times*, April 17, 1937, 1, 3.

102. Pendergest, 175-176.

103. Abella, *Nationalism, Communism and Canadian Labour*, 17.

104. Ibid., April 17, 1937, 1.

105. Abella, *Nationalism, Communism and Canadian Labour*, 17-18. Abella claims it was "the first conference telephone call in Canadian history."

106. Ibid., 23.

107. *Toronto Daily Star*, April 19, 1937, 3.

108. *The Globe and Mail*, April 19, 1937, 1.

109. *Toronto Daily Star*, April 19, 1937, 3.

110. Ibid., April 19, 1937, 3.

111. *The Globe and Mail*, April 19, 1937, 1.
112. Ibid., April 19, 1937, 1.
113. *Toronto Daily Star*, April 19, 1937, 2.
114. *The Globe and Mail*, April 19, 1937, 2.
115. *Toronto Daily Star*, April 19, 1937, 2.
116. Ibid., April 19, 1937, 2.
117. Ibid., April 19, 1937, 2.
118. Ibid., April 19, 1937, 2.
119. Abella, *On Strike*, 116.
120. *The Globe and Mail*, April 19, 1937, 1.
121. Ibid., April 19, 1937, 1.
122. Ibid., April 19, 1937, 1.
123. Ibid., April 20, 1937, 7.
124. Hall and Hepburn had been trading insults in the press, and Hepburn had accused Hall of owing the province money dating back to when he had been removed as a Crown attorney. *Toronto Daily Star*, April 16, 1937, 2.
125. *Toronto Daily Star*, April 20, 1937, 1, 7.
126. Frederick Griffin's account started on page 1 and continued over 6 columns on page 7. It is available online and is also archived here: https://solinet.ca/oshawa-strike-1937/. The details of the meeting and quotes from speakers are all taken from this article.
127. *The New York Times*, April 21, 1937, 10. "According to the Mayor, Homer Martin, president of the U. A. W. A., approved these proposals, and Mr. Thompson pretended to approve them, but arranged with his supporters in the meeting to "intimidate" the rank-and-file of strikers to vote against the plan in a show of hands at a time when the press was excluded from the meeting."
128. *Oshawa Daily Times*, April 21, 1937, 1.
129. Walter P. Reuther Library, The George F. Addes – UAW Secretary-Treasurer Collection, Series 1, Box 1, Folder 5 – Minutes of the General Executive Board April 19-May 6, 1937, 1.
130. *Toronto Daily Star*, April 16, 1937, 1. Martin made this statement en route to Oshawa, believing settlement was close.
131. *The New York Times*, April 21, 1937, 10.
132. Minutes of the General Executive Board April 19-May 6, 1937,
133. Ibid.
134. Ibid.
135. *Toronto Daily Star*, April 21, 1937, 2.
136. *Oshawa Daily Times*, April 19, 1937, 1.
137. Ibid., April 20, 1937, 7.
138. Abella, *Nationalism, Communism and Canadian Labour*, 20.
139. *Toronto Daily Star*, April 20, 1937, 1, 2.
140. *The New York Times*, April 21, 1937, 10.
141. *The Globe and Mail*, April 21, 1937. 2.
142. Provincial Archives of Ontario (PAO), Hepburn Papers, cited by Pendergest, 186.
143. *Toronto Daily Star* (April 20, 1937, 1) said "a dozen," *The New York Times* (April 21, 1937, 1) reported "eleven."
144. *Toronto Daily Star*, April 20, 1937, 1, 2.
145. *The Globe and Mail*, April 21, 1937, 2.
146. Abella, *Nationalism, Communism and Canadian Labour*, 20.
147. *The New York Times*, April 21, 1937, 1, 10.

148. Ibid., April 21, 1937, 1.

149. *Toronto Daily Star*, April 21, 1937, 1.

150. Ibid., April 20, 1937, 1, 8.

151. Ibid., April 22, 1937, 1.

152. Ibid., April 20, 1937, 2.

153. Oscar Cole-Arnal, *To Set the Captives Free: Liberation Theology in Canada* (Toronto: Between the Lines, 1998), 135.

154. Eric Havelock, "Forty-Five Years Ago: The Oshawa Strike," *Labour/Le Travail* 11, 1983, 119-124.

155. *The Globe and Mail*, April 21, 1937, 3.

156. *Toronto Daily Star*, April 21, 1937, 1.

157. Ibid., April 21, 1937, 2.

158. *The New York Times*, April 21, 1937, 10; *The Globe and Mail*, April 21, 1937, 3.

159. *Toronto Daily Star*, April 22, 1937, 3.

160. Ibid., April 22, 1937, 3.

161. *Toronto Daily Star*, April 22, 1937, 1.

162. Ibid., April 22, 1937, 1.

163. *The New York Times*, April 22, 1937, 1.

164. Ibid., April 22, 1937, 11.

165. *Toronto Daily Star*, April 22, 1937, 1.

166. *The New York Times*, April 23, 1937, 14.

167. *Toronto Daily Star*, April 22, 1937, 2.

168. Ibid., April 22, 1937, 2.

169. Ibid., April 17, 1937, 2.

170. *The New York Times*, April 22, 1937, 1.

171. *Toronto Daily Star*, April 22, 1937, 3.

172. *Toronto Daily Star*, April 22, 1937, 3.

173. *The New York Times*, April 22, 1937, 11.

174. Ibid., April 22, 1937, 11.

175. Abella, *Nationalism, Communism and Canadian Labour*, 20.

176. Abella, *On Strike*, 119.

177. Ibid., 119.

178. *Toronto Daily Star*, April 22, 1937, 2.

179. *The New York Times*, April 22, 1937, 11.

180. *Toronto Daily Star*, April 22, 1937, 2.

181. Ibid., April 22, 1937, 1.

182. *The New York Times*, April 23, 1937, 14.

183. Ibid., April 22, 1937, 2.

184. *The New York Times*, April 23, 1937, 14.

185. Ibid., April 23, 1937, 14.

186. *Toronto Daily Star*, April 23, 1937, 4.

187. Ibid., April 23, 1937, 4.

188. Ibid., April 23, 1937, 4.

189. Descriptions are from the *Toronto Daily Star*, April 23, 1937, 1, 2; and *The Globe and Mail*, April 24, 1937, 1, 2, 3.

190. *Toronto Daily Star*, April 23, 1937, 1.

191. *Toronto Daily Star*, April 23, 1937, 1. This is another detail that Abella got incorrect. He claimed that Millard had ordered picketers to pack up before the vote started. Abella, *On Strike*, 119.

192. *The Globe and Mail*, April 24, 1937, 2, 3.

Chapter 6: Winners, Losers, and Lessons
1. *The Globe and Mail*, April 24, 1937, 6.
2. *Toronto Daily Star*, April 24, 1937, 2.
3. Pendergest, 190.
4. *The Globe and Mail*, April 26, 1937, 1.
5. Ibid., April 26, 1937, 2.
6. Ibid., April 26, 1937, 1.
7. Ibid., April 26, 1937, 2.
8. Ibid., April 26, 1937, 2.
9. *Financial Post*, May 8, 1937.
10. *Toronto Daily Star*, April 24, 1937, 6.
11. Appendix A, from Pendergest 377-379.
12. Appendix C. The February 11, 1937 agreement is Appendix B.
13. Mortimer, 143.
14. Fine, 323.
15. Ibid., 323, 324.
16. Homer Martin's Speech April 16, 1937, 3, Walter P. Reuther Library, Homer Martin Collection, 3-11.
17. Fine, 324.
18. Appendix B.
19. Appendix A, 377.
20. Appendix C, 3.
21. Fine, 325.
22. Fine, 305.
23. Ibid., 3.
24. Ibid., 4.
25. Appendix A, 377..
26. *The New York Times*, April 23, 1937, 14.
27. Appendix A, 379.
28. Appendix C, 3.
29. Ibid., 4.
30. *The New York Times*, April 23, 1937, 14.
31. Appendix D, from Veres, 126-129.
32. Veres, 128.
33. *Daily Clarion*, April 26, 1937, 1-2.
34. Ibid., April 28, 1937, 1.
35. Appendix E.
36. Abella, *Nationalism, Communism and Canadian Labour*, 20.
37. Abella, *On Strike*, 118.
38. Pendergest, 138.
39. *Toronto Daily Star*, April 10, 1937, 1.
40. *The New York Times*, April 23, 1937, 14.
41. Pendergest, 191.
42. Abella, *On Strike*, 119.
43. Ibid., 120-121.
44. Ibid., 120-121.
45. MacDowell, "After the Strike."
46. Ibid., 692.

Conclusion: Lessons and Legacy

1. "The Labor Movement Needs to Learn Its History," An Interview with Toni Gilpin, *Jacobin*, March 7, 2020.

2. The RCMP weekly report on "revolutionary organizations and agitation in Canada" highlighted the activity of Communists in support of the Oshawa GM strike. R.C.M.P. Security Bulletins, No. 852, April 21, 1937.

3. Yates, 29.

4. *War Worker* volume 1, no. 4, November 29, 1943, 1.

5. Yates, 72; McLaughlin, "Producing Memory," 19-21.

6. Yates, 98-99.

Notes on Sources and Bibliography

1. Nelson Lichtenstein, *Walter Reuther: The Most Dangerous Man in Detroit* (Urbana and Chicago: University of Illinois Press, 1995). Walter Reuther was an important and controversial figure in the history of the UAW, and Lichtenstein tends to give Reuther the benefit of the doubt on issues of dispute with his critics.

2. Henry Kraus, *The Many and the Few: A Chronicle of the Dynamic Auto Workers* (Los Angeles: The Plantin Press, 1947); Henry Kraus, *Heroes of Unwritten Story: The UAW 1934-39* (Urbana and Chicago: University of Illinois Press, 1993); Sidney Fine, *Sit-down: The General Motors Strike of 1936-1937* (Ann Arbor: University of Michigan Press, 1969).

3. Wyndham Mortimer, *Organize! My Life as a Union Man* (Boston: Beacon Press, 1971); Len De Caux, *Labor Radical: From the Wobblies to CIO, A Personal History* (Boston: Beacon Press, 1970).

4. Walter Linder, *How Industrial Unionism Was Won: The Great Flint Sit-down Strike Against General Motors 1936-1937* (Brooklyn: Progressive Labor Party, 1970). Linder said of the workers who carried out the Flint sit-down: "Once inside they set about organizing one of the most effective strike apparatuses ever seen in the United States." Linder, 98.

5. William Weinstone, *The Great Sit-Down Strike* (New York: Workers Library Publishers, 1937).

6. Roger Keeran, *The Communists and the Auto Workers' Unions* (New York: International Publishers, 1980), 13, 16.

7. John Manley, "Communists and Autoworkers: The Struggle for Industrial Unionism in the Canadian Automobile Industry, 1925-36," *Labour/Le Travail*, 17 (Spring 1986), 105-133.

8. Ibid., 133.

9. James Napier, *Memories of Building the UAW*, (Toronto: Canadian Party of Labour, 1975).

10. Stephen Endicott, *Raising the Workers' Flag: The Workers' Unity League of Canada, 1930-1936* (Toronto Buffalo London: University of Toronto Press, 2012).

11. John Manley, "Canadian Communists, Revolutionary Unionism, and the "Third Period": The Workers' Unity League, 1929-1935," *Journal of the Canadian Historical Association* 5 (1994) 167-194.

12. Tom McEwen, *The Forge Glows Red: From Blacksmith to Revolutionary* (Toronto: Progress Books, 1974).

13. Tim Buck, *Yours in the Struggle: Reminiscences of Tim Buck* (Toronto: NC Press, 1977).

14. William Z. Foster, *American Trade Unionism: Principles and Organization Strategy and Tactics* (New York: International Publishers, 1947).

15. Robert W. Dunn, *Labor and Automobiles* (New York: International Publishers, 1929).

16. Pamela Sugiman, *Labour's Dilemma: The Gender Politics of Auto Workers in Canada, 1937-1979* (Toronto Buffalo London: University of Toronto Press, 1994).

17. August Meier and Elliott Rudwick, *Black Detroit and the Rise of the UAW* (New York Oxford: Oxford University Press, 1979).

18. Steve Babson, *Building the Union: Skilled Workers and Anglo-Gaelic Immigrants in the Rise of the UAW* (New Brunswick and London: Rutgers University Press, 1991).

19. Ibid., 3.

20. Irving Abella, "The CIO, the Communist Party and the Formation of the Canadian Congress of Labour 1936-1941," *Historical Papers/Communications historiques 4(1)* (1969) 112-128; Irving Abella, "The CIO: Reluctant Invaders," *Canadian Dimension* vol. 8 No. 6 (March-April 1972) 20-23; Irving Abella, *Nationalism, Communism, and Canadian Labour* (Toronto: University of Toronto Press, 1973); Irving Abella, "Oshawa 1937," in *On Strike: Six Key Labour Struggles in Canada 1919-1949*, edited by Irving Abella (Toronto: James Lewis and Samuel, 1974).

21. James Pendergest, *Labour and Politics in Oshawa and District 1928-1943*. Unpublished MA thesis, Queen's University, 1973. Pendergest's thesis is available at the Oshawa Public Library and at the Oshawa Museum. The Pendergest Fonds at the Oshawa Museum include his notes of *Oshawa Times* articles, which is of value because many of the originals were lost in the fire of 1970.

22. Donald Wells, "Origins of Canada's Wagner Model of Industrial Relations: The United Auto Workers in Canada and the Suppression of 'Rank and File' Unionism, 1936-1953," *Canadian Journal of Sociology*, 20(2) 1995.

23. Charlotte Yates, *From Plant to Politics: The Autoworkers Union in Postwar Canada* (Philadelphia: Temple University Press, 1993).

24. Laurel Sefton MacDowell, "After the Strike—Labour Relations in Oshawa, 1937-1939," *Relations Industrielles* (Québec, Québec) 48 (4) (1993) 691–711.

25. Ibid.

26. Christine McLaughlin, *The McLaughlin Legacy and the Struggle for Labour Organization: Community, Class, and Oshawa's UAW Local 222, 1944-49* (unpublished MA thesis, 2008); Christine McLaughlin, "Producing Memory: Public History and Resistance in a Canadian Auto Town," *Oral History Forum d'histoire*, 33 (2013) 1-31.

27. Carole Condé and Karl Beveridge, *Oshawa—A History of CAW Local 222 (1982-83)* multimedia installation. Interviews from Library and Archives Canada: Carole Condé and Karl Beveridge fonds http://central.bac-lac.gc.ca/.redirect?app=fonandcol&id=190381&lang=eng. (Cited in this book as Condé and Beveridge Interviews)

28. Ibid., in particular the interviews with J.B. Salsberg, Art Shultz, Bill Rutherford, Ethel Thomson, and George Burt.

29. The *Toronto Daily Star* and *The Globe and Mail* can be accessed online through the Toronto Public Library. *The Daily Clarion* is available on microtext at the Toronto Public Library – Toronto Reference Library, and the Scott Library at York University. *The New York Times* is available online via the Timesmachine: https://timesmachine.nytimes.com/

30. Irving Abella, *Nationalism, Communism and Canadian Labour*, 15.

31. In 1943 the Local 222 publication was called *The War Worker*. The name *The Oshaworker* was chosen in a contest for Local members and used starting in January 1944. It is still published.

32. *Where Was George Burt?* (Windsor: UAW International Union Education Department, 1968), no author.

Appendices

    1. PAO, Hepburn Papers, from Pendergest, 377-379.

    2. From author's collection.

    3. From author's collection.

    4. Veres, 126-129. The Windsor GM plant was in the former municipality of Walk.
erville.

    5. WRL, UAW Region 7: Canadian Office Records, Series V, Subseries A, McKinnon
Industries Ltd., St. Catharines (Local 199). McKinnon Industries was a subsidiary of
General Motors of Canada.

Index

Keeran, Roger, 35, 36, 64, 66, 70; *The Communist Party and the Auto Workers' Unions*, 219
Kelly, Ivers, *164*
Kelsey Wheel plant strike, 80–82
Ketcheson, Georgia, 55
Kingbury, James, *164*
Knight, Joseph, 39
Knights of Labor: establishment of, 12; growth of, 24–25, 26–27; legacy of, 212; memorabilia of, *25*, 250n11; position on strikes, 25
Knudsen, William S., 129, 131, 132, 138, 206
Kraisman, Sam, 101, 205
Kramer, Claude, 183, *193*, 205
Kraus, Dorothy, 69
Kraus, Henry, 65, 66, 219, 255n33
Krawchuk, Paul, *60*

Labor and Automobiles (Dunn), 220
Labour and Politics in Oshawa and District 1928-1943 (Pendergest), 222, 266n21
Labour/Le Travail, 176
labour movement: call for unity, 37, 55, 63, 75, 214, 259n13; Cold War and, 215–216; Communists in, 15, 16; conflicts within, 13; corporate agenda and, 216; history of, 23–31, 219–222; industrial unionism, 214; organizing activities, 85–86; purge of the left, 215–216; rank-and-file-democracy and, 72–73, 76; resurgence of, 216–217; Soviet Union and, 36, 44, 58–59, 61; strategies of, 36–37, 221; weakening of, 38
Labour Party, 13, 176
Labour's Dilemma (Sugiman), 221
Ladies' Auxiliary, 68, 113, *137*, 209, 212, 223
Lapointe, Ernest, 122, 139
Lauchland Tannery, 24, 26
Lawrence, Sam, 104

Lawrie, R., 201
L.A. Young Spring and Wire, 72
Lazarus, Felix, 129
left-wing movement: Communists and, 16, 63; ethnic minorities and, 51; industrial unionism and, 13, 44, 54, 119; influence of, 109, 214; principles of, 37; purges of, 16, 38, 216
Lemeu, George, *32*
Levitt, Joe, *59*
Lewis, John L.: Hepburn and, 157, 158; as leader of CIO, 17, 57, 58, 65, 139, 141, 151; Oshawa strike and, 122, 161; arrest threat of, 133
Lewisism, 189, 190
The Lexicon of Labor (Murray), 13
Lichtenstein, Nelson, 116; *Walter Reuther*, 219
Life, 68, 69
Linder, Walter, 68; *How Industrial Unionism Was Won*, 219
Liptrott, Clinton, 201
Local 174 of UAW, 80, 81–82, 256n82
Local 195 of UAW, *80*, 80–82, 110, 141
Local 199 of UAW, 82, 110, 201, 267n5
Local 200 of UAW, 116, 222
Local 222 of UAW: affiliation with TTLC, 131–132; AFL and, 40, 41, 64; communist influence in, 214; contracts with supplier companies, 113; Ed Hall and, 105, 109, 132, 205; Executive Board, *77*; formation of, 88, 90, 113, 223; GM recognition of, 194–195; influence of, 23, 223; leading figures of, 28, 77, 98, 214, 256n65; membership meetings of, 106–107, 109, *124*, *162*, 163–168, *167*, 194, 204–205, 211–212; minute book entry, *105*; Open Forum of, 214; protest against Hepburn's private militia, 141, *142*; stewards of, 108, 113; Thompson's letter to, 95; UAW charter, 10, 20, 23, *89*
Local 248 of UAW, 14, 119

Printed by Imprimerie Gauvin
Gatineau, Québec